The Celestial Journey of the Soul
Zodiacal Themes in the Gospel of Mark

The Celestial Journey of the Soul

Zodiacal Themes in the Gospel of Mark

Bill Darlison

Zodiacal Illustrations by Dan Hodgkin

© Bill Darlison 2017

All rights reserved

No parts of this publication may be reproduced, stored in a retrieval system, or transmitted in any form or by any means, electronic, mechanical, photocopying, recording, or otherwise without prior permission of the copyright owner.

First Published in 2008 by Dublin Unitarian Church

Original illustrations of the zodiac symbols © Dan Hodgkin

Some scriptural verses have been taken from the Holy Bible, NEW INTERNATIONAL VERSION®
© 1973, 1978, 1984, International Bible Society.
NEW INTERNATIONAL VERSION® and NIV® are registered trademarks of International Bible Society.
Use of either trademark for the offering of goods or services requires the prior written consent of the International Bible Society.

ISBN: 978-1-326-92697-7

Acknowledgments

Thanks to:

Dan Hodgkin for his lovely illustrations of the individual zodiac signs, and to Duckworth for permission to use these and other items of copyright material.
The Dublin Unitarian congregation who listened patiently, perceptively and uncomplainingly to these sermons over a whole year.
Tony Brady who recorded them all for broadcast on the Dublin Unitarian Church website.
Numerous correspondents world-wide who have been listening over the internet and who have sent me their comments and criticisms.
Wikipedia for some of the illustrations.
Paul Spain for his boundless expertise.
My wife, Morag, for her patience.

For my friends Janet and John Walker
'Some people are too great for fame.'(Emerson)

CONTENTS

Introduction	1
What's the Good News?	3
Chapter 1: Aries	10
Pick up your Bed and Walk!	11
Who is my Mother	19
Chapter 2: Taurus	26
Nurturing the Seed	27
Letting the Light Shine	34
Chapter 3: Gemini	42
'I Contain Multitudes'	43
Waking Up	51
How do we wake up?	61
Chapter 4: Cancer	69
Feeding all the People	70
Opening Up	80
Chapter 5: Leo	88
Who do Men say that I am?	89
If you can! The Meaning of Faith	97
Chapter 6: Virgo	105
Service and Simplicity	106
Beginner's Mind	114
Chapter 7: Libra	121
Getting the Balance Right	122
Distractions	130
Chapter 8: Scorpio	138
Into the Depths	139
The Ransom	146
Chapter 9: Sagittarius	155
Where two Roads meet	156
Moving Mountains	165
Chapter 10: Capricorn	173
Rendering to Caesar	174
Call no man Father	183
Chapter 11: Aquarius	192
Standing out from the Crowd	193
'O Brave New World'	201

The Age of Aquarius	211
Chapter 12: Pisces	217
The King must die	218
Pisces/Aries: Resurrection	229
Bibliography	236

Everybody wants to change the world.
Nobody wants to change himself.
(Tolstoy)

Introduction

This book contains the text of 27 sermons delivered in the Dublin Unitarian church between Easter 2007 and Easter 2008. The sermons are based on my book *The Gospel and the Zodiac: The Secret Truth about Jesus*,[1] and reflect that book's contention that individual sections of Mark's Gospel are informed by ideas and imagery corresponding to a particular sign of the zodiac, and that these 'zodiacal' sections would have originally been read and studied throughout the solar year, beginning at the spring equinox. These sermons are an attempt to present this radical reassessment of the Gospel of Mark in an informal and accessible way. Although there is some inevitable overlap, this volume is less concerned than *The Gospel and the Zodiac* with presenting the scholarly case for the thesis, and much more concerned with exploring the spiritual lessons carried by the individual Gospel sections.

The sermons are based on the assumption that the Gospel story is not just about a man called Jesus, who may or may not have lived 2,000 years ago, but about the passage of each individual through the various stages necessary in order to achieve 'enlightenment' or 'salvation' – hence the book's title, *The Celestial Journey of the Soul*. The Gospel story is about you and me; the stages of the human spiritual journey correspond with the stages of Sun's yearly journey around the zodiac.

Each sermon is prefaced by my own translation of a passage from the Gospel and Mark, and by a classic spiritual story illustrating one of the main lessons of the Gospel text. Readers with time and inclination may want to read the various sections of Mark in their entirety and should be able to find a copy of the Gospel without too much difficulty. The New International Version or the Revised Standard Version are recommended, but some readers may prefer the beautiful, if rather archaic, prose of the Authorised Version. The Gospel of Mark is the shortest of the four Gospels and can be read through in an hour.

Although the 27 sermons can obviously be read at any time of the year, it may be instructive to follow the sequence throughout

---

[1] Published by Duckworth/Overlook, 2007

the solar year, starting at the spring equinox, and reading the relevant sections as the Sun enters the individual zodiacal signs. So, the first two sections would be studied at the end of March, the next two when the Sun enters Taurus around 21st April, and so on through the year. The specific dates mentioned in the sermons relate to the solar year beginning on March 21st 2007.

For those who are unfamiliar with the sequence and approximate dates of the Sun's presence in each of the zodiacal signs, the table below might be helpful. It also includes the chapter and verse divisions of the corresponding sections of Mark's Gospel.

Sign	Approximate Dates	Section in Mark
Aries	March 21st – April 19th	1:1 – 3:35
Taurus	April 20th – May 20th	4:1 – 4:34
Gemini	May 21st – June 20th	4:35 – 6:29
Cancer	June 21st – July 22nd	6:30 – 8:26
Leo	July 23rd – August 22nd	8:27 – 9:29
Virgo	August 23rd – Sept. 22nd	9:30 – 9:50
Libra	September 23rd – Oct. 23rd	10:1 – 10:31
Scorpio	October 24th – Nov. 21st	10:32 – 10:52
Sagittarius	November 22nd – Dec. 21st	11:1 – 11:26
Capricorn	December 22nd – Jan. 19	11:27 – 12:44
Aquarius	January 20th – Feb. 19th	13:1 – 14:16
Pisces	February 20th – March 20th	14:17 – 16:18

Although there are a few minor changes and additions to the original text in this 2017 edition, the sermons are given here pretty much as they were delivered, and no attempt has been made to modify their informal style.

Bill Darlison

What's the Good News?

Mark 1:14-15

> After John was arrested, Jesus went to Galilee preaching the good news about God. He was saying that the appointed time had come; the kingdom of God was close by. 'Change your mind and your ways and believe the good news.'

Story: The Smuggler

> Every day Nasrudin took his straw-laden donkey across the border, but one day he was stopped by a customs officer, who eyed him suspiciously. 'What have you got in that straw?' he asked. 'Are you carrying any contraband goods across the border? If you are, you'll have to pay a fee.'
> 'Look for yourself,' replied Nasrudin. 'I'm hiding nothing!'
> The customs officer poked about in the straw on the donkey's back, but he couldn't find anything. Reluctantly he let man and donkey through.
> The next day the same thing happened, and the next day, and the next. Every day, the customs officer stopped Nasrudin and searched the straw on the donkey's back, but he never discovered any contraband goods. Sometimes he would look in the donkey's mouth, sometimes he would even have a look under the donkey's tail. Sometimes he would search Nasrudin himself, but each time his search proved fruitless. Nevertheless, the customs officer still suspected Nasrudin of smuggling, and vowed never to stop searching until he had evidence.
> This went on for ten years until the customs officer finally retired with the case unsolved. But even though he was no longer working he would occasionally think about the clever

smuggler, and wonder whether he might have caught him out if he'd searched even more thoroughly. Maybe Nasrudin was smuggling diamonds and he'd hidden them in the metal shoes on the donkey's feet. He'd never thought of that at the time. Drat! Maybe Nasrudin was smuggling gold dust and he'd spread it very fine on the donkey's fur. He'd not thought of that either. 'He had some devious scheme. I could see it in his face!' thought the retired customs officer.

One day, as he was walking through the market place, he noticed a familiar face in the crowd. It was Nasrudin, without his donkey. 'Hey, you! Come here! You are the man who came to the border every day with a donkey laden with straw, aren't you?'

'Yes, I am,' said Nasrudin.

'And you were smuggling weren't you? I'm convinced you were. I searched you every day, but I couldn't find anything, because you were very crafty. But you can tell me now. Were you smuggling?'

'Yes I was,' said Nasrudin.

'I knew it! What were you smuggling?'

'Donkeys!' said Nasrudin, with a big smile.

I found, when I was teaching religious studies, that it often came as a shock to young people to discover that the word 'gospel' means 'good news'. 'What's good about it?' some would ask. 'It didn't do St. Peter any good. He was crucified upside down; and St. Paul had his head chopped off; and all the other apostles seem to have met a similar, grisly fate.' As the discussion developed, they would really start to list what they considered to be the negative aspects of the Christian enterprise. (Children, even children of pious parents, can be very irreverent!)

After reciting the litany of problems endured - and caused - by Christians throughout the world and throughout the ages, they would look at the impact of Christianity on their own lives. Far from it being 'good news', they saw it as little more than an arbitrary collection of rules designed to stop them having a good time. William Blake had made much the same point centuries ago:

> And priests in black gowns
> Were walking their rounds,
> And binding with briars
> My joys and desires.

I can remember developing similar attitudes when I reached adolescence and began to question received wisdom a little. Our priests told us that Jesus died for us because he loved us, and this seemed like a decent thing for someone to do, but when we were told that the sacrifice was necessary because God the Father demanded it in payment for human sin it began to appear grotesque. And sin seemed to be everywhere; we had to be constantly on our guard against the temptations of the devil because just one slip-up at the wrong time could put our souls in jeopardy. There were sins of omission and sins of commission; venial sins and mortal sins; sins crying out to heaven for vengeance; sins of thought, word, and deed. There may only have been seven 'deadly' sins but there were thousands of others which could wound grievously. They were all deliciously appealing, of course, but were also capable of putting that black mark on the soul that would mean eternal hell for the really unfortunate, and aeons in purgatory for the rest. In school we talked about the categories of sin and the degrees of sinfulness and culpability. For example, when was stealing a mortal sin and when was it a venial sin? (In the fifties, £5 seemed to be the significant sum. Below £5 and it was venial; above £5 and it was mortal. What about four pounds nineteen shillings and eleven pence? Or five pounds and a penny? And what about inflation? Generally, we were told to shut up at this point.) And then, of course, there were inappropriate thoughts, 'dirty' thoughts. Were they sinful? Could I go to hell for entertaining those thoughts that were more entertaining than any others, and which seemed to my adolescent mind to be constantly present? Yes, was the disappointing answer.

And, we were told, God was looking all the time; maybe you could fool your mother or the police, but you couldn't fool God. He had a little book and he was noting it all down. We prayed for the grace of final repentance, that death wouldn't take us by surprise with unconfessed sins on our soul. The really scrupulous people –

and I've known plenty over the years - could find themselves living in a perpetual state of anxiety.

How good was that news?

The Protestants didn't fare much better. They didn't have to go to church every week, or eat fish on Fridays, or go to confession to tell the priest the intimate details of their life, but they seemed to have equally onerous tasks to perform – reading the Bible, for example, which we Catholics didn't seem to bother about – and some mysterious things called 'being born again', and 'entering into a relationship with Jesus Christ', all of which seemed to leave them with that dutiful joylessness, which had inspired the 19th century British poet Algernon Swinburne to write of Jesus,

> Thou hast conquered, O pale Galilean
> And the world has grown grey from thy breath.

So, the Protestants with their grey world didn't seem to be the recipients of good news either.

I often envied my father. He was not a churchgoer but it never seemed to bother him. He didn't have to worry about all the details concerning sin and God and judgement, nor did he seem to regret their absence from his life. I asked the teacher about my dad, and about my friends who were similarly unconcerned by religious scruples. 'Would they go to heaven?' The reply was instructive. 'Catholics have the best chance of heaven, but if a person lives a good life, according to the dictates of their conscience, and according to the extent of their knowledge of the laws of God, then it might be possible that they could be saved.'

It was a reasonably humane reply, but it got me thinking. If sins were only sins if you knew they were sins, then surely it would be better not to know? I'm actually at a disadvantage, I began to think. The unchurched majority in our own society, and the billions of people who had never heard about God and Jesus and the 'good news' were really better off than I was! I was going to church every week just to hear stuff that was doing little more than increasing my chances of going to hell! And missionaries, far from being benefactors of the human race, as I'd been told, were actually its enemies. Leaving the pagans in ignorance would mean that they could enjoy their present life to the full and escape punishment after death. The good news was actually bad news! My adolescent mind savoured the paradox.

Many years ago, Peter Cook and Dudley Moore performed a sketch about this particular problem. It ends with the pair musing about a group of 'Ephiscans' settling down to breakfast before going off for a day at the seaside. They are full of anticipation and excitement when a knock comes at the door. It's the postman. He's brought a letter from St. Paul. 'Oh no!' they say. 'Trust Paul to spoil everything!' And, sure enough, on opening the letter they find Paul's simple instruction: 'Dear Ephiscans, Stop enjoying yourselves. God's about. Signed, Paul.'

Not terribly good news for the Ephiscans, either!

The problem is that Christianity has not really convinced us that the kingdom of God – which is what the good news is supposed to be about – is really all that appealing. Some say that the kingdom is to be built on earth as a kind of economic and political utopia, others that it is a state of blessedness with God after death; but, either way, there is always the implication that it is a kind of colourless existence, under the watchful all-seeing eye of a celestial potentate who will bully us into joyless conformity and punish us for disobedience.

But this was never the original message of Jesus. His message, his 'good news', was very simple: the longed for kingdom of God is *here already*.[2] Of course, if Jesus was promising an economic or political utopia, he was completely mistaken; if anything, things were to get worse for the Jews, and, two thousand years later, a just and equitable political system still eludes us. But the kingdom of God, as Jesus understood it, is a state of being, not a social arrangement. Entry into the kingdom requires a complete change of mind, a willingness to re-orientate our perceptions. This is the meaning of the Greek word *metanoia*, which is generally translated as 'repentance', but which involves much more than regret for past actions, and it certainly doesn't mean 'confessing our sins'. It implies a resolution to begin again from the beginning, *to make a fundamental alteration to the way one looks at the world*, which St.

---

[2] Mark 1:15

Paul calls 'transformation by the renewing of the mind'.[3] Luke's Gospel tells us that 'The kingdom of God does not come visibly, nor will people say, "Here it is," or "There it is", because the kingdom of God is within you'.[4] From the Gnostic Gospel of Thomas we learn, 'The kingdom of the Father is already spread out on the earth, *and people aren't aware of it*',[5] which means that the kingdom of God is not something that we can create with political action and economic redistribution (important though these may be), nor is it something that will be imposed upon us by divine intervention; it is, instead, something we can discover *by correcting our eyesight*.

      The Sufis, Islam's mystics, tell the story of how Nasrudin, the 'holy fool', would take his donkey across a frontier every day, its panniers loaded with straw. The customs inspector suspected the increasingly prosperous Nasrudin of smuggling, but despite regular and extensive searches, he could never find any contraband. Years later, when both were retired, they met in the marketplace. 'I know you were smuggling something,' said the customs officer. 'What was it? You can tell me now.'

      'Donkeys,' replied Nasrudin.

      The story illustrates the Sufi contention - shared by Jesus - that the mystical goal, the kingdom of God, is nearer than is generally realised. In fact, it is here, 'at hand', but we are so busy looking for something else that we never find it. The mystic poet and painter William Blake, who stands in a similar esoteric tradition, writes:

> To the eyes of a miser a guinea is far more beautiful than the Sun, and a bag worn with use of money has more beautiful proportions than a vine filled with grapes. The tree which moves some to tears of joy is in the eyes of others only a green thing which stands in the way. As a man is, so he sees. As the eye is formed, such are its powers ....
> 'When the Sun rises, do you not see a round disc of fire, somewhat like a guinea?' 'O no, no, I see an innumerable

---

[3] Romans 12:2
[4] Luke 17:21
[5] Saying 113

company of the heavenly host crying, "Holy, holy, holy is the Lord God Almighty'" ... ... If the doors of perception were cleansed everything would appear to man as it is, infinite.
For man has closed himself up, till he sees all things through narrow chinks of his cavern....
For everything that lives is holy.[6]

    To see the world as Blake saw it is to become a citizen of the Kingdom of God, and the good news is not that the kingdom is something to build, or something to 'get into' when we die, it is something to discover while we are still alive. And, what's more, it is possible to discover it, to open up those narrow chinks in the caverns of our minds, to cleanse the doors of perception. And when we do, our individual and communal lives will be immeasurably enriched.

    This is the real promise of the Gospel. This is the real 'good news', and the Gospels themselves are guidebooks to the journey of transformation. They are not history for us to believe or to become sentimental about. It is my belief that the original Gospel message gave us a map of the road towards transformation based on the metaphor of the Sun's passage through the signs of the zodiac. The document that we call the Gospel of Mark preserves this original sequence. It begins in the spring, and throughout the coming year I will be giving sermons which point out the various spiritual lessons that the Gospel of Mark teaches us. The first of these sermons will be on 25th March, and will concern the first three chapters of Mark, which, I believe, are related to the zodiac sign of Aries, the sign of the springtime.

---

[6] Haddon, pages 12-13

Chapter 1: Aries
21st March – 19th April

Aries is the sign of the springtime and so signifies new beginnings, new life. The very first word of the Gospel in Greek is 'beginning',[7] and the theme of 'newness' pervades the whole section. The Twelve Apostles are the 'new Israel', and Jesus revives three men from conditions which imply powerlessness – paralysis, a withered hand, and leprosy – thus giving them new life. Aries is associated with the element Fire and its symbol is the Ram or Lamb. It is related to the head and to the tops of things in general and was called 'The Lord of the Head' by the Egyptians. (The paralyzed man is lowered down through *the roof* to Jesus).[8] The Babylonians called Aries 'The Hired Man' (James and John leave their father with the *hired men*).[9] Nearby constellations are Cassiopeia, *The Reclining Woman* (Peter's mother-in-law is said, oddly, to be *'reclining* with a fever')[10] and Perseus, *The Bridegroom* (can the wedding guests fast while the bridegroom is with them?' asks Jesus).[11]

The 'ruler' of Aries (the planet associated with it) is Mars; its colour is red.

---

[7] ἀρχή without the definite article
[8] Mark 2:1-12
[9] Mark 1:20
[10] The Greek word is κατέκειτο (Mark 1:30)
[11] Mark 2:19

Pick up your Bed and Walk!

Mark 2:1-12

A few days after he'd gone back to Capernaum, word of his whereabouts got around, and so many people gathered that there was no room, not even by the door, and he was speaking the word to them. And four men arrived carrying a paralytic. And not being able to get near him because of the crowd, they took off the roof of the house where he was, and when they'd made an opening they let down the stretcher on which the paralysed man was lying. When Jesus saw their faith he said to the paralysed man, 'Child, your sins are forgiven.' But there were some legal experts sitting there who were asking themselves, 'Why is he speaking such blasphemy? Only God can forgive sins!' But Jesus was immediately aware of their thoughts, and he said to them, 'What's your problem? What is easier to say to the paralysed man: "Your sins are forgiven", or "Get up, pick up your stretcher, and walk"? But in order to prove to you that the son of man has authority on earth to forgive sins,' he said to the paralysed man, 'I say to you, get up, pick up your stretcher and go home!' And up he got immediately, and picking up his stretcher went out in front of everyone, so that they were all amazed and praising God saying, 'We've never seen anything like this!'

Story: Nasrudin and the Chillies

One day Nasrudin was feeling very thirsty. He'd been walking for a long time in the blazing Sun and there was no water to be had anywhere. 'What I need is some luscious fruit. A big melon or a couple of oranges would be perfect,' he said to himself. As he turned the corner he saw a fruit and vegetable stall. His prayers had been answered!

'How much are your oranges?' he asked the stallholder, looking at the mountain of juicy oranges.

'Fifty cents each,' replied the man. 'Three for one euro.'

Nasrudin looked at the few coppers in his hand. Not enough for even one orange. And his thirst was burning! 'How much are your melons?' he inquired, optimistically.

'Seventy-five cents each, and cheap at the price.'

Disappointed but not defeated, Nasrudin looked at the rest of the stall, and some shiny little red pods caught his attention. They looked wonderfully refreshing. 'How much are those?' he asked excitedly.

'Three cents each,' replied the man.

'I'll take ten!'

Nasrudin handed over the thirty cents - all the money he had - and then he sat down in a nice shaded place and began to munch the red pods. He devoured the first one with no trouble, but mid-way through the second his eyes began to water and his mouth began to burn. 'These are the hottest fruits I've ever tasted,' he thought. But he still carried on eating.

Just then, a passer-by saw Nasrudin's distress. 'What on earth is the matter?' asked the concerned woman.

'I'm eating some fruit,' replied Nasrudin, 'but I've never tasted any like this before! They're hot!'

The woman looked closely at what Nasrudin was holding in his hand. 'No wonder they're hot!' she laughed, 'those are chillies! They're not for eating, they're for cooking. You put them in curries!'

But Nasrudin carried on eating. Tears were streaming down his bright red face, and his throat was burning unmercifully. 'You must stop eating them at once!' ordered the woman, 'or you'll make yourself very ill! I'm telling you, they're not fruit!'

'Oh I know they're not fruit,' said Nasrudin, 'but I've paid for them so I'm going to finish them. I'm not one to waste my money!'

'There's a time for departure, even when there's no certain place to go.'
Tennessee Williams (born March 26th 1911)

Last Wednesday was the first day of spring. It wasn't such a pleasant day in England; it was windy and cold, with the odd flurry of snow and sleet, but, despite the inclement weather, the evidence of new growth was everywhere, as it has been for a few weeks: the daffodils are blooming, the trees budding, the days lengthening. This is the season of new life, celebrated throughout human history with great rejoicing; the long sleep of winter is over, the sap is rising; it's when 'a young man's fancy turns to thoughts of love' (and 'an old man's stomach turns!') It is an optimistic time, when, according to Chaucer, 'folk long to go on pilgrimages'; it's when we start to make our plans, change our jobs, sell our houses. Forget January 1st, with its dreary darkness and its forced bonhomie; this is the real 'new year' and has been acknowledged as such in the northern hemisphere since human beings appeared on earth. The ancients believed that the creation of the world took place at this time of the year (as well they might), and the Jewish people said that the Exodus occurred in springtime, the waking of the earth from its winter sleep providing a powerful metaphor for casting off the shackles of slavery in Egypt and moving on to freedom in the Promised Land.

The Sun has entered the zodiac sign of Aries, the sign of the Ram or Lamb, and it is this sign that is reflected in the first three chapters of Mark's Gospel. Aries is the sign of the springtime, the sign of new beginnings, vigour, activity, and impetuosity. People who are born under Aries are often confrontational, somewhat aggressive, fiery, individualistic – like the ram itself, attacking head-first, butting all those who would oppose it out of the way. One of the most characteristically Aries people of the modern world was Ian Paisley (born on April 6th 1926). He was fiercely individualistic, an initiator *par excellence* and, until the last years of his life, incapable of negotiation or compromise. Life for Ian Paisley was a battle, and 'No surrender!' his constant battle cry. This is how he expressed his disapproval of the pope's visit to the European Parliament in Strasbourg in 1988:

> This is the battle of the Ages which we are engaged in. This is no Sunday school picnic; this is a battle for truth against the lie, the battle of Heaven against hell, the battle of Christ against the Antichrist!'[12]

General William Booth, the founder of the Salvation Army, was born on 10th April 1829, and while considerably less disputatious and confrontational than Ian Paisley, the motto he chose for his organisation – 'Blood and Fire' – combines two combative Aries images. Unlike Paisley, his battle was not with the pope in Rome but with poverty among the wretched and indifference among the rich. However, his rhetoric was no less militaristic than Paisley's, as this little piece, part of a speech delivered in the Royal Albert Hall in London just before his death in 1912, demonstrates:

> 'While women weep, as they do now, I'll fight; while little children go hungry, as they do now, I'll fight; while men go to prison, in and out, in and out, as they do now, I'll fight; while there is a drunkard left, while there is a poor girl upon the streets, while there remains one dark soul without the light of God, I'll fight – I'll fight to the very end!'[13]

Richard Dawkins – born on 26th March - is another Aries. He is Darwin's champion, fearlessly challenging religion, even resurrecting the old idea of 'warfare' between religion and science.

---

[12] Cooke, page 4
[13] See 139581.gridserver.com/2012/05/09/ill-fight-100-years-since-booths-final-address/

His equally disputatious colleague, Daniel Dennett, who is beating the anti-religious drum in America, was born just a year and two days after Dawkins, on 28th March, 1942. Christopher Hitchens, born on 13th April, 1949, entered the fray in 2007 with his book *God is not Great*, and Sam Harris, probably America's most celebrated atheist, was born on April 9th, 1967. These four, sometimes called 'The God Busters' or 'The Four Horsemen of New Atheism' were all born under Aries. Here they are together, probably sharing a birthday party.

The Four Horsemen of New Atheism
(left to right: Hitchens, Dennett, Dawkins, Harris)

Madalyn Murray O'Hair, militant feminist and the founder of American Atheists, was born on 13th April 1919, but we shouldn't infer from this cluster of famous God-Debunkers that there is an intrinsic connection between Aries and atheism. Not all people born in the springtime are atheists, but they do seem to share a tendency to challenge the status-quo, and fearlessly to break away from what Aries poet Seamus Heaney (born 13th April, 1939) calls 'the implacable consensus'.

Of the great spiritual figures born under Aries, none is more typical or more appealing than the wonderful Teresa of Avila, who was born on 28th March, 1515. She's one of my very favourite saints. There's nothing wishy-washy about Teresa. Her earliest desire was to become a martyr, and when she was a little girl she ran away from home just so that she could be captured and executed by the Moors!

Fortunately, her uncle saw her trying to escape and brought her back. She'd only gone down the road. Her love for God was passionate, expressed by her in unambiguously erotic terms, and the famous Bernini statue of Teresa shows her lost in almost orgasmic rapture. Although she was a nun, and although at times she was said to levitate when lost in ecstasy at mass, she was certainly no recluse: she founded and ran a religious order, travelling by cart in Spain's scorching heat to the various convents under her jurisdiction, suggesting improvements, disciplining backsliders, dealing with finances, all the while writing the most startling religious prose. She deliberately avoided marriage, which she considered a kind of slavery, making her into one of the great feminist figures of the past, and one of a number of Aries women who have fought the battle for female rights down the ages (the other sign with more than its fair share of feminists is Aquarius).

Among the most characteristically Arien figures in the Bible is John the Baptist, the very first person we are introduced to in the Gospel of Mark. Mark doesn't tell us very much about him, except to say that he was dressed in no-nonsense Aries style – a garment made from camel's hair – and his diet didn't have too many frills either; he existed on locusts and wild honey! In the Gospels of Matthew and Luke he lambastes the religious people of his day, calling them 'a brood of vipers' and threatening them with all manner of calamities if they don't mend their ways. His plain speaking eventually brings

The Zodiacal Man
Aries is shown ruling the head

about his downfall. His fearless, but rather foolhardy, rebuke of King Herod for marrying his sister-in-law, Herodias, gets him beheaded – a most Arien death, since Aries was said to govern the head and was even called 'The Lord of the Head' by the Egyptians.

The figure of Jesus that we meet in these early chapters of Mark is equally confrontational. He goes into battle against his religious opponents with breath-taking fervour and more than a dash of rashness. He takes on the Pharisees and the Scribes, and even tackles good old Satan himself, casting the devil out of various disturbed people, and claiming that the kingdom of Satan has been brought to an end. Maya Angelou, a great contemporary Arien figure (born 4th April 1928), says, 'I love to see a young girl go out and grab the world by the lapels; life's a bitch; you've got to go out and kick ass,' which is exactly what Jesus is shown to be doing. 'Gentle Jesus meek and mild'? Forget it! That's just religious sentimentality. This is Jesus kicking ass, and his ass-kicking provokes the religious authorities so much that even sworn enemies, the patriotic Pharisees and the collaborative Herodians, are prepared to join forces to plot his death.

So, what are the spiritual lessons of Aries? There are a number of them, but, unfortunately we can't deal with them all. Today I want to look briefly at two.

The first is found in those passages where Jesus calls his first disciples. They read very strangely as history. Jesus simply says 'Follow me!' to James and John, and later to Levi, the tax collector, and, without further ado, they all leave everything behind and impetuously follow him. No lengthy conversations, you notice; no police checks on his background; no, 'Give us a little time to think about it Jesus'. None of this; just, up and off. (Incidentally, James and John leave their father Zebedee in the boat 'along with the hired men'.[14] 'The Hired Man' was the name of the constellation Aries in ancient Babylon, a fact I discovered long after I'd developed my theory of Mark, but which made the hairs stand up on the back of my head when I discovered it!)

These passages teach us that procrastination has no part to play in the spiritual life. If we dither around telling ourselves that we

---

[14] Mark 1:20

will begin our journey of self-transformation – which is what 'living a spiritual life' means – when circumstances are favourable, when we've found a congenial path, when we have more time, when the kids are grown, when we retire, then we might as well forget it. The Hindu sage, Sri Ramakrishna, tells the following story which illustrates this very point:

> A wife once spoke to her husband, saying, 'My dear, I am very anxious about my brother. For the last few days he has been thinking of renouncing the world and of becoming a Sannyasin (a wandering holy man), and has begun preparations for it. He has been trying gradually to curb his desires and reduce his wants.' The husband replied, 'You need not be anxious about your brother. He will never become a Sannyasin. No one has ever renounced the world by making long preparations.' The wife asked, 'How then does one become a Sannyasin?' The husband answered, 'Do you wish to see how one renounces the world? Let me show you.' Saying this, instantly he tore his flowing dress into pieces, tied one piece round his loins, told his wife that she and all women were henceforth his mother, and left the house never to return.[15]

That's the way to do it! As St. Paul says, '*Now* is the acceptable time; *now* is the day of salvation!'[16] That's lesson one: stop wasting time; stop kidding yourself that once you've sorted out the historical problems of Christianity to your own satisfaction, and come to satisfactory conclusions about the existence of God and the nature of Jesus, you'll start the process. Because you won't. The path beckons. Get on it.

Lesson two deals with another important aspect of the same procrastinating syndrome, and is brought out in the story of the paralysed man which we heard as our second reading this morning. You remember what happens: Jesus is teaching in somebody's house, but the place is crowded; even the doorway is packed with people. Four men carrying a paralysed man on a stretcher find that

---

[15] Ballou, page 81
[16] 2 Corinthians 6:2

their way to Jesus is barred, so they go up on the roof, make a hole in the thatching, and lower the man down to Jesus. (Remember: Aries represents the head – or the roof!) Jesus is amazed by the faith of all concerned, and he tells the man that his sins are forgiven, but this so incenses the Pharisees ('How dare he presume to forgive sins!' they say), that Jesus changes his tactics. 'Okay,' he says, 'I won't say "Your sins are forgiven", I'll say "Pick up your stretcher and walk!"' which the man proceeds to do.

When we stop bothering ourselves about the theological implications of the expression 'Your sins are forgiven', we can make some sense of this lovely story. It simply means, stop letting the past paralyse you. The man on the stretcher is you and I. We are all paralysed by the past, or, in the words of Aries writer Ram Dass (born April 6th 1931), 'we are too busy holding on to our unworthiness'. We like the past, sins and all, because we are safe there. We know where we are with our habits and traditions. We may be, in fact we probably are, like Nasrudin in our children's story, chewing ferociously on hot peppers, simply because that's what we've always done. 'Habit is a great deadener' says Arien Samuel Beckett (born April 13th 1906) in *Waiting for Godot*. But now is the time to stop, to let the past go, to break with the comforting habits of thought and action we've allowed to cripple us for so long.

Pick up that stretcher and walk!

And do it today!

These are two important lessons of Aries.

Who is my Mother?
Mark 3:31-35

> And his mother and brothers came and were standing outside. They sent someone in to summon him. And a crowd was sitting around him and they said to him, 'Your mother and your brothers and your sisters are outside; they are looking for you.' Jesus responded by saying, 'Who is my mother and my brothers?' And looking at those sitting in a circle round him, he said, 'Look. Here are my

mother and my brothers. Whoever does the will of God is my brother, my sister, and my mother.'

Story: The Farmer, the Sheep, and the Robbers

A farmer went to market one day with the intention of buying a sheep. He soon found a beautiful specimen and set off home with the sheep walking by his side. On his journey through the deserted countryside he was spotted by some robbers who were hiding in the bushes. 'That sheep would make us a lovely supper,' said one.

'Let's take it from him,' said another.

'I have a better idea,' said a third. 'There's no need for violence. Let's trick him out of it!' And with that he explained his plan to his cronies … …

One of the robbers approached the farmer and said, 'Good afternoon, sir. Are you going hunting?'

'What makes you think I'm going hunting?' asked the farmer.

'Because you've got your hunting dog with you. I thought you might be going to catch some rabbits with it.'

'This is not a dog. It's a sheep,' said the bewildered farmer. 'That man must really have poor eyesight if he can't tell the difference between a sheep and a dog,' he said to himself as the robber walked away. A little further on, a second robber came upon the farmer. 'Don't let that dog get too close to me,' he said. 'I'm terrified of big dogs!'

'This isn't a dog. It's a sheep!' shouted the exasperated farmer. 'Can't you see? It has a woolly coat and it says "Baa, Baa."'

The second robber walked off, leaving the farmer so perplexed that he was beginning to doubt his own eyes. Then a third robber appeared. 'My goodness, that's a fine dog,' he said. 'I used to have one like that. He was my guard dog. Is he your guard dog?'

'But it's not a dog …. … it's a sheep,' said the farmer, but without conviction. As the third robber took his leave, the farmer said to himself, 'I've been swindled! I thought I'd bought a sheep, but they've obviously sold me a dog! I don't need another dog!' With that he left the sheep by the roadside and continued on alone.

The robbers enjoyed their supper.

There are a number of incidents recorded in the Gospels in which, we are told, Jesus seems to act 'out of character'. The most famous one, of course, is of Jesus casting out the money changers in the temple, a scene which does not fit our image of him as a passive man of peace. John's Gospel tells us that he took a whip to them, and even though this might have been more of a symbolic gesture than a frenzied attack, his actions don't correspond terribly well with his words in the Sermon on the Mount about loving our enemies and turning the other cheek. Another example is the way he treats the Gentile woman who begs him to cure her disturbed daughter. 'It's not right to give the children's food to the dogs,'[17] he says, meaning that he was only prepared to heal the people of his own nation – 'the dogs' were all non-Jews. He eventually does heal the girl, but only after her mother has won him over with a smart rejoinder.

However, to say that on these and similar occasions Jesus was acting 'out of character' is really rather misleading. Our character comes out in what we do and what we say, and if Jesus said and did these things then they were part of his character. What we really mean is that Jesus seems to be acting in ways which don't quite square with the image of him that we carry around in our heads; but this image has been built up more from pious sermons, sentimental films, and apocryphal stories than from an actual close reading of the Gospel texts. According to the Gospels, Jesus was not always 'Mr. Nice Guy'; sometimes he could be extremely unpleasant. I have never found the Jesus of John's Gospel to be an appealing person at all. There are places where he seems to be arrogant, patronising, and self-righteous. On one occasion, in chapter 7, he even seems to be deceitful. 'You should go to Jerusalem to celebrate the Feast of Tabernacles,' say his brothers. 'No, I'm not going to go,' replies Jesus dismissively; but then he goes! And when he later tells his

---

[17] Mark 7:27

apostles that they are his friends *if they do what he tells them*,[18] I find myself losing patience with him as a genuinely sympathetic and humane person.

But then, the Gospels were never intended to present a sentimental picture of the perfect man, in touch with his feminine side, a kind of prototype of St. Francis of Assisi, or Mahatma Gandhi. The Gospels are not character studies. Whatever conventional Christians say, the Gospels do not give us a rounded portrait of a person to emulate. In his words and actions, Jesus is demonstrating and expounding important spiritual principles, and these sometimes demand what, to us, appear as inconsistency.

Nowhere is this more in evidence than in a little passage which occurs at the end of what I have called the Aries section of the Gospel, in which Jesus seems to be repudiating his family. 'Who is my mother, and who are my brothers?' he asks.

This is quite shocking isn't it? And it is particularly shocking to Catholics who have elevated Jesus's mother Mary to the status of goddess, and who have presented to us a picture of Jesus as a dutiful, obedient son within the 'holy family'. And it is also shocking to Catholics because it tells us unequivocally that Jesus had brothers and sisters, demolishing at a stroke the Catholic doctrine of the perpetual virginity of Mary, at least in so far as it is meant to be understood biologically.

But the embarrassment is not only to the Catholics. This passage calls into question Christendom's general portrait of Jesus as a man who upholds 'family values', so beloved by the American Christian right, although how one could ever assume that an unmarried, childless man whose mother was a virgin and whose father was a ghost could represent a typical human family has always puzzled me.

The tension between Jesus and his immediate family is illustrated a little earlier in Mark's Gospel, where we learn that his family members thought that he was out of his mind,[19] and the other Gospels say nothing to contradict it. From the early chapters of Luke's Gospel, we learn of a twelve-year-old Jesus listening to the wise men in the temple rather than returning home with his parents,

---

[18] John 15:14
[19] Mark 3:21

and in Matthew chapter 10, Jesus says, with almost unbelievable directness:

> Do not suppose that I have come to bring peace to the earth. I did not come to bring peace, but a sword. For I have come to turn a man against his father, a daughter against her mother, a daughter–in–law against her mother-in-law; a man's enemies will be the members of his own household. Anyone who loves his father or mother more than me is not worthy of me; anyone who loves his son or daughter more than me is not worthy of me.[20]

This is very unsettling stuff, which is probably why we don't hear it read aloud too often, but it is not a rant against monogamy or the nuclear family; it is not even a plea for more tolerance of alternative lifestyles. These passages are intended to alert us to an extremely important spiritual principle: that discovering and establishing one's identity, one's true individuality, within a communal context, and particularly within the family context, is extraordinarily difficult, but it is so important that nothing, not even those things demanded by our closest intimacies, can ever take precedence over it.

These incidents teach us that anyone intent on following the spiritual path has to break away from some pretty restricting and oppressive social conditioning, and the most effective agency of this conditioning is the family. We learn our earliest and most enduring lessons about life and relationships at our mother's knee; we inherit the family religion, or lack of it; we imbibe the family's values before we are weaned; we build a social identity by processing the thousands of messages which accumulate daily from the overt and subtle words and actions of our parents and our siblings. The family itself has its own dynamics, from the obvious age relationships among brothers and sisters - which usually requires the oldest child to be competent, the middle one to be troublesome, and the

---

[20] Matthew 10:34-38 (NIV)

youngest to be spoiled - to the designated roles which are apportioned early and which seem impossible to shake off.

The Australian psychologist Dorothy Rowe says that when we get beneath the cosy facade that most families tend to present to the world we find some pretty disturbing dynamics, particularly in regard to the allocation of roles. 'You have been given a role in the family which is yours for life,' she says. 'You cannot escape it.' She is the intelligent one, he is the sensitive one, she is the daydreamer, he is ambitious. Rowe says that the greatest compliment her mother could give to anyone was, 'He is always the same.'

But these disturbing words of Jesus tell us unequivocally that we must not allow the prejudices of our family to determine the course of our spiritual life. As the novelist Sue Monk Kidd says,[21] we have to pull away from the Collective They, to 'stand before the bare mystery of our own being.' 'I came to understand,' she writes, 'that there is an Authentic "I" within, an "I Am," or divine spark within the soul', and that this 'true identity' transcends the outer roles which have been bequeathed to us by our family and our culture. To discover this true identity, the mark of God upon us, something as distinctive and unique as our fingerprints, is the *raison d'être* of our existence, and the only guarantee of personal fulfilment and of collective harmony. Ignoring this, mistaking uniqueness for madness, in ourselves or in others, is what Jesus calls 'the unforgivable sin'. It's unforgivable because in committing it we have missed the whole point of our existence. In the works of the Sufi sage Rumi, we find it expressed thus:

> It is as if a king had sent you to a country to carry out one special, specific task. You go to the country and you perform a hundred other tasks, but if you have not performed the task you were sent for, it is as if you have performed nothing at all. So man has come into the world for a particular task, and this is his purpose. If he doesn't perform it, he will have done nothing.[22]

---

[21] Beliefnet.com Inspirational Story 7th April 2007
[22] Rinpoche, page 127

Each of us is responsible for bringing to birth that authentic self which lies buried beneath those layers of prejudice which stifle its emergence with their insistence on conformity, homogenisation, prosperity, celebrity, and a hundred and one other culturally sanctioned distractions. This is why the passage from Mark's Gospel in which Jesus is shown dissociating himself from his immediate family occurs where it does, in the Aries section of the Gospel, which would have been read and discussed at this time of the year, when the very trees and flowers around us are emerging from winter's collective homogeneity and beginning to express their individuality and uniqueness. 'Doing the will of God' does not mean behaving yourself, going to church on Sunday, living a respectable life; it means discovering and expressing the unique and precious part that only you can play in the great drama of existence. 'Who is my mother, and who are my brothers?' asks Jesus. He goes on, 'Those who do the will of God are my mother, my sisters and my brothers,' by which he did not mean that his biological family were disreputable people – they were probably anything but - but that true nurture can only be provided by those who have themselves broken away from the Collective They, and who are concerned to help you find your authentic, creative, unique self.

The Jews tell of a certain Rabbi Susya who used to say, 'When I die, God will not ask me why I wasn't Abraham, or why I wasn't Moses; he will ask me why I wasn't Susya.' The same is true of you and me. The success or otherwise of my life will not be determined by how rich I become, or how famous I become, or how influential I become, or how popular I become. It will not even be assessed by how well I have kept the rules, or how closely I have emulated the life of some great spiritual figure. God will not ask me why I haven't been another Jesus, or another Francis of Assisi. He will ask me why I allowed my inherited cultural and religious prejudices, and my desire for conformity and respectability, to prevent me from becoming Bill Darlison.

Chapter 2: Taurus

20th April – 20th May

Taurus is an Earth sign, and the Pleiades, a beautiful group of stars in the shoulder of the Bull, which has been called 'The Hen with her Chickens' by many cultures throughout history, was used by ancient farmers to mark their seeding time. This section of Mark uses the Greek word for 'earth'[23] (translated here variously as earth, ground, soil etc.) nine times, and nowhere else in the Gospel do we find such a wealth of agricultural imagery and vocabulary. In the ancient world Taurus was also associated with light, and was called The Bull of Light by the Egyptians, probably because in and around the constellation are some of the most beautiful sights in the night sky. Orion, one of the constellations near Taurus, was called The Light of Heaven by the Babylonians.

---

[23] γñ (gé)

Nurturing the Seed

Mark 4: 1-20

'Listen! Look! The sower went out to sow, and while he was sowing some seed fell by the roadside and the birds came along and ate it. Some fell on the rocks where there wasn't much soil; it sprang up very quickly because there was no real depth of soil, but when the Sun rose it was scorched and it withered because it didn't have any root. Some fell among the thorns, but the thorns came up and choked it and so it yielded no crop. But some fell on good soil where it grew and throve, yielding an abundant crop - When they were alone, those close to him, along with the twelve, began to question him about the parables, so he said to them, 'The mystery of the kingdom of God has been given to you, but to those on the outside, everything is expressed in parables so that although they may look they won't see, and although they may hear they won't understand in case they would need to turn around and forgiveness be given to them.

He said to them, 'If you don't understand this parable, how are you going to understand all the other parables? The sower is sowing the word. The seed that falls on the roadside represents those who hear the word but no sooner do they hear it than Satan comes along and takes it away from them. The seed that falls on the rocks are those people who hear the word and receive it with joy but they don't have any staying power, so they continue for a while but as soon as they encounter trouble or persecution on account of the word they let things slide. Then there are those represented by the seed among the thorns. They are the ones who hear the word but the cares of the time, the enticements of wealth and desires for all kinds of other things overwhelm them and choke the word so that they cease to be fruitful. But the seed that is sown on the good ground represents those who hear the word, receive it and produce fruit - thirtyfold, sixtyfold, and a hundredfold.'

Story: The Persistent Frog

Once upon a time there were two very inquisitive frogs. They liked nothing better than to go exploring the nooks and crannies of the riverbank, and sometimes they would venture even further on to the land in search of adventure. One day, as they were hopping around, they saw something they hadn't seen before: a big silver bucket.

'What's in this, I wonder?' said one

'I don't know,' said his friend, 'but let's go and look!'

Fortunately, the bucket was beside some steps, so it was easy for the two frogs to hop up the steps and peer into the pail. It was filled with milk! The frogs had never seen milk before, but it looked cool and inviting and, what's more, it looked good enough to drink, so they hopped off the top step and plunged into the bucket full of milk.

At first they were very happy. The milk was indeed good to drink, and they slurped and slurped until they could drink no more. But it wasn't too long before they were bored. They'd seen all they wanted to see, and drunk all they wanted to drink. 'Let's get out of here,' said one.

But that was easier said than done. They tried to jump out of the milk but they couldn't jump over the side of the bucket. Sometimes they would get near the top but then they would slide down the sides back into the milk. They tried and tried for a long time, but then one of them said, 'I can't do this anymore. I'm worn out.' He gave up and, sadly, he drowned in the bucket of milk.

The other frog was determined not to be beaten. 'I'm never going to give up,' he said to himself. He continued to paddle with his little feet and to attempt a jump every now and then but, as before, he just hit the slippery side of bucket and slid back down into the milk. He was really tired by now, and almost ready to give up, when he felt something solid under his feet. He stepped onto this solid platform, jumped, and he was out of the bucket!

What had happened?

'Consistency, Madam, is the first of Christian duties.'
Charlotte Bronte (born 21st April 1816)

On our recent daily walks through St. Stephen's Green, Morag and I have been noticing the dramatic changes occurring in the trees and shrubs. A month or so ago, there was the budding: shoots pushing tentatively through the hardened, frosty soil, embryonic leaves scattered among the still skeletal trees. But now, the place is awash with colour, and the pathways are submerged under a canopy of green. The ducks on the lake are squawking busily, the birds are building their nests, and young couples are lazing on the grass, whispering sweet nothings as they enjoy the returning sunshine.

Spring has really taken hold. Every day brings new delights; trees seem to blossom overnight, and the bare branches of yesterday are today wrapped in pink and gold. The Sun has entered Taurus, the sign of growth, profusion, opulence, sensuality, pleasure. The ancient symbol for this sign was the priapic, fertile, but languid bull, who scatters his seed where he may, who seems to have no purpose other than copulation and procreation, and who guards his own territory and his own females with jealous ferocity.

Taurus is the first of what the old astrologers called the Earth signs, and it is indeed the most 'earthy' of them all. People who are strongly Taurean are aware of, and sometimes obsessed by, their own physicality, and by the material nature of the universe. They are 'ruled' by Venus, the goddess of love and beauty, and they rejoice in the flesh and its appetites, although Chaucer's sensual Wife of Bath laments the fact that being born under Taurus has brought her nothing but trouble: 'Taurus rising, with Mars therein, Alas, alas, that ever love were sin!' she cries.

But Taurus is not only about sensuality and sex. More philosophers seem to be born under Taurus than under any other sign. In the summer of 2005, BBC Radio 4 held a poll to find out Britain's favourite philosopher. The results were, to me at least, quite astonishing. The winner was Karl Marx, born on May 5th; the runner up was David Hume, born on 26th April; and in third place was Ludwig Wittgenstein, also born on 26th April. Immanuel Kant, born on 22nd April was sixth. All of these were born under the sign of Taurus. In fact, since no one knows the birthdays of Socrates, Plato, Aristotle, and St. Thomas Aquinas, only two of the top ten – Karl Popper (Leo), and Friedrich Nietzsche (Libra) - were certainly *not* born under Taurus. Although we don't know the birthday of Thomas Aquinas, the fact that his student peers called him 'The Dumb Ox' would certainly indicate Taurus, and May birthdays have been suggested for both Socrates and Plato. This means that seven of the top ten were certainly or probably born under Taurus. This is a remarkable statistic, and although it may be dismissed as 'coincidental' by mathematicians (who, by the way, are a strongly Taurean body, too), it should come as no surprise to students of astrology. Taurus is the sign which symbolises our relationship with the material universe, and so its sons and daughters should have a particular interest in attempting to define the nature of that relationship, which, on one level at least, is the function of philosophy.

It is the sign of the builder, and it is surely not without significance that some of the human race's grandest and most enduring structures – including Stonehenge, Newgrange, and the pyramids of Egypt - were erected during the astrological age of Taurus (c. 4,000 – c. 2,000 BCE). [24]

The ancient writers weren't terribly kind to people born under Taurus, considering them best fitted for agricultural work. A Taurus man is a 'dull, honest ploughman', according to the Roman writer Manilius, fit for tilling the ground and manuring the field, and while the Taurean philosophers don't often spend their time spreading manure (except figuratively, perhaps!), they do tend to expound one version or another of 'no nonsense' materialism – 'if

---

[24] For an explanation of Astrological Ages see Chapter 11: The Age of Aquarius below.

you can't see it, touch it, taste it, hear it, or smell it, it doesn't exist' - which Britain's pragmatic and sceptical Radio 4 listeners seem to find so congenial. Marx's 'dialectical materialism', John Stuart Mill's Utilitarianism, and David Hume's scepticism, all bear the unmistakeable signature of Taurus. Thomas Reid, another Taurean, was called 'the common sense philosopher'; Bertrand Russell, yet another, was a thoroughgoing materialist, prepared even to reduce human thought to chemistry; and Wittgenstein, who, in true Taurus style, designed and built a house in Vienna for his sister, summed up the anti-metaphysical bias of Taurus when he said, 'Whereof we cannot speak, thereof we must be silent'. The sons and daughters of Taurus certainly seem to have their feet on the ground.

There is another very important link between Taurus and the earth. The constellation Taurus contains the Pleiades, one of the most conspicuous and beautiful sights in the night sky, six or seven stars (depending on your eyesight) closely packed together, which have probably inspired ancient poets and mythmakers more than any other stellar grouping. But they were also used by farmers throughout the ancient world to mark the times of planting and of harvesting. Virgil says that any farmer who doesn't use the Pleiades to tell him when to plant his crops, will undoubtedly pay a heavy price.

All of which helps us to understand why, in this second section of his Gospel, Mark has given us a number of parables which are based almost entirely on agricultural imagery, the principal one being the Parable of the Sower, which we heard as our second reading today, which teaches us how we should approach those important aspects of life which are symbolised by Taurus.

Remember the story. The Sower, who stands for God, sows his seed on four different types of ground: by the roadside, on rocky soil, among thorns, and on good soil. The seed that falls by the roadside is soon pecked up by the birds; the seed that falls on the rocky ground grows quite quickly, but it has no real roots and is scorched by the Sun; the seed which falls among the thorns grows for a while, but is choked by the thorns; only the seed which falls on the good soil yields an abundant crop.

The parable describes four different ways of responding to the spiritual call, the call to a transformed existence. Some will barely hear it; others will receive the message gladly, and will even make a very promising start on living the spiritual life, but they will burn out before too long, especially when the going gets tough as it inevitably will (a bit like the beautiful magnolia tree, which blossoms spectacularly, but only for a couple of weeks); some are so distracted by their carnal appetites and their desire for material possessions that any spiritual impulse they might have felt is completely overwhelmed by the cares and concerns of the world. Only the fourth group, the persistent ones, will show any real fruitage. (Only consistent effort by the frog in our story will churn the milk into butter!)

The lesson is very simple: the impulse to embark on a life of self-transformation – that impulse symbolised in the Aries section of Mark's Gospel by the apostles impetuously following Jesus - is not enough. All of us will feel that impulse at some time or another, at a moment of transcendent joy such as the birth of a child, perhaps, or when overcome by the beauty of some aspect of the natural world. Maybe something we read, something we hear, or someone we meet will plant the seed. Often, it will be when things don't seem to be going right, and we begin to ask the big questions. 'Is this all there is?' 'Is it just eat, drink, and be merry for tomorrow I die?'

And we'll answer such questions for ourselves, concluding perhaps that there *is* something more than this, that, to quote the great Taurean mystic Rabindranath Tagore, 'the world holds a deeper meaning than what is apparent', and we'll want to pursue it, to find out what the meaning is, to discover who we intrinsically are, and what our life is really about. And it's a fine and noble impulse, and all of us here have felt it, in fact we wouldn't be here *unless* we had felt it, but the Parable of the Sower warns us that the impulse alone is virtually worthless. The circumstances which give rise to the impulse are fleeting, whatever we might think at the time and, when our circumstances change, our resolve can evaporate as we become embroiled in the market place once more, 'getting and spending', convincing ourselves that a little more money, a better job, a bigger house, a better car, more holidays, more status, winning the lottery, will turn our life around and make us happy.

Such things – mammon, material possessions – are what the Book of Job calls the 'sweet delights' of Taurus,[25] and they can choke the spiritual life. In the Jewish scriptures, the material world is symbolised by Egypt, the place where the belly is full but where the spirit is enslaved. When the Children of Israel escape into the wilderness, into freedom, they are constantly complaining that they want to go back to the 'flesh pots'

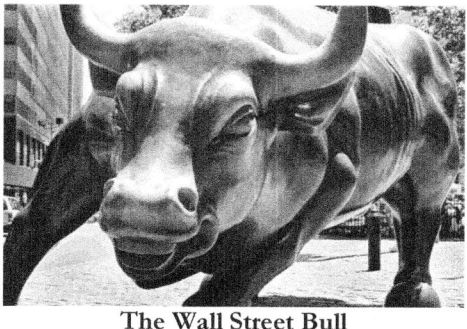

The Wall Street Bull

of Egypt. They have their freedom, but they don't want it, and would gladly trade it for a varied diet, even though this would mean returning to slavery, making bricks from straw – a beautiful Taurean image! And what do they do when Moses leaves them for a while to meet God on the mountain? They build a golden calf and worship it. It's strange, isn't it, how the ancient images crop up in our modern culture? The 'bull market' is the investor's delight, when stocks and shares are increasing in value and, on Wall Street, at the very heart of the Western economic system, there is the great big Taurean bull, introduced no doubt unconsciously, but demonstrating the power of these ancient symbols to transcend cultures and ages.

According to the Parable of the Sower, what we need to cultivate in order to overcome the temptations of Taurus is the great Taurean virtue, steadfastness. The astrological writer Isabella Pagan tells us that:

> The chief characteristic of the highly developed Taurean type is his stability of character and of purpose. He is the steadfast mind, unshaken in adversity, and his the power of quiet persistence in the face of difficulties ... in hard circumstances

---

[25] Job 38:31

his patience and perseverance are marvellous.'[26]

Persistence in the spiritual life is what we are all called upon to exercise. The seed has been planted, but it has to be nurtured – consistently and carefully. Last Friday, as Morag and I were taking our walk around St. Stephen's Green, we came across Chris Tormey,[27] and we spoke briefly about the beauty and profusion of the trees and the shrubs that surrounded us. 'That reminds me,' said Chris, 'I must go home and water my plants.' Chris has got it right. It's no good just planting a seed and hoping for the best. The plant has to be fed and watered.

So it is with the things of the spirit. They, too, must be watered. Do you remember the story of the manna in the book of Exodus?[28] Manna was the food that God provided for the Israelites. It came daily, and there was just enough. Any that was left over began to rot and stink. This is a perfect image of spiritual nurture. It is a daily affair. We have to keep our spirits alive by consistent care, ensuring that *daily* prayer, *daily* meditation, a *daily* period of withdrawal and silence, *daily* acts of kindness are built into our lives. Only then can the impulse take root and grow.

Only then will there be any hope of an abundant harvest.

Letting the Light Shine

Mark 4: 21 - 34

> And he said to them, 'You don't bring in a lamp and then put it under a measuring basket, or under the bed? No, you put it on a lamp stand, don't you? So, there's nothing hidden that will not be revealed; and what's been carefully concealed will be brought into the open. Use your ears and take notice of what I'm saying.'

---

[26] Pagan, page 23
[27] Chris is a member of the Dublin Unitarian congregation.
[28] Exodus 16

And he said to them, 'Take notice of what you are hearing; 'What you receive by way of increase will be in proportion to what you give out; and to him who has it will be given and to him who has not, what he has will be taken from him.'

And he said, 'The kingdom of God is like a man who scatters some seed on the ground and he sleeps by night and gets up by day and the seed sprouts and grows, but how it happens he doesn't know. Things grow by their own power; first the shoot, then the ear of grain, then the full head of corn. And when it is ready, he puts in the scythe because it's time for the harvest.

And he said, 'With what can we compare the kingdom of God? What comparison can we use to describe it? It's like a grain of mustard seed which, at the time that it's sown in the ground is smaller than all the seeds of the earth, but after it's sown it grows and becomes bigger than all other plants and produces branches so massive that the birds of heaven can nest in its shade.

And using many parables like these he told them just as much as they were able to grasp. Indeed, he didn't speak to them except by means of a parable, but he explained everything privately to his disciples.

Story: The Dog in the Hall of Mirrors

There once was a dog who wondered into a room filled with mirrors. The dog looked around and seeing all of the other dogs, growled and showed his teeth. Upon seeing all of the other dogs do the same, he got frightened and cowered. When he noticed the other dogs cowering, he once again growled and started barking. A similar reaction from the others made him cower and become very frightened once again. This continued over and over until the dog finally fell over, dead from emotional and physical exhaustion. One must stop and consider what would have happened if the dog had only once wagged its tail. The world is merely a reflection of our attitude toward it.

Two weeks ago I was speaking about the Parable of the Sower, which can be found in the fourth chapter of Mark's Gospel – the chapter which I believe reflects the zodiacal sign of Taurus, the first of the so-called Earth signs. The imagery of this chapter is almost entirely agricultural, and the lessons of the section concern growth in the spiritual life. Today I want to have a cursory look at some of the other parables which can be found in this section, but first I want to talk about parables in general: what are parables, and why are they such a popular means of instruction among the world's great spiritual teachers?

The word 'parable' comes from the Greek, and it means 'thrown beside'. A parable is something – usually, but not necessarily, a story – which is placed beside something else for the sake of comparison. The parable is an attempt to explain in simple narrative terms something that would otherwise appear complicated or abstruse, and spiritual teachers have used them since the beginning of time for three main reasons. First, they have the natural appeal of all stories. No matter how old we are, or how sophisticated we consider ourselves to be, we are all captivated by the words, 'Once upon a time ...' Stories cannot fail to get our attention. The second reason is that stories engage our imagination and our judgement in ways that theological discourse does not. With a story we are obliged to come to our own conclusions, and these conclusions may differ according to the individual, so there is an 'open-ended' quality to a story, and room for the imagination to roam around.

The third, but by no means the least important reason, is that stories are memorable; generally speaking, we only need to hear a story - or a joke - once before we are ready to tell it, and once it is fixed in the memory it can be accessed even years later without too much trouble. Contrast this with mathematical theorems, chemical formulae, historical dates, geographical features, theological propositions and the like, which stay in our memory just long enough for us to use them in the examination before disappearing without trace. Sarah Tinker, our minister in Kensington, tells how she recently met up with a group of old school friends and they discussed what they could remember about their years of secondary schooling. The only thing they had a clear memory of from a dozen years of schooling was the formation of an ox-bow lake. It's a common experience, which our educators, with their growing concern to impart a 'body' of knowledge, would do well to take notice of. But, for all that these women have forgotten the facts, I'll bet they can remember the stories their teachers told them, or read to them. I can certainly recall the ones that I was told. I can still remember, well over fifty years ago, listening while the teacher read us the *Labours of Hercules,* or *The Adventures of Wurzel Gummidge,* or *Peter Pan,* or *Children of the New Forest.* Facts disappear: stories stick.

The power of the story was not lost on Jesus. When asked – as reported in Luke's Gospel – 'Who is my neighbour?'[29] by a man who wanted to put him to the test, Jesus did not reply with a philosophical or sociological definition, like: 'In popular usage, your neighbour is the person who lives in close proximity, usually next door. But, taken in a wider sense, it refers to anyone who may be in need of your assistance.' No. Jesus told a story. 'A certain man was travelling from Jerusalem to Jericho ....' he began, and he went on to tell the story of the Good Samaritan, one of the most important and memorable stories in the whole of religious literature. And at the end of the story, Jesus's questioner was asked to draw his own conclusions, thereby producing an impact on the listener that would be impossible with a lengthy and convoluted argument.

But the spiritual story was not the invention of Jesus. In the Jewish scriptures we read how Nathan the prophet brought King David to repent his shameful treatment of Uriah the Hittite by telling him a story. David was taking the air on the roof of his house one day when he spied the beautiful Bathsheba, whose husband Uriah was away at the wars. David seduced her and, on learning that she had become pregnant, arranged for her husband to be killed. He then took her as his own wife. The prophet Nathan came to David and told him the story of a poor man who had just one lamb, which he treated like one of his own children. However, a rich man, with plenty of sheep, had an unexpected visitor, and so he took the poor

---

[29] Luke 10:29

man's lamb and slaughtered it. 'What do you think should happen to such a man?' asks Nathan. 'He is deserving of death,' thundered an indignant David. 'You are that man,' says Nathan, fearlessly. 'Stealing the wife of Uriah the Hittite was even more reprehensible than what this rich man did.' Nathan's parable alerted David to the monstrous nature of his sin.[30]

The stories I tell the children here on Sundays are for the most part similar spiritual parables, and the fact that they are taken from all of the world's spiritual traditions – Buddhist, Hindu, Jewish, Christian etc. – underlines the ubiquity of the story as a vital aid in spiritual teaching. Today's story, the Dog in the Hall of Mirrors, from the Zen Buddhist tradition, illustrates one of the oldest and most widespread spiritual teachings of all: the principle of karma, or the notion that the external world reflects the internal disposition. If you perceive the world as hostile it is because you yourself are harbouring hostility; remove your own hostility and you'll find that the external world will cease to threaten you. This principle is also found in chapter four of Mark's Gospel, although it does not appear in story form. 'What you give out will be what you get back,' says Jesus.

How strange then, in the light of all this, that Jesus says something very odd about parables in the Gospel of Mark. He doesn't say that he tells parables because they are pithy, engaging, memorable, or powerful, as we might expect. He says that he tells them *in order to keep the truth from people*.

> When he was alone, the Twelve and the others around him asked him about the parables. He told them, 'The secret of the kingdom of God has been given to you. But to those on the outside everything is said in parables, so that "they may be ever seeing but never perceiving, and ever hearing but never understanding otherwise they might turn and be forgiven."'[31]

---

[30] See 2 Samuel 11-12
[31] Mark 4:10-11 (NIV)

What is implied here is that there is a secret teaching which is only imparted to a certain few – those 'inside the house'; to those 'on the outside' everything is given in parables.

We can only guess the nature of that secret teaching, but I am sure that it had something to do with the approach to Mark's Gospel which we are studying in these sessions: that there is a 'hidden' meaning behind all the Gospel stories, and that this meaning will only be imparted to those who are ready to receive it. The rest will have to be content with parables.

But this 'hidden meaning' will not remain hidden for ever. In the verses which immediately follow the Parable of the Sower, Jesus says,

> Do you bring in a lamp to put it under a bowl or a bed? Instead, don't you put it on its stand? For whatever is hidden is meant to be disclosed, and whatever is concealed is meant to be brought out into the open. If anyone has ears to hear, let him hear.[32]

This is the only 'parable' in this section which does not use agricultural imagery, and when I began investigating the zodiacal structure of Mark, I wondered what possible connection it could have with the sign Taurus. I considered the possibility that it was an interpolation – that is, a passage slipped in by a later editor. But when I studied the astronomy and the mythology associated with Taurus I realised that it was precisely where it should be. In the ancient world, Taurus was always associated with 'light' principally because in and around the constellation Taurus are some of the most spectacular sights in the night sky. Orion, which dominates the winter sky and is probably the one constellation which everyone can identify, is close by Taurus, and Taurus itself was called 'The Bull of Light' by the Babylonians. In the shoulder of the Bull are the Pleiades, which have inspired more poetry and song than any other stellar grouping, and, as I mentioned last time, were used by farmers in the ancient world to determine when they would plant and harvest their crops.

---

[32] Mark 4:21-23 (NIV)

But what the ancient sky watchers found so intriguing about the Pleiades was the fact that there was no agreement about how many stars the naked eye could see. Some authors say that you can see six, some say you can see seven. Consequently, the mythology of the Pleiades concerned seven daughters, six of whom were married to gods, and so became immortal, but one of whom was married to a mortal; so, while six immortal stars shone brightly, the mortal one was only dimly visible, and only occasionally seen. Now we can understand why this little piece occurs where it does in Mark: 'For whatever is hidden is meant to be disclosed, and whatever is concealed is meant to be brought out into the open.'

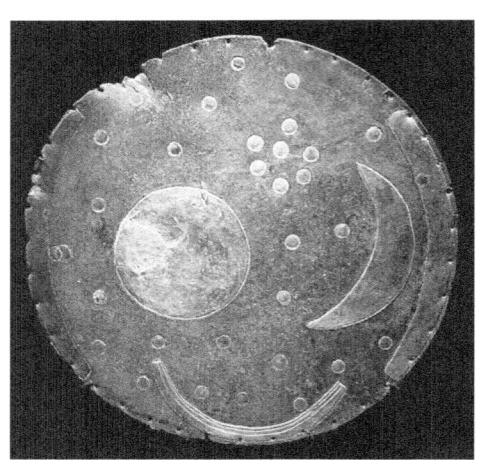

The Nebra Disk (c.1660 BCE)
(The Pleiades are top right)

We must be careful not to misinterpret this little saying of Jesus. It is not a threat of exposure and embarrassment: it is a promise of enlightenment. Jesus is not saying that God, like some celestial Big Brother, is spying on us and that every one of our secret vices will be made known to the world at some time in the future; he is saying that the deepest and most obscure truths about the nature of the world and the purpose of human life can and will become clear to us. How will that occur? Jesus says that we don't know how, any more than we know how it is that the seed which the farmer scatters on the ground eventually becomes a plant. The farmer simply does what he has to do and trusts that the mysterious process of transformation will take place.

So it is with our own enlightenment. It does not require us to engage in some self-conscious and narcissistic activity called 'spiritual development'. The promise is that it will come to us, unbidden, as we go about our daily life in a spirit of wakeful attentiveness. Listen to this piece by Taurean writer, Annie Dillard:[33]

> Then one day I was walking along Tinker Creek thinking of nothing at all and I saw the tree with the lights in it. I saw the backyard cedar where the mourning doves roost charged and transfigured, each cell buzzing with flame. I stood on the grass with the lights in it, grass that was wholly fire, utterly focused and utterly dreamed. It was less like seeing than like being for the first time seen, knocked breathless by a powerful glance. The lights of the fire abated, but I'm still spending the power. Gradually the lights went out in the cedar, the colors died, the cells unflamed and disappeared. I was still ringing. I had my whole life been a bell, and never knew it until at that moment I was lifted and struck. I have since only rarely seen the tree with the lights in it. The vision comes and goes, mostly goes, but I live for it, for the moment when the mountains open and a new light roars in spate through the crack, and the mountains slam….."[34]

When the seed of the Spirit is nurtured and watered by constant care; when we trust in the power of the Spirit to transform our lives in its own way and in its own time, then we may begin to hear the divine voice within the apparently chaotic and cacophonous sounds of the world. We may not be able to articulate what we discover; we will certainly not be able to put it into a creed or a series of propositions; but when we suddenly realise that 'the thorn-bush by the wayside is aflame with the glory of God',[35] we will know that our world has been transformed and the kingdom of God has arrived.

---

[33] Annie Dillard, born April 30th, 1945
[34] Annie Dillard, *Pilgrim at Tinker Creek*
[35] From a prayer by Walter Rauschenbusch.

Chapter 3: Gemini

21ˢᵗ May – 20th June

Gemini, the Twins, is the first of the Air signs, and concerns duality, fragmentation ('my name is Legion, for we are many' says the man with the demons), communication (Jesus sends out the apostles to preach), brothers and sisters (Jesus's siblings are named in this section). Gemini's strength is versatility, its weakness duplicity. The two principal stars in the constellation are Castor and Pollux, the gods to whom Greek sailors would appeal when in distress at sea. The Gemini section begins with an account of a storm on the lake in which the distressed apostles make an appeal to Jesus. Notice the unusual construction of the story of Jairus' Daughter and the Woman with the Blood Flow: it's the only 'double' miracle in the Gospel, and these two miracles emphasise the need to reawaken the feminine, the neglected polarity. In this section, the apostles are sent out 'in twos' and told not to take 'two coats' with them. This is the only place in the Gospel which mentions Sodom and Gomorrah, 'the twin cities of the plain'. The story about Herod's encounter with John the Baptist shows Herod to be 'in two minds' (he likes and respects John the Baptist but he nevertheless orders him to be killed). Herod offers the daughter of Herodias 'half his kingdom' as a reward for her dancing.

I Contain Multitudes

Mark 5: 1- 20:

They came to the other side of the lake into the land of the Gerasenes, and no sooner was he out of the boat than a man with an unclean spirit approached him. This man was living among the tombs in the graveyard and he was so out of control that no one could subdue him or even chain him. In the past he'd been bound hand and foot, but he'd pulled the chains apart and smashed the shackles. Night and day among the tombs and on the mountains he was crying out and bruising himself with stones. When he saw Jesus in the distance he ran and fell on his knees, paying him homage and shouting at the top of his voice, 'What's your business with me, Jesus, son of God Most High? I beg you in God's name don't torment me!' He said this because Jesus was ordering the unclean spirit to come out of him. Jesus asked, 'What is your name?' He replied, 'My name is Legion; there's a whole gang of us.' He kept begging Jesus not to send them all out of that region.

There was a great herd of pigs feeding on the hillside, and the demons shouted out, 'Send us into the pigs! We want to go into them!' Jesus gave them permission, and the unclean spirits came out and entered the pigs, and the herd of about two thousand dashed headlong down the steep slope into the sea where they drowned. The herdsmen ran off and told the story so that people came from town and country to see what had happened. They came to Jesus and they looked at the man who'd been possessed by the legion of demons, and when they saw that he was now dressed and sane they were terrified. Those who had witnessed it related what had happened to the possessed man and to the pigs, and they began to implore Jesus to leave their neighbourhood. When he got into the boat, the man who'd been possessed begged that he might go along with him, but Jesus wouldn't allow it, and said to him, 'Go home to your family and tell them what the Lord has done for you and how he's taken pity on you.'

Story: What colour would you be?

One day, a teacher asked her class, 'If all the good people in the world were blue, and all the bad people were yellow, what colour would you be?'

Without hesitation, the children began to shout out their answers.

'I'd be blue,' shouted one. 'My mother says I'm a little angel.'

'I'd be blue, too,' said another 'I try my best to behave myself.'

'I'd be yellow,' said one girl, who thought herself a bit of a tearaway.

Mary didn't put up her hand with the rest. She just sat there, pondering the question. 'What about you, Mary? What colour would you be?' asked the teacher.

'I think I'd be green,' said Mary.

Last week the Irish tabloids went to town on the case of a Catholic priest who had been tricked into revealing details of his homosexuality to a journalist. Pictures of the priest in his underpants appeared in the press midweek and the poor man has had to take temporary leave of absence, but it is doubtful that he will ever be able to return to the parish that he has served so well for so many years. 'I'm so ashamed says gay priest', runs the headline in the *Irish Daily Mail*, and inside there is the regulation stuff about homosexuals in the clergy, and the Catholic Church's celibacy laws, plus conflicting views about whether a man who has broken his vows is fit to minister. All perfectly predictable, of course, but the debate was given an added dimension because this man (whom I refuse to name) had been an exemplary pastor, much loved by his people, who, in a high profile incident four years ago, had been a source of comfort and solace to a young family who lost a child in tragic circumstances.

The *Irish Daily Mail* tried to be fair – in so far as devoting the front page and two inside pages to a case like this in which no laws have been broken can ever be considered fair – by printing an article by Roslyn Dee with the headline 'This man needs sympathy not sanctimony' to balance the 'I'm sorry but his actions are sinful' rant by Hermann Kelly. But the intention of this kind of journalism is always to leave us shaking our heads as we pose the question, 'Can a man with unusual sexual tastes be a caring and effective counsellor and friend? Can a sinner be a good priest?' 'Is he this, or is he that?'

The answer is, he's both, and a good deal besides. He's a complicated, flawed human being, neither blue nor yellow, but green, just like you and me, just like the *Sun* journalist who 'exposed' him and who now can, presumably, sleep comfortably in his bed, secure in the knowledge that he has protected the community from yet another sex fiend, while at the same time banking a sizeable cheque from his editor.

How we long to sum someone up in a sentence or two, or even a word or two. But the fact is that we can't really give a comprehensive definition of anybody. Each of us, celebrity and nonentity alike, is a complex mixture of contradictory features. Mother Theresa, champion of the poor, supped with oppressive dictators; Gandhi, dedicated to celibacy, slept with young women 'to test his resolve'; Dickens, whose works relentlessly attack cruelty and injustice, treated his first wife abominably; Hitler, the 20th century's most reviled man, was a vegetarian and would weep at the music of Wagner; Martin Luther King, a contemporary saint and martyr, found it difficult to keep his trousers buttoned, as did the influential theologian Paul Tillich. When I spoke on this topic before – at the beginning of 2004 – the previous day's paper, rather coincidentally, furnished two more examples: an article about Ronnie Biggs, the great train robber, written by his son, entitled, 'My Beloved Father, the Train Robber', and a review of a biography of Carl Jung, which appeared under the headline, 'A Man in Two

Minds', told us that he was 'never quite sure which of the two versions of himself he was most impressed by, the inspired, tormented eccentric, or the respectable, assured, bourgeois professional'. Jung, undoubtedly one of the most remarkable spiritual writers of modern times, was called by Freud 'a snob and a mystic' and Freud was right on both counts. Jung's lifelong quest for God did not eliminate his equally lifelong obsession with glamorous cars.

Tolstoy, whose novels delineate human motivation with unparalleled sensitivity, was, we are told, quite indifferent to his wife and family, and Tolstoy himself expresses this paradoxical quality of the human being in his last novel, *Resurrection*:

> One of the most widespread superstitions is that every person has his or her own special definite qualities: that he or she is kind, cruel, wise, stupid, energetic, apathetic, and so on. People are not like that. We may say of a man that he is more often kind than cruel, more often wise than stupid, more often energetic than apathetic, or the reverse, but it would not be true to say of one man that he is kind and wise, and another that he is bad and stupid. And yet we always classify people in this way. And this is false … …Every person bears within him or herself the germs of every human quality, but sometimes one quality manifests itself, sometimes another, and the person often becomes unlike him or herself, while still remaining the same person.[36]

To be human is to be complex and inconsistent, and one would expect that the spiritual writers of the past should be alert to such a conspicuous – and troublesome - feature of our nature. And so they are. Mark's Gospel deals with it in the third section, what I have called the Gemini section, which would have been read and discussed at this time of the year, when the Sun has entered the sign of Gemini. Gemini is the Twins, the first of those signs which modern astrologers call 'Mutable' – changeable – but which the ancient Greek writers called 'two-bodied'. These signs – Gemini,

---

[36] Tolstoy, Page 211

Virgo, Sagittarius and Pisces – come in between the four seasons of the year and so each of them bears the qualities of two states of weather. Gemini comes between spring and summer, and has characteristics of both. Its symbol is the twin poles joined at top and bottom (♊), expressing the duality of the season and, according to the old theory, the duality inherent in all of us, but especially in those who are born at this time of the year.

The two stars of the constellation Gemini are Castor and Pollux which, in mythology were said to be the protectors of sailors. A poem attributed to Homer refers to the 'great twin brethren', who, he said, would swiftly come to the aid of sailors in distress, lulling the storm and enabling the mariners to 'plough the quiet sea in safe delight'. Now we can understand why Mark introduces this third section of his Gospel with the story of the Calming of the Storm. But this is not the story I want to concentrate on today (I'll be dealing with it next week). Today I'm more interested in the episode which follows it, the story of the man possessed by 2000 demons, since this deals with the idea of human inconsistency in a particularly vivid way.

This man, often referred to as the Gerasene Demoniac, had been living among the tombs, and no one could bind him or restrain him.[37] 'What is your name?' asks Jesus. The man's reply is strange: 'My name is Legion, for we are many,' he says. Jesus casts out the demons, sending them into two thousand pigs which go hurtling down the steep bank and drown in the lake.[38]

This incident with the pigs always used to trouble me, especially in former times when I believed that the Gospels were history of a sort; the story would probably vex animal rights activists even now. But I no longer waste my energies asking mundane, practical questions of spiritual stories. The story has no historical basis, but it does have a psychological one: this man with the demons is you and I. Each of us has a number of warring elements within our psyche, and the pig, which, according to the Book of Leviticus[39] is unclean to Jews *because it has a split hoof, completely divided,*

---

[37] In a parallel story, Matthew has *two* demoniacs (Matthew 8:28-34)
[38] A Roman legion typically consisted of 6,000 soldiers. The 2,000 in Mark's story is another Geminian reference.
[39] Leviticus 11:7

symbolises this fragmentation; the division of the pig's foot mirrors the multiple divisions in the human mind.

With the benefits of modern psychiatric knowledge, we cannot fail to see in the man with the two thousand demons an example of that most Geminian of conditions, schizophrenia, or split-personality. In fact, the term 'multiple-personality' would be a better description. This is an actual mental disorder, but we do not need to restrict the use of the term to describe those in whom the symptoms manifest so dramatically. We are all 'split-personalities', since, as Aldous Huxley tells us, the complex human personality is made up of 'a quite astonishingly improbable combination of traits'. He goes on:

> Thus a man can be at once the craftiest of politicians and the dupe of his own verbiage, can have a passion, for brandy and money, and an equal passion for the poetry of George Meredith and under-age girls and his mother, for horse-racing and detective stories and the good of his country – the whole accompanied by a sneaking fear of hell-fire, a hatred of Spinoza and an unblemished record for Sunday church-going.[40]

The character and career of British publisher Robert Maxwell (born 10th June, 1923) provide a spectacular example of this. Following his death in November 1991, *The Guardian* newspaper printed an assessment of the man by British journalist Geoffrey Goodman. Goodman asked how it had been possible for Maxwell to fool so many people for so long. He continues:

> My own theory from observations of the man at close quarters during the year and a half I worked for him at the *Daily Mirror* is that he was at all times at least 20 different people at once. It was usually impossible to know which one I was dealing with at any one moment - and I later came to the conclusion that he wasn't sure either. The 20 different personalities were in constant struggle with each other.... [41]

---

[40] Huxley, page 48
[41] *The Guardian*. December 6th 1991, page 21

The practitioners of Assagioli's system of personality integration, Psychosynthesis, often refer to the crowd-like nature of the human psyche. And Geminian Salman Rushdie (born 19th June, 1947), writes:

> O, the dissociations of which the human mind is capable, marvelled Saladin gloomily. O, the conflicting selves jostling and joggling within these bags of skin. No wonder we are unable to remain focused on anything for long; no wonder we invent remote-control channel-hopping devices. If we turned these instruments on ourselves we'd discover more channels than a cable or satellite mogul ever dreamed of.[42]

Peter Ouspensky, who was a disciple of the Russian mystic Gurdieff, likens the ordinary human being – you and me – to a house full of servants without a master or a steward to look after them. 'So, the servants do what they like; none of them does his own work. The house is in a state of complete chaos, because all the servants try to do someone else's work which they are not competent to do. The cook works in the stables, the coachman in the kitchen, and so on. The only possibility for things to improve is if a certain number of servants decide to elect one of themselves as a deputy steward and in this way make him control the other servants. He can do only one thing: he puts each servant where he belongs and so they begin to do their right work.'[43] This, says Ouspensky, is the beginning of the creation of a 'controlling I'; until that time we are a great many disconnected I's, divided into certain groups, some of which don't even know each other.

Walt Whitman (born May 31st 1819) puts it more succinctly than all of them:

> Do I contradict myself?
> Very well then, I contradict myself.
> (I am large, I contain multitudes.)[44]

---

[42] Rushdie, page 519
[43] Ouspensky, P., page 137
[44] Whitman, W. page 72 (*Song of Myself*, section 51)

Walt Whitman

We can all say, 'My name is Legion' with the demon-possessed man, or 'I am large, I contain multitudes' with Walt Whitman. 'When a man lacks discrimination, his will wanders in all directions, after innumerable aims,' says the Hindu classic, *The Bhagavad Gita*. But the spiritual writers do not stop at mere observation; the object of all spiritual practice, whatever the tradition, is the transformation of Legion into Union, the reduction of the many to the one, the fashioning of singularity and simplicity from duality and complexity. This difficult movement towards simplicity, and not the pleasant cultivation of 'nice feelings' is what, in large part, any genuine spiritual practice attempts to effect. Aldous Huxley maintains that the saint is characterised by simplicity and singularity of purpose, qualities which are completely at odds with the lifestyle and appetites of sophisticated and mentally active people like ourselves, who constantly seek novelty, diversity, and distraction. The actions of the saints, says Huxley, 'are as monotonously uniform as their thoughts; for in all circumstances they behave selflessly, patiently, and with indefatigable charity'. Their biographies, he goes on, are of no interest to us because 'Legion prefers to read about Legion';[45] complexity and contradiction fascinate us; simplicity leaves us unmoved

Becoming 'simple', or becoming saintly, requires effort, and it may well be that, for most of us, it is an unappealing prospect. I

---

[45] Huxley, page 55

seem to be quite content in my diversity, so I cannot recommend that you take inordinate steps to reduce your own. I'm not ready to cast out my demons, so maybe I'm not ready for sainthood yet! (It is important to point out, I think, that we need to *control* our diverse elements, not destroy them.) But Ouspensky, who devised a complicated system specially designed to bring about a psychic unity, tells us that the first stage on the way to transformation is the *realisation* of one's own fragmentation, and the *acceptance* of it as a reality, and this can only come with constant self-observation. I am certainly prepared to do this. Learn to become aware of your own inconsistency, your own automatic reactions to circumstances, because each time we make ourselves aware of these things, says Ouspensky, their hold upon us is weakened. We may not wish to go further than observation, but this is probably enough to make a significant difference to our self-understanding, and it will certainly help to check our tendency to make simplistic, partial, unkind, and hypocritical judgements about the behaviour of others.

Waking Up

Mark 4:35-41

> On the evening of the same day, he said to them, 'Let us cross over to the other side.' So, leaving the crowds they took him as he was in the boat, and other boats were with him. A great windstorm blew up and the waves were beating against the boat, so that it was already filling up. Jesus was sleeping in the stern with his head on a cushion, so they woke him up and said to him, 'Teacher, don't you care that we're going down?' He got up and rebuked the wind and said to the sea, 'Quiet! Be silent!' And the wind subsided and a great calm descended. He said to them, 'Why are you so timid? Are you still without faith?' And they were very scared and said to one another, 'Who is this man? Both the wind and the waves obey him!'

Mark 5:21-43

When Jesus had crossed over again to the other side, a large crowd thronged around him as he stood on the shore. When one of the rulers of the synagogue, a man called Jairus, saw Jesus, he threw himself at his feet. 'My little daughter is dying. Come and lay your hands on her so that she can be healed and live,' he begged. So Jesus went with him.

A great crowd pressed upon him. There was a woman who'd had a flow of blood for twelve years, and who'd undergone a lot of suffering at the hands of many doctors, but despite spending all her money on medical treatment, none of the doctors had been able to help her and her condition hadn't improved at all; in fact, it had deteriorated. She'd heard about Jesus and, coming up behind him in the crowd, she touched his clothing, because she'd told herself, 'If I can only touch his coat I'll be healed!' Straightaway the flow of blood dried up and she felt in her body that she'd been cured of her condition. But Jesus, sensing that power had gone out of him, turned round to the crowd and said, 'Who touched my clothes?' His disciples said to him, 'You see the crowd milling around you and you say, "Who touched me"!' But Jesus kept looking around to see who had done it. The woman, conscious of what had happened to her, and trembling with fear, fell down before him and told him the whole truth. He said to her, 'Daughter, your faith has saved you. Go in peace and be free of your sufferings.'

While he was speaking to her, some people came from the ruler of the synagogue's house and said, 'Your daughter has died; why bother the teacher anymore?' Jesus overheard, and he said to the ruler of the synagogue, 'Don't be afraid. Just have faith.' He allowed no one to accompany him except Peter, James, and James's brother John. They went into the house of the synagogue ruler, and he saw a great commotion, people crying and wailing. Going inside he said to them, 'Why are you weeping and making such a racket. The little girl is not dead; she's asleep.' They laughed at him, but he threw them all out and taking the child's mother and father along with his companions he went in to the child's room. Holding her hand, he said to her, '*Talitha koumi*,' which means 'Little girl, I'm telling you to wake up!' The girl got up immediately and started walking around. She was twelve years old. And they were overcome with astonishment, but Jesus ordered them all to keep quiet about it, and he told them to give the child something to eat.

Story: Shaydoola

Shaydoola was tired of working every day. 'How happy I would be if I didn't have to slave away in the fields from dawn to dusk, sweating in the summer, freezing in the winter, all for just a few miserable coins!' he would say to himself, and to anyone else who would listen. 'I want to be rich so I never have to work again. Then I'll be able to sit in the shade and eat and drink while I watch other people working!'

One day, he decided he would go to the forest to find the wise man who lived there and ask him if his luck would ever change and if he would ever become rich. He hadn't gone very far before he met a scrawny-looking wolf lying by the side of the path. 'Where are you going?' asked the wolf.

'I'm going to find the Wise Man of the Forest to ask him if I'll ever become rich. I'm sick and tired of working all the time.'

'If you find the Wise Man of the Forest, would you ask him why I am so weak and miserable? I used to have lots of energy, but now my fur is falling out and my body is getting thinner every day. Soon I won't be able to stand up.'

'Yes, I'll ask him,' replied Shaydoola, as he went on his way.

A little further along Shaydoola came upon an apple-tree, but even though it was summer time there were no apples on the tree. 'Where are you going?' asked the tree.

'I'm going to find the Wise Man of the Forest, to ask him if I'll ever be rich. I don't want to work, I just want to enjoy myself,' said Shaydoola.

'If you find him, will you please ask him why I don't seem to be able to produce any apples? There used to be lots of apples on my branches but for a few years not even a single one has appeared.'

'Yes, I'll ask him,' replied Shaydoola, as he hurried on.

Nearing the end of his journey, Shaydoola came to a river, and he had no alternative but to swim across. Half way over, a big fish approached him. 'Where are you going?' it croaked in a barely audible voice.

'I'm going to find the Wise Man of the Forest, to ask him if I'll ever be rich. I want to live in a big house with lots of servants!'

'If you find him, will you ask him why I can't speak properly?' asked the fish. 'I used to be able to talk to all the travellers as they swam across the river, but now my voice Is very faint and my throat hurts when I talk.'

'I'll see what I can do,' replied Shaydoola as he pulled himself out of the water and on to the river bank.

It wasn't long before he came to a clearing in the forest where the wise man lived. 'Why have you come to see me, Shaydoola?' asked the Wise Man of the Forest.

Shaydoola was so amazed that the wise man knew his name, and so nervous to be in the presence of such an important person, that he shouted out all his questions at once: 'I want to know when I'll become rich. The fish wants to know what's wrong with his throat. The apple tree wants to know why it hasn't any apples, and the wolf wants to know why she is so weak and thin!'

'Tell the fish that there is a huge diamond stuck in its throat. It needs someone to reach inside and pull it out; then the fish will be able to talk without any pain. Someone has buried a treasure chest underneath the apple-tree and this is interfering with the tree's roots. If someone were to dig the treasure up the tree would start producing apples again. And if the wolf were to eat the next lazy fool who passes by she would start to regain her strength,' said the Wise Man of the Forest.

'What about me?' asked Shaydoola. 'When will my life change?'

'Go on your way Shaydoola. What must be must be!' replied the Wise Man of the Forest, enigmatically.

Excited by the wise man's promise, Shaydoola set off eagerly for home. While he was swimming over the river he spotted the fish and called out, 'The wise man says that there's a big diamond stuck in your throat. Just get someone to reach in and pull it out and then you'll be fine. Got to hurry. Can't stop!'

Rushing past the apple-tree, he shouted: 'There's a chest of treasure buried under you. If you can persuade someone to dig it up, your branches will start to produce apples again. Bye!'

Eventually he came to the miserable looking wolf. 'Did you ask the Wise Man of the Forest about me?' he asked.

'Yes I did,' replied Shaydoola. 'He said that you had to eat the next lazy fool who comes along and then you'll start to become strong again,' said Shaydoola. Mustering all his remaining strength, the wolf did as he had been advised and he gobbled up Shaydoola.

And so indeed, it was just as the Wise Man of the Forest had said. What must be must be.

The story I wanted to tell the children this morning is the story of the world's politest man. It's the very first story in my book *The Shortest Distance*, and so I thought that they – and you - would all be familiar with it. But for those who aren't, or who have forgotten, let me refresh your memory.

It takes place in the City of Fools, where a lecture is to be delivered by the politest man in the world. He is to talk about the importance of politeness, the development of etiquette, and how he gained the prestigious title of The World's Politest Man.

Some citizens of the City of Fools are taking the morning air when they spot a stranger sitting on a bench, reading a newspaper. 'I'll bet that's him,' says one citizen to his companion. 'I'll bet that's the politest man in the world, the man who is going to give a lecture tonight. I think I'll go and ask him.' He goes up to the man and says, 'Excuse me, sir, but are you the politest man in the world, the one who is going to give us a talk on the importance of politeness?'

The stranger looks up from his newspaper and says, 'How dare you interrupt me when I'm quietly reading? Why are you bothering me with your impertinent questions? If you don't get out of my sight this minute I'll punch you on the nose, you ignorant oaf!'

The citizen leaves as instructed and returns to his friend who asks, 'Well, was he the politest man in the world?'

'I don't know, he didn't say.'

This story comes from the Sufis – Islam's mystics – and, like so many Sufi stories, it seems like a joke. But it makes an extremely serious point – as does the story of Shaydoola, which I actually did tell the children. The City of Fools is everywhere. It's where human beings live. And we are fools because we can't read the signs. We are oblivious to the very simple and obvious messages that are presented to us daily, but we are so immersed in the irrelevant minutiae of life that we constantly miss them. It's as though we are half asleep.

In fact, one of the clearest and most emphasised teachings of the world's spiritual traditions is precisely this: we are asleep. Even the busiest and most energetic among us is walking in his sleep; indeed, it is one of the paradoxes of the spiritual life, that those who seem to be the most active are often the sleepiest of all. Expressions like, '24/7', 'work hard, play hard', 'burning the candle at both ends' – expressions which one may be encouraged to use in a job interview just to impress potential employers – are clear indicators of people who are asleep. Another sure sign is the human being's apparent willingness to surrender control of his or her life and thought to inherited and largely unexamined belief systems – secular and religious – which ensures that we think, act, speak, and aspire within narrow, culturally sanctioned parameters.

It's also emphatically taught by our spiritual mentors that unless we do something about our sleepiness we'll never even begin to sort out our problems. This is what distinguishes the spiritual approach to life from the purely secular, political one. The political and economic solutions to human problems from right and left suggest that by increasing our gross national product, redistributing wealth, making serious noises about peace, increasing education, making life more comfortable, we will contribute substantially to the sum of human happiness. The ambiguous results of that approach are everywhere in evidence around us. There is as much war as there has ever been. Slavery, outlawed by Britain 200 years ago, is as prevalent now as it was in days gone by; we may have got rid of child labour and sweatshops in the developed West, but we've simply removed them to China and India where they no longer offend our delicate sensibilities. Prosperity brings its own problems, as does peace. In Shakespeare's *Coriolanus*, in one of those short scenes which we tend to ignore, two minor characters – 'Servingmen' – are discussing the relative merits of war and peace. One says, 'Let me have war, say I; it exceeds peace as far as day does night; it's sprightly, waking, audible, and full of vent. Peace is a very apoplexy, lethargy, mulled, deaf, sleepy, insensible....' 'Aye, and it makes men hate one another,' says a second. And why, 'Because they then less need one another,' says a third.[46] Why are there wars? These minor characters in Shakespeare know very well that it's because in some way, deep down, in our unawakened state, we actually like them.

Happiness has not kept pace with material advances in the developed world – recent surveys suggest that British people are no happier now than they were in the fifties, and the 31 million prescriptions for antidepressants issued in Britain in 2006 would seem to support this conclusion.[47] Why are these things so? Because economic and political agendas are, according to the human race's spiritual teachers, merely cosmetic attempts to solve a much more

---

[46] Coriolanus, Act IV, Sc.5

[47] In 2015 there were 61 million prescriptions. The figure doubled in a decade. (See *The Guardian*, 5th July 2016)

radical problem. And the radical problem is that the vast majority of the human race is asleep, lulled into slumber by numerous cultural soporifics which effortlessly seem to discourage us from behaving, thinking, or speaking with any measure of depth or originality. To quote the Hindu sage Krishnamurti, many of our earnest political efforts are ineffective simply because they are devoted to 'decorating the prison walls'. Jesus puts it simply, too. 'Seek ye first the kingdom of God,' he says, 'and everything else will be given to you.' And where or what is the kingdom of God? Well, it's certainly not some imaginary economic utopia brought into existence by a political saviour, either divine or human. It's the awakened, enlightened state. When we reach it – or when a significant number of people reach it – our political and economic problems will take care of themselves.

'Awakening' is central to all forms of Buddhism, which postulates that each of us has a Buddha nature, buried deep within, which needs to be aroused. Buddhists tell the story of how the Buddha himself was questioned by some seekers after truth.

> 'Are you a god,' they asked him.
> 'No, I am not a god,' he replied
> 'Are you an angel, then?'
> 'I am not an angel.'
> 'Well, what are you which makes you so different from the rest of us?
> 'I am awake.'

The word 'Buddha' simply means, 'one who is awake'. Buddha-hood is a state of consciousness potentially attainable by us all. Gautama – the one we call 'The Buddha' - is just one of many who have attained this exalted state.

Henry David Thoreau expresses this need for awakening in less overtly religious terms in his book *Walden*:

> Moral reform is the effort to throw off sleep … … The millions are awake enough for physical labour, but only one in a million is awake enough for effective intellectual exertion, only one in a hundred millions to a poetic or divine

life. To be awake is to be alive. I have never yet met a man who was quite awake. How could I have looked him in the face? We must learn to reawaken and keep ourselves awake, not by mechanical aids, but by an infinite expectation of the dawn, which does not forsake us in our soundest sleep.[48]

The Christian stories also warn us of the dangers of sleep. Two stories in this third section of Mark's Gospel – what I call the Gemini section – are concerned with awakening. Why should they occur here? One reason is that Gemini represents the lively, butterfly mind of the intellectually curious and the perennially busy; people who are strongly Geminian are constantly active, nervously restless, betraying that very busy-ness which is often a counterfeit of genuine alertness; the externally hectic life is frequently a sign of interior turmoil. In addition, as we said last week, Gemini is associated with lack of focus, fragmentation, splitting within the psyche, from which we are all in differing measure suffering, but of which most of us are blissfully unaware.

The first of the Gospel's 'sleep' stories occurs right at the beginning of the section, at the end of chapter four. It's the account of the Stilling of the Storm. The Geminian elements within this story are so numerous that I won't even try to list them. Suffice it to say that the twin stars of the constellation Gemini were considered the patrons of seafarers in the ancient world, and mariners would pray to these gods when they were in distress. Mark is capitalising upon his reader's ability to make this connection; but, of course, he is doing more than this. He is showing how … well … think about it for yourself. You don't need me to spell it out for you! Ask yourself, who or what is the 'master' who is sleeping in the stern of the boat? Is it the historical Jesus of 2000 years ago? Is it the heavenly Jesus of much Christian preaching today? Or is it a power which lies deep within your own psyche which can be roused and which can help to calm your own life's turbulence?

The second story is the story of Jairus' Daughter. The first thing to notice about this story is the strange way in which it is told: *it is the only miracle story in the Gospels which is broken into by another*

---

[48] Thoreau, H.D., page 172

miracle story, the story of the Woman with the Flow of Blood. Two stories told together, a clear indication of Gemini. Mark (or whatever he or she was called) was so clever! This Gospel, which is almost universally considered to be the least sophisticated of the four Gospels, is actually a masterpiece of construction.

However, more pertinent to our present purposes, the story introduces us to Jairus. Jairus is the 'ruler of the synagogue', so he is an important figure within he Jewish community, and his daughter is moribund. Indeed, as the story proceeds, we learn that she is dead. But Jesus goes into the girl's room, takes her by the hand, and says, 'Talitha Koumi', an Aramaic phrase which means, 'Little girl, I'm telling you to wake up!' The girl duly awakes, and Jesus tells her parents to give her something to eat.

This story is conventionally interpreted as yet another miracle story, another incident which demonstrates the amazing power of Jesus, but such an interpretation generates numerous problems, especially in these sceptical times. But what is a problem to the intellect is a delight to the imagination. Let your imagination play with the story and what does it yield? Mine yields this: the daughter of the synagogue ruler is dying, maybe she's dead already. Judaism, represented by Jairus, is in danger of losing its soul, its 'feminine', intuitive side. It is controlled by 'masculine' laws, rules, and regulations which are strangling the life out of it. The feminine needs to be revived, and needs to be fed if Judaism is to be a source of spiritual nurture to the people. Jesus uses the Aramaic phrase 'Talitha koumi', not as some have sentimentally proposed because Peter or some other figure was remembering the actual words of Jesus, but because the author of the Gospel wants to emphasise them. What he's saying is, 'I'm putting these words in a different language to draw your attention to them'. This message is to everyone: 'Wake up!' As we shall see, Mark does the same thing in the next section of the Gospel.

When we awake, what then? Geminian Ralph Waldo Emerson (born May 25th 1803) says, 'When the torpid heart awakes it will revolutionise the world....(it) will give new senses, new wisdom of its own kind; that is, not more facts, nor new combinations, but ... direct intuition of men and things.'[49] Awakening the 'torpid heart' – not filling our heads with metaphysical speculation - is the function of all true religion. We are here to help one another to wake up.

Waking up the feminine, intuitive, poetic side of the psyche, the side that has been dormant for so long, which has been outlawed and suppressed for so long, is the urgent religious task of our time, as it was the urgent task of Jesus's time. When we rouse it from slumber we will gain a comprehensive, rounded and complete response to life. It will transform the City of Fools into the City of God.

How do we wake up?

Story: The Magic Pebble

Once upon a time, while aimlessly browsing through some library books, a man discovered a folded piece of parchment, which had been slipped between the pages of an ancient volume. The writing was minuscule, and the ink had faded, but, with the aid of a magnifying glass, he was just able to make out these words: 'On the shores of the Black Sea, there is a pebble which will turn everything it touches into gold. This magic pebble looks like every other pebble, but there is a difference: while the other pebbles feel cold, the magic pebble feels hot.'

The man was overjoyed at his good fortune. 'Just imagine,' he thought, 'a pebble which will turn everything it touches into gold! I must have it! I shall be richer than anyone else alive!' He immediately resigned from his job, sold everything he owned, borrowed some money from his relatives and friends, and set off to the Black Sea to find the magic pebble, and make his fortune.

He soon discovered that it would be a daunting task, because the shore was covered with millions of virtually identical pebbles. But the man set about it with great

---

[49] Emerson, R.W., *The Preacher*

enthusiasm. Each day he would go down to the beach at dawn and spend the day picking up pebbles and feeling their temperature. If a pebble was cold, he would discard it, but in order to make sure that he didn't pick up the same pebble again, he didn't throw it back on to the beach, he threw it into the sea. This went on hour after hour, day after day, week after week, month after month. At the end of a year he hadn't found the magic pebble, but he wasn't discouraged. He travelled back home, borrowed some more money with which to keep himself alive, and then returned to the beach to resume his search.

On and on he went. The same process, day after day. Lift a pebble; feel its temperature; throw it into the sea. But he still could not find the magic pebble.

Then, one evening, just as he was about the finish for the day, he picked up a pebble. It was hot, but through sheer force of habit, he threw it into the Black Sea.

Last Sunday I was speaking about the story of Jairus' daughter in the Gospel of Mark, and I said it should be understood as an exhortation to us to 'wake up', to cast off the slumber induced by habit and respond to life in a new way. I said that this was the consistent testimony of all the spiritual traditions, and that 'waking up' was the primary objective of the spiritual life. Naturally, such statements prompt the question, 'Well, what is the awakened state, and how exactly do we reach it?' - the very questions I was asked over coffee by Annie, and so important are these questions that I have decided to postpone the topic originally announced for today's sermon – Stories and Truth - and to address the practical issues involved in the process of waking up.

I've dealt with this topic before, on numerous occasions, and those of you who have been attending for some time will be familiar with what I am going to say, but this is so important a topic that a little bit of recapitulation will not go amiss. We can all do with a little gentle reminding about something so central to spiritual living.

Five years ago today I was in hospital in Leeds. I had been diagnosed with cancer of the kidney, and so extensive was the cancer that the doctors in Tallaght hospital thought that an operation would be pointless. I was given just over a year to live, but it was thought that immunotherapy just might work (there was a 1 in 10 chance) and so I found myself in St. James' hospital in Leeds on the weekend of my birthday, preparing to receive this relatively new treatment. I remember asking the nurses on the evening of the 10th June if it would be okay for me to go for a few pints to the pub across the road because, I said, this might be the last birthday I ever celebrate.

It's strange to be told that you are going to die quite soon. It doesn't quite register in the way that you think it will when you are well. There is dreadful sadness at the prospect of leaving the people you love, of course, and those expected feelings of regret for lost opportunities, but something else occurs, something perhaps that one doesn't quite expect. How do you think you would respond?

This was a question that was posed in the summer of 1922 by a Parisian newspaper, which invited its readers to consider how they would react to the news that some great cataclysm was about to destroy the world.

The responses to the question were just as one might suppose. One man said that the news of impending calamity would drive people either into the nearest bedroom or the nearest church; a woman correspondent thought that people would lose all their inhibitions once their actions had ceased to carry long-term consequences; and a third person declared his intention to devote his final hours to game of bridge, tennis, or golf.

All very predictable, and some variation on these conventional responses I would have given myself before I was told of my impending death. But, in the event, I responded quite differently and quite surprisingly. In fact, I responded pretty much as Marcel Proust had predicted in his reply to the newspaper's question. This is part of what he wrote:

> I think that life would suddenly seem wonderful to us if we were threatened to die as you say. Just think how many projects, travels, love affairs, studies it – our life – hides from us, made invisible by our laziness which, certain of a future, delays them incessantly … … But let all this threaten to become impossible for ever, how beautiful it would become

again! The cataclysm doesn't happen, (and) we find ourselves back in the heart of normal life, where negligence deadens desire. And yet we shouldn't have needed the cataclysm to love life today. It would have been enough to think that we are humans, and that death may come this evening.[50]

'Life would suddenly seem wonderful .... how beautiful it would become again!' This exactly mirrors my experience. Watching the sunrise, experiencing the intense colours of the flowers – as if for the first time –, talking with friends, standing on the pier at Whitby with Morag, listening to the birds, all of these things and countless more took on an incredible freshness. The commonplace became thrilling; dross was transformed into gold; a new mind was born within me, a new aliveness which was overwhelmed by the beauty, the strangeness, and the mystery of even the most ordinary sight, the most humdrum experience. This is the paradox of grief: as we feel our own life – or the life of one who is close to us – ebbing away, we become aware of life's depth and its delights with a new intensity. This is why the Sufi mystic Jelaladin Rumi says that 'grief is a gift'. He doesn't mean that grief is pleasant, or even that it is to be desired; he means that it inevitably sharpens our perceptions, breaks the deadening power of habitual thought and action, and brings us to a new level of awareness.

It is this new level of awareness that the spiritual life calls us to nurture, without having to rely on tragedy or grief to confer it briefly. This is 'the awakened life', 'the resurrected life', 'eternal life', 'the kingdom of God', 'abundant life', as opposed to the dreary, sleepy, and unsatisfying life that most of us lead most of the time; lives, in the words of Thoreau, of 'quiet desperation'. Life is not – or should not be – as some have suggested, cynically, a long process of dying; it is, rather, a long process of becoming awake.

We may never reach this state. Some suggest that it takes many lifetimes to reach it. Some people think that we can only reach it by arduous spiritual practice necessitating withdrawal from the world into some sort of monastery, and the renunciation of normal human activity – frugality in diet, celibacy, hours and hours of

---

[50] de Botton, A., page 5

prayer and meditation. If this is the case, then it is foreclosed to all of us here. But the Sufis, and others, tell us that this state is not beyond the reach of the ordinary person pursuing the normal activities of life. We don't need to change our life circumstances too radically; *we just need to change our attitude to our life circumstances.*

There are numerous ways of doing this, and, as I said last week, a significant part of why we come to this church is so that we can teach each other how to do it. One way is to make a conscious effort to break the habit patterns which blunt our perceptions. After all, it was sheer habit which caused the man to throw the magic pebble into the sea. 'Habit,' says Samuel Beckett in *Waiting for Godot*, 'is a great deadener'. A contemporary Buddhist says that we should try to do some of the following:

> When in company act as if alone
> When alone act as if in company
> Spend one day without speaking
> Spend one hour with eyes closed
> With eyes closed, have someone you are close to take you on a walk
> Think of something to say to someone particular. Next time you see them, don't say it.
> Go somewhere particular to do something. When you get there, don't do it.
> Walk backwards
> Upon awakening, immediately get up
> Get dressed to go somewhere, then don't go
> Just go out immediately, as you are, anywhere
> Do what comes next
> Walk on![51]

Here are three more things we can all do which will take us a little further on the road towards awakening.

The distinguishing characteristic of the awakened life is that it is a grateful life. The awakened person is one who readily gives thanks, who appreciates the giftedness of life, whatever its

---

[51] Cassetari, S., pages 37-8

circumstances, whatever its vicissitudes. But we live in a culture of comparison, and instead of expressing thanks for the incredible gift of life, we spend our time lamenting that we are not taller, richer, thinner, younger, more intelligent than we are, blighting our experience with envy and dissatisfaction, and fomenting all manner of personal conflict and communal strife. Learning to appreciate what you have and what you are is the foundation upon which the spiritual life is built. Stop worrying about the deal the other person is getting. God has been gracious to you; accept the gift and resist the petulant response of the spoiled child who is constantly complaining that his sister has received a bigger slice of the pie. Your day should begin and end with a moment of thanksgiving. Immediately upon waking I say the first line of E.E. Cummings's ode to spring: 'I thank you God for most this amazing day!' and I end the day with these lines from G.K. Chesterton:

> Here dies another day
> During which I have had eyes, ears, hands,
> And the great world about me;
> And with tomorrow begins another.
> Why am I allowed two?

The awakened life is also a reflective life. Thoreau advises that part of our reflection should involve just 'sauntering'. How strange that a word associated with purposeless meandering should be employed to describe a positive spiritual practice! But 'sauntering' comes from the French 'Sainte Terre', Holy Land, and 'saunterers' was a name applied to certain people in the Middle Ages who would beg money to take them to the Holy Land on pilgrimage. Whether they ever got there, or whether they even intended to go, is doubtful, but, says Thoreau, we must go there. Every day we must be 'saunterers', headed for the Holy Land, in a daily walk, in the countryside if possible, and free from the distractions of the personal stereo and the desire simply to stretch our legs. This is not entertainment, or passive relaxation, or exercise, but a conscious, determined, and deliberate attempt to become aware of the sights and sounds of the world which is full of the life of God, but which we are ordinarily too busy to imbibe. Some time, too, should be spent in quiet contemplation. This does not mean drifting into reverie; still less does it mean thinking about our problems or trying to puzzle out the meaning of existence. It simply means striving to be aware, learning to pay attention.

Thoreau says that he was for many years a self-appointed inspector of snow storms and rain storms, and he did his duty faithfully. What can you appoint yourself an inspector of?

One of the problems of the contemporary busy world is that we don't take our silence seriously. It embarrasses us. Radio and television dominate our lives, and we don't know what to do with quiet. Anne Morrow Lindbergh says that even those of us who practise some form of silent contemplation don't take it seriously enough to make it sacrosanct. 'If one sets aside time for a business engagement, a trip to the hairdresser, a social engagement, or a shopping trip, that time is accepted as inviolable. But if one says, "I cannot come because that is my time to be alone", one is considered rude, egotistical or strange. What a commentary on our civilisation, when being alone is considered suspect; when one has to apologise for it, make excuses, hide the fact that one practices it – like a secret vice.'[52] Honour the quiet time is good advice for one who wishes to awake.

The awakened life is also a compassionate, generous life. I'll have more to say on this when we look at the next section of Mark's Gospel, but it is important to mention it in passing here because every day we should make an opportunity to behave in a way which expresses our concern for others. This does not mean interfering in people's lives like some busybody, and it is best done anonymously anyway. Each day try to do something for which you cannot possibly be rewarded, even if this means picking up some litter from the street and putting it in the bin, smiling at babies, saying 'thank you' to shopkeepers, giving money to those in need. These are ways in which we can flex our social muscles, make ourselves more aware of those who share the joys and sufferings of life with us.

Finally, and above all, the awakened life is a joyful life; not always happy. One doesn't have to go around with a ridiculous beaming smile all day, pretending to be free from problems, but

---

[52] Quoted in Andrews, B.M., page 50.

gratitude, reflection, and generosity work a silent magic on our psyche and enable us to cope with life's vicissitudes, and to radiate a sense of peacefulness and calm which can have extremely positive effects on those around us.

I can't promise you that doing these things will bring you to a state of nirvana, but I can confidently assert that practising these simple things faithfully will raise your level of awareness, and will have a dramatic effect on the way you live your life.

Chapter 4: Cancer
21ST JUNE – 22nd JULY

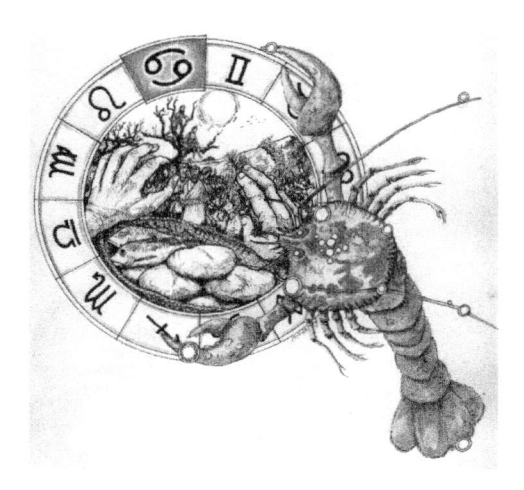

Cancer is the sign of the summer solstice, when the Sun begins to reverse its direction. The symbol of Cancer is the crab, a curious, scuttling creature which has its skeleton on the outside and which carries its house on its back. Cancer symbolises the urge to protect and to nourish and is associated with the family, the nation, traditions, memory. Its virtue is loyalty, its vice clannishness, its motto, 'Blood is thicker than water'. Even Jesus is shown to be acting and speaking in a narrow 'insular' fashion in his encounter with the Gentile woman. Nearby stars have been likened to crumbs falling to the dogs from a table (see note on page 83). Cancer is said to govern the stomach, hence the two 'feeding' stories which appear here. The name of one of Cancer's stars, *Ma'alaph* means 'numbered thousands'. Nearby constellations are Ursa Major and Ursa Minor, the Great Bear and the Little Bear, two linked groups, one smaller than the other, like the 5,000 and the 4,000 fed by Jesus. Argo, 'the ship that conquered the waters' is close by, too. Jesus conquers the waters by walking on them! Notice the strange 'crab-like' journey Jesus makes in 7:31.

Feeding all the People

Mark 6:30-44

The apostles came back to Jesus and told him everything they'd done and taught. There was so much to-ing and fro-ing that they'd not had a chance to eat, so he said to them, 'Come. Go off by yourselves to a secluded place and rest for a while.' They went off in the boat by themselves to a deserted spot, but many people who'd seen and recognised them as they were setting off ran on foot from all the towns and arrived at the place before them. When Jesus disembarked he saw a huge crowd and he was moved with pity for them because they were like sheep without a shepherd. He began to teach them many things. It was already late and his disciples came up to him and said, 'This place is off the beaten track and it's getting late. Send the crowds away so that they can go into the surrounding towns and villages to buy themselves something to eat.' Jesus replied, 'You give them something to eat.' They said, 'It would cost six months' wages to feed them all!' He said to them, 'Go and see how many loaves you have.' When they'd found out they said, 'Five, and two fish.' He told the people to sit in groups on the green grass, so they sat down in groups of fifty or a hundred, looking like so many garden plots. Taking the five loaves and the two fish and looking up to heaven, he blessed and broke the bread and gave it to his disciples to distribute. He also divided up the two fish. They all ate their fill and, after five thousand men had eaten, there was enough bread and fish left over to fill twelve baskets.

Mark 8:1-10

In those days, when once again there was a big crowd of people with nothing to eat, he called his disciples and said to them, 'I'm concerned about the crowd because they've been with me three days and they've not eaten. If I send them off home hungry they'll faint on the way, and some of them come from far away. His disciples replied, 'Where can anyone get enough bread to satisfy these people in this lonely place.' Jesus asked them, 'How many loaves have you got?' 'Seven,' they said. He gave orders to the crowd to sit down on the ground, and taking the seven loaves he gave thanks, broke them, and gave them to the disciples who distributed them to the crowd. They also had a few little fish, and when he'd blessed them he told them to distribute these too. They ate their fill, and they collected up seven baskets full of leftovers. There were about for thousand men. Finally, he let them all go.

Story: The Monkeys and the Caps

Aurangzeb sold caps for a living. He would travel to a village, set up his stall in the market place and sell his caps to the locals. One day, while travelling from one village to the next, he was very tired. The Sun was shining, and he'd had a busy morning, so he put down his heavy sack of caps and sat down in the shade of a mango tree for a snooze. After an hour or so he woke up refreshed, but when he picked up his sack he found that it was empty. 'Where are my caps?' he thought. 'I'm sure this sack was nearly full when I went to sleep.' Just then he looked up into the tree and he saw a gang of monkeys each with a cap on its head. 'Hey, those are my caps!' shouted Aurangzeb. 'Give them back to me!' But the monkeys just seemed to mock him, imitating his shout. So he pulled a funny face, and each of the monkeys pulled a funny face, too. But they wouldn't give him back his caps. He picked up a stone and threw it at the monkeys. They responded by throwing mangoes at him. He was really angry now, and in his frustration, he took off his own cap and threw it to the ground. The monkeys took off their caps and threw them to the ground! They were imitating him! Without further ado, Aurangzeb picked up all the caps from the grass, put them in his sack, and went on his way, thinking how clever he'd been to outsmart the monkeys.

Fifty years later, Habib, Aurangzeb's grandson, was selling caps. He'd inherited the family business. He was travelling from one village to the next on a hot day, and he felt he needed a rest. He sought out the shade of a mango tree, put down his sack of caps, and sat down for a snooze. He woke refreshed after an hour, but when he picked up his sack he found it was empty. 'Where are my caps?' he asked himself. 'I'm sure this sack was nearly full when I went to sleep.' Then he looked up into the trees and saw dozens of monkeys, each with a cap on his head. How could he possibly get them back? Then something stirred in his brain. He remembered a story his grandfather had told him many years ago, about how he'd outwitted some monkeys by getting them to imitate him. So Habib stood up. He put up his right arm; the monkeys put up their right arms. Habib put up his left arm; the monkeys did the same. Habib scratched his nose; the monkeys scratched their noses. He pulled a face, rocked from side to side, stood on one leg. Each time the monkeys copied him. Then … … Habib took off his cap and threw it to the ground. The monkeys didn't respond. So Habib tried again. He put up his right arm, his left arm; he scratched his nose, he pulled a face, rocked from side to side, stood on one leg. Each time the monkeys imitated his actions. Once again he put his hand to his head, took off his cap and threw it to the ground. No response from the monkeys.

Feeling miserable, Habib picked up his empty sack and began to walk back home. He hadn't gone far when he felt a tap on his shoulder. He looked round and saw a monkey with a big smile on its face.

'Do you think you're the only one with a grandfather?' asked the monkey.

'War is God's way of teaching Americans Geography.'
Ambrose Bierce

Last Thursday, the 21st June, would have been my father's one hundredth birthday. He was born on 21st June 1907 but, sadly, he died just a little short of his 72nd birthday, in April of 1979. The 21st of June is also the anniversary of my ordination as a Unitarian minister. I became a minister on 21st June 1994 at a ceremony held in Unitarian college Manchester, where I had been a student.

So, the 21st June has special significance for me. But the significance of the day extends beyond my own parochial concerns. June 21st is the day of the summer solstice, the longest day of the year, the day on which the Sun seems to change direction. Since last December, the Sun has been moving higher and higher in the skies of the northern hemisphere; now it begins its slow journey downwards, the days becoming gradually shorter and shorter until, on December 21st, when there is barely any daylight, it will change direction once again

These two solstice points – along with the two equinoxes - always had great significance for our ancestors, who were much more aware of these celestial cycles than we are, and who celebrated the 'stations' of the Sun with parties and bonfires, singing and storytelling. Ancient sites in Ireland and Britain testify to the importance of the solstices to ancient peoples. Newgrange is primarily associated with the winter solstice, but Stonehenge marks the summer solstice, and there would have been plenty of activity around these two sites on Thursday last, as well as on the Hill of Tara in Co. Meath, and at Dowth in the Boyne valley. In some parts of the world there have been revivals of ancient dances, in which men and women move in snake-like procession through the streets, imitating the undulating movements of the Sun in its yearly cycle through the heavens.

Today, Sunday the 24th June, is St. John the Baptist's Day, exactly six months before Christmas Eve because, you remember,

St. John the Baptist was said to be six months older than Jesus, and the Gospels consistently contrast these two figures, associating them, in my opinion, with the two solstices. Jesus, 'the light of the world', is born when the light is born in December; John is associated with the midsummer, when the light starts to decline. As John himself says in the Fourth Gospel, 'He (meaning Jesus) must increase, but I must decrease'.[53]

On the day of the summer solstice the Sun enters the zodiacal sign of Cancer, the Crab, but the crab is only one of a number of creatures that have been used as images of this sign: the tortoise, the crayfish, and the lobster have at various times and in various cultures been used to represent Cancer. These creatures have one thing in common; they seem to be embodiments of the principal of reversal, because they appear to be constructed inside out. The crab's skeletal system is on the outside – as anyone who has tried to eat one will be aware. What's more, the crab moves in a strange way, scuttling rather than walking directly, moving forwards, backwards, and sideways in an apparently random fashion. This may give us a clue as to why Jesus is shown making such an apparently ridiculous journey in chapter 7 of Mark's Gospel. The text tells us that he went from the region of Tyre and Sidon to the Sea of Galilee through the middle of the Decapolis. If you consult a map of the area (see page 79), you will see how strange this journey is; it has been compared with travelling from London to Cornwall via Manchester, and it has given scholars no end of trouble for centuries, and fuelled numerous theories. It shows that Mark didn't know his geography too well, they say, or that he was probably not a native of the area. But, in reality, it is a little joke by the Gospel's author. It shows a crab-like, scuttling, to-ing and fro-ing movement, and it is Mark's way of putting yet another Cancerian signature on this section of his Gospel.

The zodiacal sign Cancer reflects the crab in a number of curious ways. People born at this time of the year often present a hard shell to the world, as a means of protecting an extremely vulnerable inside. Cancerian people are highly emotional, but guarded and defensive, with a strong sense of family identity, an

---

[53] John 3:30

appreciation of traditional values, and a concern for history and ancestry. The past has an enormous influence on the strongly Cancerian person, and it is absolutely appropriate that the world's greatest literary celebration of the past, Marcel Proust's *A La Récherche du Temps Perdu* – Remembrance of Things Past – should have been written by a Cancerian. Proust was born on July 10th 1871, and, according to his biographers, he spent much of his time wrapped, crab like, in a cocoon of blankets.

Cancerians are nurturers and protectors, figuratively putting their arms around those close to them, in an attempt to shield them from life's vicissitudes.

America, 'born on the 4th of July', is a Cancerian country. This sounds absurd to the modern ear: 'How can a whole country be represented by a single image, and have a collective identity?' we ask. And yet, on one level, these attributions do seem to be appropriate. The iconic images of American life – 'the flag, mom, and apple pie'- are all connected with Cancer, as is food in general, and popcorn, another iconic American image, is itself an expression of the Cancerian desire to eat forever and never get full or fat! In the figure of the zodiacal man, Cancer is shown as being associated with the stomach. (Incidentally, archetypal Cancerian Proust was constantly plagued by his stomach. Apparently he informed his doctor that he couldn't even drink a whole glass of Vichy water at bedtime without being kept awake by intolerable stomach pains. And what is it that sparks off the remembrance of things past? A *madeleine*, a plump little cake which looks as if it had been moulded in a scallop shell! And what job did Proust say he would like to do if he weren't a writer? Bake bread! Cancer again. The universe is a strange place!)[54]

The Crab manifests in other ways in the American psyche, and I was amused in the 1980s when President Reagan began proposing his 'star-wars' project, whose intention was to place a 'protective shell' around America to keep out all enemy missiles:[55]

---

[54] See *How Proust Can Change Your Life*, by Alain de Botton.
[55] Before the presidential election of 2016, Republican candidate Donald Trump spoke about 'building a wall' to keep out the Mexicans, an idea which seemed to strike a chord in the American psyche and no doubt contributed to his eventual victory.

'protective shell' was the actual term used. The so-called Monroe Doctrine – American isolationism – is another political expression of Cancer, as is the persistent call for those 'family values' which all American politicians must claim to espouse if they are to have any success whatsoever at the polls. Even the apparent obsession of American visitors to Europe with discovering their ancestry, and explaining with some precision that they are one eighth English, two fifths Danish and three tenths Cherokee, reflects the sign Cancer, and it is strange to think that Mormonism, the one major world religion which can claim a uniquely American birth, has a preoccupation with genealogy as one of its distinguishing characteristics. You may be inclined to retort, rationalists that you are, that the American obsession with genealogy is simply a feature of their colonial past. A good try, but it won't work. You don't find nearly the same preoccupation with ancestry among Australians and New Zealanders.

And, of course, we may tend to think of Americans as great world travellers, but, in reality, they are not. Only 21% of Americans hold passports. While researching this figure on Google, I came across the following on a website called Yale Global:

> As the world becomes accustomed to the American way of life, Americans are tuning out the rest of the world. US citizens have paid less and less attention to foreign affairs since the 1970s ... The number of university students studying foreign languages has declined, and fewer Americans travel overseas than their counterparts in other developed countries. News coverage of foreign affairs has also decreased. Why are Americans withdrawing from the global village?

'Withdraw into your shell.' It's a perfect image of Cancer. Yesterday, having completed this sermon, I settled down to read the *Guardian*, and what did I find? An article by the American novelist Sara Paretsky which reinforces this very point.

> In America today, we seem to prize the self-reliant ideal more than ever. In fact, so much do we prize it that we don't want

to pay taxes to support the common good. In one hyper-wealthy Silicon Valley town, where houses commonly sell for more than $2m, the streets are full of potholes: when I visited, I was told that town residents would rather ruin their own cars than pay taxes so that someone else could drive in safety.

The American dream is of a private home with a private yard, in which each child has their own room, their own iPod, their own computer, and, by the time they're 12 or even younger, their own mobile phone. We spend our waking moments plugged into our Game Boys. We seem to withdraw as far as possible from each other encased in our own worlds.[56]

Strange, isn't it, that another great icon of America, *Walden*, by Thoreau, which every American child has to read, and which has become a Bible of self-reliance describes a withdrawal from normal society and an attempt to live in virtual isolation. Thoreau was born on 12th July 1817, making him a Cancerian.

Withdrawal, ancestry, traditions, clannishness, food; these are all associated with the sign Cancer – although I must stress that they are not the exclusive concerns of people born in late June and early July; they are *human* preoccupations and tendencies, and all human beings have to come to terms with them. These are the principal themes of this little section of Mark's Gospel as even a cursory glance will show. The only episode that seems a little out of place is the account of Jesus walking on the Water, but even this relates to Cancer, since Cancer is a Water sign and Jesus's ability to walk on the water is a symbolic account of the spiritually evolved person's dominance over the turbulent emotions symbolised from time immemorial by the waves of the sea. In addition, one of the decans of Cancer, that is, one of its surrounding constellations, is Argo, the magical ship of Jason and the Argonauts which was said by the Roman writer Manilius to be 'the ship that conquered the water'. Here Jesus, whose name, by the way, is just another variation of the name Jason, is shown making a symbolic conquest of his own.

---

[56] The *Guardian Review*, 23rd June, 2007

But the dominant image of this whole section concerns food. It begins with the account of the Feeding of the Five Thousand (which occurs, you notice, after Jesus asks the apostles 'to withdraw' for a while), and it goes on to discuss the Jewish obsession with dietary laws, the tradition of ritual cleansing before food, and later it deals with 'the leaven' or yeast of the Pharisees. We've only got time today to look very briefly at the feeding stories. Notice, there are two of them. This has given headaches to traditional commentators for many years, some scholars suggesting that Mark included two accounts of the same event, showing himself to be less than a competent historian – just as Jesus's strange journey shows Mark to be a poor geographer. Liberal scholars who view the Gospel as 'exaggerated history' will often explain these stories by saying that all the people really had food hidden away, but they were too mean to advertise the fact; but after listening to Jesus they were ashamed of their selfishness and willingly shared what they had and everyone was satisfied. But this kind of explanation – harmless enough in its way – is rather patronising to the Gospel's author, implying that he allowed evangelistic piety to cloud his judgement.

But the author of this Gospel was no fool to be patronised, still less was he a poor historian or a poor geographer. In my view he was nothing short of a genius, and he knew perfectly well what he was doing. He deliberately has *two* feeding stories because he wants to make a very important point relating to Jewish clannishness. The stories are indeed the same except for a few details. But the details are crucial to a proper understanding of their meaning. Bread and fish are used in both – for reasons which we will discuss on another occasion[57] - but while the feeding of the Five Thousand takes place in Jewish territory, the feeding of the Four thousand occurs in a predominantly Gentile area. And the numbers are significant. In the feeding of the Five Thousand, the predominant numbers are 5 and 12 – 'Jewish' numbers – the 'five' reflecting the five books of Moses, the Pentateuch, considered to be Judaism's holiest books; and the 12 representing the twelve tribes of Israel. So, in this incident, Jesus is shown feeding the Jews. The predominant numbers in the other incident are 7 and 4, readily

---

[57] See 'The Age of Aquarius' below

identified as 'Gentile' numbers: the Jews believed that there were 70 Gentile nations (the zero is irrelevant in this kind of numerology) scattered around the 'four corners' of the earth.

So, the two stories show that God's spiritual 'manna' is to be distributed to all people, not just to the Jews, and read together, they constitute an attack on the narrow exclusivism and parochialism which characterised much Jewish thinking at the time the Gospel was written, and which have characterised much religious thought and practice before and since that time. Taken together, these stories ask the same question the monkey asked in the story I told the children this morning: 'Do you think you're the only one with a grandfather?' Or, to put it another way: Do you think that your people are the only people who have traditions? Do you think that God only speaks through your prophets and your religion? We will explore these vital issues again next week when we will have another look at the Cancerian section of Mark's Gospel.

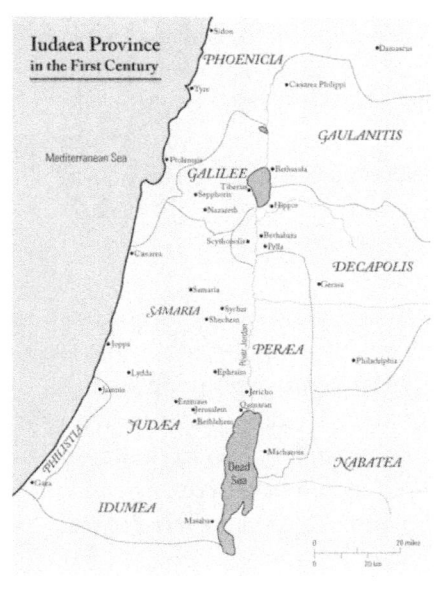

Jesus's Strange Journey: *'Leaving the region of Tyre he went through Sidon to the Sea of Galilee, up through the middle of the Decapolis' (Mark 7:31, my translation) This roundabout journey, which has been compared with travelling from London to Cornwall via Manchester, has given literalist commentators untold headaches. The general consensus seems to be that it shows Mark's lack of geographical knowledge and probably indicates that he was not a native of the area. However, it is quite obviously a joke by Mark – a reference to the scuttling crab's inability to get directly to its destination. The NIV tries to make sense of it by translating it: 'Then Jesus left the vicinity of Tyre and went through Sidon, down to the Sea of Galilee and into the region of the Decapolis' but this is not completely faithful to the Greek.*

Opening Up

Mark 6:45-52

Straight afterwards, Jesus urged his disciples to get into the boat and go on ahead to Bethsaida while he was releasing the crowd. Taking his leave of them he went into the mountain to pray. It was evening and the boat was in the middle of the sea, and he was alone on the land. At about three o'clock in the morning, seeing that they were struggling to make headway because of a contrary wind, he went towards them walking upon the sea, as if he meant to go past them. Those who saw him walking on the water took him for a ghost and screamed out, because they all saw him and were very frightened. But he began to speak to them straightaway. He said, 'Take heart! It's me! (Greek: *ego eimi*, literally 'I am'). Don't be frightened!' He went up to them in the boat and the wind abated and they were all utterly astonished., because they hadn't understood about the loaves and their hearts were hard.

Mark 7:24-37

From there Jesus went to region of Tyre and went into a house where he hoped to escape notice. But it wasn't possible for him to remain hidden for long, and a woman whose daughter was possessed by an evil spirit heard about him and she came and fell down at his feet. She was a Greek – a Syrophoenician – and she begged him to cast the demon out of her daughter. He said to her, 'Let the children be fed first; it's not right to take the children's food and throw it to the dogs.' She replied, 'Yes, Lord, but the dogs under the table eat the children's scraps!' And he said to her, 'Because of what you've just said, go on your way. The demon has left your daughter.' When she went home she found the child lying on her bed, and the evil spirit had gone.

Leaving the region of Tyre, he went through Sidon to the Sea of Galilee, up through the middle of the Decapolis. And they brought to him a deaf man with a speech impediment and they begged Jesus to lay his hand upon him. Taking him privately, away from the crowd, he placed his fingers in his ears, and touched his tongue with spittle. Looking up to heaven he sighed aloud as he said, 'Ephphatha!' (which means, 'Be opened!') The man's ears were opened, his tongue was loosed, and he began to speak correctly. Jesus ordered them not to tell anyone, but the more he told them to keep quiet, the more they proclaimed it. They were completely amazed, saying, 'He's done everything well; he makes the deaf hear and the dumb speak!'

They came to Bethsaida where they brought a blind man to him, begging him to touch him. Taking the blind man by the hand, he led him outside the village. He spat into his eyes, put his hands on him and said, 'Can you see anything?' The man looked up and said, 'I can see men, but they look like walking trees!' Then Jesus put his hands on the man's eyes once more. This time his sight was restored and he could see clearly. So Jesus sent him home and told him not to enter the village.

Story: When has the Night ended?

> A rabbi gathered his students together very early one morning, before the Sun had risen. 'How do you know when the night has ended and the day has come?' he asked them.
>
> One student answered: 'When you can see an animal in the distance and you can tell whether it is a sheep or a goat.'
>
> 'That's not the answer,' said the rabbi.

'When you can tell whether a distant tree is a fig tree or an apple tree,' said another.

'No,' replied the rabbi. 'That is wrong, too.'

A few more students had a try, but each time the rabbi shook his head. 'Tell us, then,' said one student, 'when do we know that the night has ended and day has come?'

'When you can look at the face of any man or woman and see them as your brother or your sister. If you cannot do this, it is still night, no matter what the time of day,' said the rabbi.

'It is well to remember that the whole universe, with one trifling exception, is composed of others.' (John Andrew Holmes)

Last week I explained how the zodiacal sign Cancer was associated in the ancient world with the stomach and food and how it also symbolises the natural tendency of the human being to be isolated, to build a barrier keeping out unfamiliar experience and unfamiliar ideas. And it is this aspect of the sign's symbolism that I want to look at today.

The traditions we inherit and pass on, the prejudices we develop, our natural instincts, act like the crab's shell to cut us off from what we consider to be alien or strange. It is probably a survival mechanism, built into our genes, but one objective of the spiritual life is to identify and then try to eliminate those instinctive factors which work to give us short term survival advantages, but which have now outlived their usefulness and which actually impede our development as a species

The visceral – 'gut' – reactions, which all human beings exhibit in the presence of the unfamiliar, are a feature of our emotional life. They come unbidden, up from the depths, and we have little immediate or conscious control over them. We instinctively prefer those people who look like us, talk like us, and who share our assumptions and our outlook. This is why the story of Jesus walking on the water is so appropriate in the Cancer section of the Gospel. It is astronomically appropriate because one of the constellations surrounding Cancer is Argo, the mythical and magical ship of the Argonauts which, according to the Roman writer

Manilius, was the ship 'which conquered the waters'. But this story is also related to the idea of overcoming our emotional reactions to things, because Water has perennially symbolised the turbulent emotional life of the individual and, by walking on the water, Jesus is demonstrating his mastery over those instinctive responses to life which will often override our intellectual convictions and which are the cause of so much emotional turbulence. Walking on the water is not a marvellous demonstration of the uniqueness of Jesus, a proof of his divinity; nor is it a misapprehension on the part of eye-witnesses who saw Jesus walking on some kind of rocky outcrop and mistook it for a miracle. It is, rather, something we are all called upon to do: we too must learn to conquer the internal emotional turmoil which militates against any genuine acceptance of unfamiliar customs and people.

There are three more miracle stories in this section, and although they seem like separate incidents, they must be taken together to get the full impact of the lesson the Gospel writer is trying to teach us.

The first one is the story of the woman who asks Jesus to cast out a demon from her daughter. It is important to remember that this woman is a Gentile – a non-Jew - and it is for this very reason that Jesus initially refuses her request. 'It's not right to give the children's food to the dogs,' he says. This, of course, is a terrible insult, and the fact that it is uttered by Jesus himself has proved quite embarrassing to conventional commentators, who try to soften it a little by saying that the word used is rather an affectionate term for a dog, and anyway, Jesus was really only testing the woman's faith. Does Jesus really come out of it better if we assume that he is playing some sort of game with this distressed woman? If she had been unable to respond cleverly to his insult by mentioning the crumbs which fall from the children's table would he have refused to heal her daughter?[58]

---

[58] 'Above Procyon are the stars of Castor and Pollux, the Twins - nearly a perfect rectangle. Sometimes this rectangle is seen as a table at which Castor and Pollux are eating; the two dogs (Sirius and Procyon) are waiting patiently for the table crumbs. These crumbs can be seen as very faint stars of magnitude 5 or 6, scattered between Gemini and Procyon.' (From *Patterns in the Sky*, by Julius D.W. Staal, page 86)

The significance of this story only becomes apparent when we read it in conjunction with the story of the deaf man, which follows. After putting his fingers in the man's ears and touching his tongue with spittle, Jesus says the Aramaic word *Ephphatha*, and the man finds himself able to hear properly and to speak coherently.

It is unusual to find Aramaic words or phrases in the Gospels. Aramaic was the first language of the Palestinian Jews, and so would have been the language of Jesus and the apostles, and commentators regularly point out that it is present in the Gospels – which were all originally written in Greek – because these would have been the actual words that Jesus said. But, as we noted in the story of Jairus's Daughter, Aramaic is almost certainly used *for emphasis* in the Gospel of Mark. The Gospel writer is saying, 'I'm writing this word in another language, so pay attention to it. It's important'.

The word *Ephphatha* means 'Open up!' (It was from this word that we took the name of our monthly magazine *Oscailt*, meaning 'open' in Irish.) What Jesus is saying to this deaf man is the Gospel's message to you and me. This man was suffering from physical deafness; we are suffering from spiritual deafness. Our ears are closed to the entreaties of those who live in foreign countries, whose skin colour is different from our own, whose way of life does not correspond with ours. We are deaf to the words even of those who live in close proximity to us, but whose traditions are different from ours. We don't hear what they are saying, and so our opinions about them and their customs are garbled and worthless. The Jewish exclusiveness displayed by Jesus in his encounter with the Gentile woman dramatically illustrates our own clannishness, our instinctive conviction that 'blood is thicker than water', that 'charity begins at home'. It's a shocking reminder of our own refusal to listen attentively to the unfamiliar voices. It is only when we are prepared to open up that our prejudices can be eroded; and only then that the impediment in our speech will be removed and our opinions will be worth listening to. We have to break the shell of our own tribalism and exclusiveness.

This theme is explored further in the final scene of this section, the Cure of the Blind Man. As Jesus enters Bethsaida a blind man is brought to him and, in response to the man's entreaties, Jesus restores his sight. This seems to be just another example of Jesus' amazing power to heal. But the story is different from all the other miracles recounted in the Gospels, because it is the only one in which Jesus is shown failing at his first attempt. He takes the man to one side, rubs spittle on his eyes, and asks him, 'What do you see?' 'I see men but they look like walking trees,' the man replies. Jesus rubs the man's eyes again, and this time his sight is restored and he can see everything clearly.

The blind man, like all the characters in the Gospels – when the Gospels are read as psychological, spiritual treatises and not as historical reminiscences - is you and I. We have received the first rub of the spittle, and we can see – that is, we have the sense of sight - but we don't quite see people, we see walking trees – or, in contemporary language, ciphers, zombies, humanoids. We recognise their general shape and their mobility, but we have yet to grant them fully human status. What we need is a second metaphorical rub of the eyes to correct our vision, to remove the residual film which prevents us seeing people as they really are, as ends in themselves, and not as means to our own ends. Einstein expresses the same sentiment as Mark, but less dramatically and more philosophically, as follows:

> A human being is part of a whole called by us 'universe', a part limited in time and space. He experiences himself, his thoughts, and feelings as something separated from the rest, a kind of optical delusion of his consciousness. This delusion is a kind of prison for us, restricting us to our personal desires and to affection for a few persons nearest to us. Our task must be to free ourselves from this prison by widening our circle of compassion to embrace all living creatures and the whole of nature in its beauty.[59]

---

[59] Goldstein, page 26

The function of all spiritual practice – from whatever tradition it comes – is to help us to narrow the gap between self-awareness and other-awareness, to remove that residual film from our eyes which is deluding our sight. But how, practically, do we achieve it? Like so many of the spiritual lessons contained in this Gospel, it takes a lifetime to learn, but I suggest, as a starter, that whenever we say the Lord's Prayer we pay particular attention to the first two words: 'Our Father'. Forget the dispute over the word 'Father' and whether it is sexist or not. This is just a distraction. The important word is 'Our'. God is *our* father', not 'my father', and throughout the prayer we ask 'give us *our* daily bread' and 'forgive us *our* trespasses' as 'we forgive those who trespass against *us*'. This prayer is written in the first person plural. It's not about me, it's about us.

Be conscious of those moments – and there will no doubt be many, no matter how spiritually evolved you consider yourself to be - when you figuratively retreat into your shell, when you act and think as Jesus is shown acting with the Gentile woman, when you cut yourself off from somebody with the thought, 'He/she/they is/are not like me. Their problem is nothing to do with me. I am white, I am Irish, I am European, I am male, I am civilised.' This happens more frequently than we might suspect. An essy in the book *All I need to know I learned in Kindergarten* by Robert Fulghum, describes a subtle example of it. It concerns a man called Nicolai Pestretsov, a Russian soldier who was stationed in Angola, whose wife was killed when she came out to visit him. Nicolai's colleagues fled after the attack, but Nicolai didn't. The South African military communiqué said, 'Sgt. Major Nicolai Pestretsov refused to leave the body of his slain wife, who was killed in the assault on the village.' What impressed Fulghum about this report was the air of disbelief that seemed to lie behind the words. It was as if the journalist were saying, 'He showed concern for his dead wife, refusing to leave her body, putting his own safety at risk – and he's a Russian! Imagine that!' As Fulghum comments, the journalist couldn't quite get beyond the words, Russian, Communist, Soldier,

Enemy, to see a person. To the journalist, Nicolai was just a walking tree.[60]

We too have to try to fight against the tendency to see people as walking trees. Try doing this. Every day select one person that you casually encounter, and make a special imaginative effort to tell yourself that this person, whose name you do not know, whose history and circumstances you do not know, is a thinking, feeling, hurting, doubting, frightened, rejoicing human being, just as you are. Wish him or her well with a silent blessing.

The Dalai Lama, born under Cancer (6th July 1935), and therefore no doubt acutely conscious of his own tendency to build a shell around himself, said, 'My religion is kindness'. Kindness has to be our religion. To be kind is to treat people as kin, as family, regardless of their genetic distance from us, and this takes practice and effort. And we can practise it daily, in the ordinary events of ordinary life.

The lesson? Make the people you encounter feel human. That's all. Then you'll be making a significant contribution to the transformation of the world.

These little exercises and practices – and others that you may devise for yourself – are designed to take us out of our natural solipsism, the feeling that I exist in a way that is different from the way that others exist, and to bring us to an appreciation of our connectedness 'in mystery and miracle, to one another and to the world'.

And it can all be summarised in that one word in Mark's Gospel 'Ephphatha: Open Up'.

---

[60] Fulghum pages 31-3

Chapter 5: Leo
23rd July – 22nd August

Leo, the Fixed Fire sign, is the sign of the sunshine, and is the only sign said by the ancient astrologers to be 'ruled' by the Sun. Charles Carter calls it 'the sign of divine splendour'. Its symbol is the lion, 'the king of the beasts' and it is associated with royalty, glory, creativity. Its principal star is Regulus, 'the little king', one of the four 'royal' stars of the ancient world. The second star in Leo is Al Giebha, said to mean 'the exalted, the exaltation' and Zosma, in the Lion's tail means 'the shining forth, the epiphany'. The Catholic Church celebrates the Feast of the Transfiguration, when Jesus's face 'shone like the Sun and his clothes became white as light',[61] on August 6th, when the Sun is in Leo.

---

[61] Matthew 17:2 καὶ ἔλαμψεν τὸ πρόσωπον αὐτοῦ ὡς ὁ ἥλιος, τὰ δὲ ἱμάτια αὐτοῦ ἐγένετο λευκὰ ὡς τὸ φῶς.

'Who do men say that I am?'

Mark 8:27-38

Jesus and his disciples went into the villages of Caesarea Philippi and on the way he asked his disciples, 'Who do men say that the son of man is?' They said to him, 'Some say John the Baptist; others Elijah, others, one of the prophets.' He said to them, 'But who do you say that I am?' Peter answered, 'You are the Christ!' And he ordered them to tell no one about him. He started to teach them that the son of man must suffer many things, and be rejected by the elders, and the chief priests and the legal experts, and be killed but after three days rise again. And he was telling them plainly. Peter drew him aside and started to take him to task, but Jesus turned, looked at his disciples, and reprimanded Peter. 'Get behind me, Satan!' he said. 'Your thoughts are men's thoughts, not God's thoughts!'

He called the crowd and his disciples together and said to them, 'If anyone wants to come after me, let him take up his cross and follow me. For whoever wants to save his soul will lose it; but whoever loses his soul for my sake and the sake of the good news will save it. What benefit is it for a man to gain the whole world and forfeit his soul? What would a man give in exchange for his soul? Whoever is ashamed of me and my words in this faithless and sinful generation, the son of man will be ashamed of him when he comes in the glory of his father with the holy angels.'

Mark 9:1-8

He said to them, 'I'm telling you the truth: there are some people standing here who will not taste death until they see the kingdom of God come in its power.

After six day Jesus took Peter, James and John by themselves up into a high mountain, where he was transfigured before them. His clothing shone with intense whiteness, a whiteness which no bleaching agent on earth could possibly match. Elijah and Moses appeared to them, and were talking with Jesus. Peter, dreadfully frightened like the others and not knowing what to say, responded with, 'Rabbi, it is wonderful for us to be here. Let us make three tents: one for you, one for Moses, and one for Elijah.' Then a voice issued from an overshadowing cloud, 'This is my son, the beloved. Listen to him!' Suddenly, looking round, they saw no one with them, only Jesus.

Story: The Eagle and the Chickens

A farmer found an eagle's egg and put it in the nest of one of his hens. When the egg hatched, the little eagle found himself among dozens of chickens. He thought of them as his brothers and sisters, and as he grew up with them he became like them. He never learned to fly. Sometimes he would flap his wings a little, just as he saw the hens doing, but, like them, he never really got off the ground. Sometimes, in his dreams, he would seem to be a great bird, carrying off small animals in a strong beak to his nest way up at the top of a high mountain, but when he awoke he would content himself with scraps from the farmer's table, and grubs from the ground.

One day, when he was old, an eagle flew over the farm. 'What's that magnificent bird?' he asked his friend.

'That's an eagle, the king of the birds. It can fly as high as the Sun, and the whole world is its playground. No other bird can match it for power and beauty, and grace.'

The eagle who thought he was a chicken looked longingly at the eagle in the sky. 'How I wish I could be like that eagle! How wonderful it would be to be free like him! But I'm just a chicken, and I'll have to live my life here on the ground, and never soar into the sky!'

So, the eagle who hatched among the chickens lived his whole life like a chicken, because that's what he'd been told he was, and that's what he thought he was.

Jesus said: 'One who knows everything else, but who does not know himself, knows nothing.'
(Gospel of Thomas, saying 67).

If you were to be asked the question, 'Who are you?' how would you answer? No doubt you *have* been asked the question many times, and you have probably responded by giving your name. 'I'm Bill Darlison,' I've said on numerous such occasions. When pressed, I could easily extend my answer by describing my physical features, giving my age, my address, mentioning the various roles I play in life – husband, brother, uncle, minister, etc. - and then maybe talking a little bit about my interests and predilections. Does this do it? Do these few sentences give an adequate account of my identity?

Some people would say that they do. I am the sum total of the roles I play and the relationships I form. I have no identity beyond these things. There is no 'Self' which stands outside, no intrinsic, internal 'I'. I am my physical actions and my brain patterns, a pretty sophisticated mechanism, no doubt, but a mechanism nevertheless.

Even those aspects of myself which I consider might tell against such a point of view – the sense that there is an interior 'I' which is in control, or the feeling that my mind transcends my physical self in some way – these, say certain philosophers and scientists, are just fictions. Your mind is simply a by-product of your brain chemistry, your sense of self an illusion. In fact, in the words of the scientist Dean Hamer, 'we follow the basic law of nature, which is that we're a bunch of chemical reactions running around in a bag.'[62] Or, as some other anonymous writer put it, even more succinctly, 'We are just hairy bags of chemicals.'

I have quite a collection of these scientific and philosophical assessments of the human being. I began to collect them when I spotted something written by Marcus Chown in the *Guardian* a few years ago: 'A total eclipse confronts us with a truth we would rather not face. The truth is that we live on a tiny clod of cold clay in an insignificant corner of an infinite cosmos. In the great scheme of things, our lives are of no importance whatsoever.' Chown's sentiments were echoed a few years later, by Jim Herrick, editor of the *New Humanist* magazine, who spoke of, 'The puniness of the self in the face of the vastness of the universe.' And George Monbiot, who writes on ecology in the *Guardian*, is no less stark in his assessment: 'Darwinian evolution,' he writes, 'tells us that we are incipient compost: assemblages of complex molecules that – for no greater purpose than to secure sources of energy against competing claims – have developed the ability to speculate. After a few score years, the molecules disaggregate and return whence they came. Period. As a gardener and ecologist I find this oddly comforting.'[63]

I was going to say that these viewpoints are almost exclusively male, but then, yesterday, curious as to whether Saturday's *Guardian* would supply me with some material for Sunday's sermon (as it has regularly done in the past!), I came across this little piece on the penultimate page of the *Review*. In a review of a new book edited by John Brockman, in which 100 eminent thinkers are asked, 'What's Your Dangerous Idea?' the psychologist Susan Blackmore is quoted as saying that her dangerous idea is that even her contribution to the book is merely the result of 'memes competing in the pointless universe'. Her idea is even considered 'chilling' by the book's reviewer, P.D. Smith.[64]

Hairy bags of chemicals. Incipient compost. Speculating complex molecules. Competing memes. Insignificant. Puny. This is who – what - you are according to these thinkers. You are a cosmic accident, a carrier of a selfish gene, which simply wants to reproduce itself. Once your reproductive life is over, you are cast

---

[62] *Time* Magazine, 29th November, 2004
[63] *Guardian*, 16th August, 2005
[64] *Guardian Review*, page 16, 4th August 2007

aside by Nature. You have outlived your usefulness. This is the new philosophical 'chic'. It's tough, but, as Richard Dawkins might say, 'It's true. So deal with it.'

I don't know whether, as a species, we are dealing with it adequately. Perhaps we can never deal with it. What price morality when, ultimately, a human being is worthless? I'm not saying that people who hold such a point of view cannot behave ethically; this would be a terrible slur on numerous such people of high moral calibre, but I sometimes wonder whether they adhere to their high principles in spite of rather than because of their philosophical convictions, and whether people like Trotsky, who declared that we must 'rid ourselves once and for all of the Quaker-Papist babble about the sanctity of human life', or Stalin who said, 'One death is a tragedy, but a million deaths just a statistic,' were not being more faithful to the contemporary scientific and philosophical ethos.

How different such points of view are from the one they are seeking to replace! The one we find in the world's spiritual traditions, which teaches us that, far from being expendable accidental products of blind natural forces, we are infinitely precious beings, 'made in the image of God',[65] intrinsic parts of the whole economy of the universe. The Psalmist puts it like this:

> For you created my inmost being; you knit me together in my mother's womb. I praise you because I am fearfully and wonderfully made; your works are wonderful, I know that full well. My frame was not hidden from you when I was made in the secret place. When I was woven together in the depths of the earth, your eyes saw my unformed body.[66]

And the writer of Psalm 8, as perplexed by the vastness of the universe as Marcus Chown or Jim Herrick, comes to the opposite conclusion:

> When I consider your heavens, the work of your fingers,

---

[65] Genesis 1:27
[66] Psalm 139:13-16 (NIV)

the Moon and the stars which you have set in place, what is man that you are mindful of him, the son of man that you care for him? And yet you have made him a little lower than the heavenly beings, and crowned him with glory and honour.'[67]

Shakespeare has Hamlet declare, 'What a piece of work is Man! How noble in reason! How infinite in Faculty! In form and moving how express and admirable! In action how like an angel! In apprehension how like a god! The beauty of the world! The paragon of animals!'(Although he does go on to say that we are also a 'quintessence of dust'.)[68]

Ralph Waldo Emerson, poet, philosopher, and one-time Unitarian minister, sums up this alternative point of view in one sentence: 'Man is a god in ruins', he declares.

So, you take your choice. Maybe we have to say that the conclusion we come to depends on when we ask the question – sometimes we feel like gods, at other times like the universe's flotsam and jetsam. Maybe we can be intellectually convinced by the scientists and emotionally convinced by the religionists. However we answer the question, we can't escape it, and this time of the year is a particularly good time to ask it, because the zodiacal sign Leo, which the Sun entered two weeks ago, is the sign which, to the ancient astrologers, symbolised the intrinsic identity of the human being. It's not too difficult to see why this is appropriate: the Sun, the 'heart' of the universe, symbolic of consciousness, is at its most powerful at this time of the year (in the northern hemisphere, of course, where this kind of thinking developed), and people born around this time do seem to display a strong sense of their own individuality and worth regardless of their philosophical convictions. Leo is the 'aristocrat' of the zodiac, and those in whom the principle operates most strongly like to be 'king' and 'queen' of their own circle, no matter how restricted. There is often a strong need for self-display, for being 'centre stage', which can manifest as superiority and bossiness. The lion, 'king of the jungle' has been

---

[67] Psalm 8: 3-5 (NIV)
[68] Hamlet, Act 2 Scene 2

associated with this time of the year for millennia.

But that sense of pride and pre-eminence is just the psychological expressions of the essence of the sign. To the ancient astrologers Leo, whose principal star is called Regulus, *the little king*, was 'the sign of divine splendour', the sign of the Sun's greatest power, its all-consuming fire and all-illuminating light reflecting the very energy, power, and might of God. All the zodiac signs were said to be 'ruled' by one of the planets, some planets ruling two signs each. But only one sign is ruled by the Sun: Leo.

How appropriate, then, that the Leo section of the Gospel of Mark — the section which, I am sure, the earliest Christians would have read at this time of the year — should deal with this question of identity. 'Who do men say that the son of man is?' asks Jesus of his apostles at Caesarea Philippi. I don't want to go into the vexed and complicated question about Jesus's role as Messiah. What I want to say this morning is that the term 'son of man', which we have learned to interpret as some kind of messianic title, really just means 'human being'. Idiomatically, in Hebrew, 'son of' means 'one who has the qualities of', so 'son of righteousness' means 'a righteous person', and 'son of perdition' means 'a rotter'. So 'son of man' means 'human being'! We heard it earlier in Psalm 8: 'What is man that you are mindful of him, and *the son of man* that you keep him in mind?' 'Man' and 'son of man' are synonyms. So Jesus' question, 'Who do men say that the son of man is?' is really 'What does it mean to be a human being?'

And what is Peter's answer? 'You are the Christ, the son of the living God!' The story of Jesus is not, as I keep repeating, the history of one man; it is the journey of the human soul on its way to enlightenment, and I venture to suggest that in the Christian mysteries which preceded the institutional church, this section of the Gospel was explained to initiates as meaning, 'You, a human being, are God's anointed one. You are God's specially chosen one. You are a son or daughter of God'. Matthew Fox, one-time Dominican priest, but now a priest of the Episcopal (Anglican) Church in America, says about this passage:

> The name 'Christ' means 'the anointed one'. All of us are anointed ones. We are all royal persons, creative, godly,

divine, persons of beauty and of grace. We are all Cosmic Christs, 'other Christs'. But what good is this if we do not know it? Everyone is a Sun of God as well as a son or daughter of God, but very few believe it or know it.'[69]

Put these things in modern dress. 'What, according to contemporary thinkers, is a human being?' Some say, 'a cosmic accident'; others 'a hairy bag of chemicals'; others, 'incipient compost'. But what do you say a human being is? This is the mystic's answer: 'A human being is an infinitely precious child of God, an irreplaceable spark of the divine, with a glorious and eternal destiny.' We are all eagles who think we are chickens.

The next scene of the Gospel ratifies Peter's answer as Jesus is transfigured before them, his clothes gleaming whiter than any bleaching agent on earth could render them, or, as Matthew's Gospel says, 'his face shining like the Sun'.[70] This is the real nature of the human being. When we see beyond the outward appearances, beyond the status and the clothing, beyond the flesh, blood, and bone, we see a vision of an eternally precious and infinitely beautiful being, the very offspring of God. This is the deepest, most consoling spiritual truth of all. It has power to transform our lives and our attitudes like no other. The English mystic Edward Carpenter writes: 'Once you really appropriate this truth (i.e. your identity with God), and assimilate it in the depths of your mind, a vast change (you can easily imagine) will take place within you. The whole world will be transformed, and every thought and act of which you are capable will take on a different colour and complexion.'[71]

This is the real meaning of these strange stories, and I'm sure the earliest Christians did approach them in this way. One clue that this is so lies in the celebration of the Feast of the Transfiguration. Do you know when it is? Tomorrow, August 6th, when the Sun is in the very centre of Leo. Tomorrow Catholics will be proclaiming the undoubted truth that Jesus was a manifestation of God; but the higher truth is that we all are.

---

[69] Fox, page 137
[70] Matthew 17:2
[71] Carpenter, page 303

'If *you* can!' The Meaning of Faith

Mark 9:14-29

When they reached the other disciples they noticed that they were arguing with some legal experts, surrounded by a huge crowd. As soon as the crowd caught sight of Jesus they were amazed and they ran towards him and began to greet him. He said to them, 'What are you arguing with them about?' One of the crowd answered, 'Teacher, I brought my son to you because he has a spirit of dumbness, and whenever it seizes him it throws him down and he foams at the mouth and grinds his teeth, and he's wasting away. I asked your disciples to cast it out, but they weren't powerful enough.' He answered them, 'O faithless generation! How long must I put up with you? Bring him here!' They brought him, and when the spirit saw him it immediately threw the lad into convulsions. He fell to the ground and was rolling about, foaming at the mouth. Jesus asked his father, 'How long has this been going on?' He replied, 'Since he was a little child. Many times it has thrown him into the fire and into the water in order to destroy him. If you can do anything, have pity on us and help us.' Jesus said to him, 'If you can! Everything is possible to someone who has faith!' Straightaway, the boy's father cried out, "I do have faith! Help my lack of faith!'

When Jesus noticed that a crowd was bearing upon them, he rebuked the unclean spirit, saying, 'Deaf and dumb spirit, I order you to come out of him, and never enter him again!' With a shriek, the spirit sent the lad into terrible convulsions, and came out. The young man looked as if he was dead, but Jesus, taking him by the hand, raised him, and he stood up. When they went into a house, the disciples asked him privately, 'Why weren't we able to cast it out?' He said to them, 'Nobody can cast out this kind except by prayer.'

Story: The Doctor's Diagnosis

A man was in bed, very sick. He had not eaten or spoken for two days, and his wife thought the end was near, so she called in the doctor.

The doctor gave the old man a very thorough physical examination. He looked at his tongue, lifted his eyelids to examine his eyes, listened to his chest through his stethoscope, tested his reflexes by hitting his knee with a little hammer, felt his pulse, looked in his ears, and took his temperature. Finally, he pulled the bed sheet over the man's head, and pronounced, in sombre tones, 'I'm afraid your husband has been dead for two days.'

At that moment, the old man pulled back the sheet, lifted his head slightly, and whispered anxiously, 'No, my dear, I'm still alive!'

The man's wife pushed his head back down again, covered him once more with the bed sheet, and snapped, 'Be quiet! Who asked you? The doctor is an expert, he ought to know!'

'Without faith, nothing is possible. With it, nothing is impossible.'
Mary McLeod Bethune

Say what you like about the internet, but when you want information quickly it's often there at your fingertips. In preparing this sermon I wanted a copy of the *Penny Catechism* – the little booklet that most Catholics over the age of fifty would have had to learn by heart – but it's not readily available these days, so I put my request into Google, and within seconds, there was the *Penny Catechism* up on my screen. I couldn't have accessed it more quickly if I'd gone to my bookcase to fetch it!

I was after the Catholic definition of 'faith', which I still vaguely remember from my own hours spent with the Catechism, but which I wanted to get right. It comes early on, at question nine:
Question: 'What is faith?'
Answer: 'Faith is a supernatural gift of God, which enables us to believe without doubting whatever God has revealed.'

A couple of questions on it asks: 'How are you to know what God has revealed?' And the answer is: 'I am to know what God has revealed by the testimony, teaching and authority of the Catholic Church.'
And then: 'What are the chief things which God has revealed?'
Answer: 'The chief things which God has revealed are contained in the Apostles' Creed.' The Apostles' Creed follows. You probably know how it goes: 'I believe in God, the Father almighty, maker of heaven and earth....'

I wanted this definition of faith because faith is a central concept of the zodiacal sign Leo which, I believe, has inspired the section of Mark's Gospel that we are currently considering. The astrological writer Charles Carter says that, 'If the keynote of the sign Cancer is "I fear", the keynote of Leo is "I have faith"'.[72] In fact, Faith is a central concept in all three of the so-called 'Fire' signs of the zodiac, Aries, Leo, and Sagittarius, and with good reason: 'Fire' is the Element which represents enthusiasm, energy, vigour, zest, power, individuality, all of which are bound up with what the Gospel of Mark means by faith.

But there is no trace of any of these things in the Catholic Church's definition. In the Catechism, faith is about believing certain propositions – propositions which have been 'revealed' to us by God and delivered to us by the authority of the Catholic Church. This is how most of us have been schooled to understand faith, and why the definition given years ago by Mark Twain that 'faith is believing what you know isn't true' is not too far wide of the mark. 'Losing' our faith is simply ceasing to accept that these propositions have any correspondence with the truth, or any relevance to life.

For many Protestants, who talk about being 'saved by faith', 'faith' means accepting Jesus Christ as Lord and Saviour and

---

[72] Carter, C., Page 71.

trusting that he has paid the price of sin. If one firmly believes this, they say, one is 'saved', that is, destined for heaven.

But neither the Catholic nor the Protestant definition of faith comes even close to what Jesus meant by the word. In the story of the Cure of the Deaf Boy, Jesus rebukes his apostles for their lack of faith, and the boy's father exclaims, 'Lord I believe, help my unbelief!' Is Jesus telling the apostles off because they don't believe the propositions of the Apostles' Creed? Is the boy's father asking for help in accepting Jesus Christ as his Lord and Saviour? Hardly. A moment's consideration will show that this cannot be the case. For Jesus, faith is not about metaphysical propositions which one has to sacrifice one's reasoning powers in order to accept. Faith is an attitude to life, a positive attitude, grounded in a strong sense of our immense powers as human beings, which we can have – or not have – regardless of the contents of our supposed metaphysical belief system. The opposite of this kind of faith is not disbelief or doubt, both of which are perfectly reasonable intellectual responses to speculative theological statements: it is apathy, cynicism, an overwhelming sense of futility and pointlessness, a feeling of being a helpless pawn in the mindless drift of an indifferent universe. Nowhere in literature is this attitude to life more succinctly or more chillingly expressed than in Shakespeare's *Macbeth*:

> To-morrow, and to-morrow, and to-morrow,
> Creeps in this petty pace from day to day
> To the last syllable of recorded time,
> And all our yesterdays have lighted fools
> The way to dusty death. Out, out, brief candle!
> Life's but a walking shadow, a poor player
> That struts and frets his hour upon the stage
> And then is heard no more: it is a tale
> Told by an idiot, full of sound and fury,
> Signifying nothing.[73]

---

[73] *Macbeth*, Act 5, Scene 5, lines 19-28

Macbeth may well have claimed that he 'believed' the contents of the Apostles' Creed, but his nihilistic observation shows that he has no faith at all.

Although Macbeth's brand of 'faithlessness' has been around since the dawn of time, it seems to be on the increase in our own day, fed by influential schools of thought which casually strip us of our personal autonomy, telling us we are simply objects in a world of objects, accidents of cosmology and history, our actions and our attitudes determined by circumstances beyond our control. I remember, many years ago, when I was a student in York, attending a lecture by a professor of psychology, at which we were told, quite blithely and with no sense of regret in her voice, that we were completely at the mercy of our genes and our environment, with the environment having the bigger influence. 'There is no freedom of the will at all,' she said.

I wondered then, and I wonder still, what such teaching does to our sense of moral responsibility, to our sense of right and wrong, virtue and vice, good and bad, honourable and despicable. Is there any room in such a system of thought for praise or blame, approval or censure? Strangely, although I have met many people who would say that they go along with such opinions, none of them has shown the slightest inclination to curb his or her tendency to criticise volubly those who have wronged them, or to heap praise on those who do them favours. Certain Marxist thinkers, who talk of human beings as pawns of history or economics, never seem tired of using the language of moral censure on people who, they believe, are simply responding as psychological, sociological and economic laws dictate. Nor is such an attitude restricted to secular philosophies. Religions often preach a type of fatalism which renders us powerless in the face of some deity's whims and diktats. So, to some Muslims, Allah has written the script and we are simply acting the parts allotted; to Christians of the Calvinist persuasion, the end of history is known in advance, and God has already separated the saved from the damned, so there's not much point in any kind of moral striving. All of which cuts clean across that deep sense we have of ourselves as moral beings with the power of choice – however limited such a power might be. We may laugh at the woman in today's children's story who believed the expert rather than her experience, but how different are we? My experiences of life may teach me that I am being with some degree of moral autonomy, but the university professor tells me I don't have any, so I must believe her. I may base my daily life on the assumption that people around me are making decisions for which they can be applauded or censured, but the intellectually respectable Mr. Grim Faced Determinist tells me that they are just acting as they must. As a consequence, faith in my own limited but real autonomy is eroded, and gradually replaced with a feeling of impotence in the face of cosmic inevitability.

In his book *Man's Search for Meaning*[74] – one of the most important spiritual books of the 20th century – psychiatrist Viktor Frankl considers the effects of such faithlessness on his fellow inmates in Auschwitz. Frankl puts it quite starkly: those without faith died first. He does not mean that those without religious belief died. Religious and non-religious people suffered in the same degree. He means that those who could see no purpose in their lives died quickly. Those who could perceive no meaning in their existence, no point to their experiences, gave in most readily. Such 'purpose' need not involve what we might call ultimate, transcendent purpose. He isn't talking about abstract or overarching meaning, such as might be given by certain kinds of religious conviction; he is talking about the specific meaning that life might have at any given moment. Quoting Nietzsche, he says that 'He who has a *why* to live for can bear with almost any *how*'.[75] Faith, for Frankl, is the *why* of life. The *why* will differ with the individual, but without it we will find ourselves in despair, regardless of our level of prosperity. Many people, says Frankl, 'have enough to live by, but nothing to live for; they have the means but no meaning'.[76]

Frankl's experiences in Auschwitz taught him that human beings, far from being the playthings of circumstances, have the potential to attain and express what he calls a 'spiritual freedom'

---

[74] Frankl, Viktor, *Man's Search for Meaning*, first published in 1946, now available in numerous editions. I used the 1984 edition, published by Washington Square Press.
[75] Frankl, page 87
[76] Frankl, page 165

which cannot be taken away, and which alone can make life purposeful and meaningful. He writes:

> A human being is not one thing among others; *things* determine each other, but man is ultimately self-determining. What he becomes – within the limits of his endowment and environment – he has made out of himself. In the concentration camps, for example, in this living laboratory and on this testing ground, we watched and witnessed some of our comrades behave like swine while others behaved like saints. Man has both potentialities within himself; which one is actualized depends on decisions but not on conditions.... man is that being who invented the gas chambers of Auschwitz; however, he is also that being who entered those gas chambers upright, with the Lord's Prayer or the *Shema Yisrael* on his lips.[77]

And this is precisely the lesson of the story of the Deaf Boy in Mark's Gospel: we are greater than we think. Jesus and his disciples have come down from the mount of Transfiguration, the mountain on which the innate divinity of the human person is graphically described. Coming down from the mountain represents coming down to earth, encountering real life once again. And what does he encounter? A man who is begging Jesus to help his troubled son. Remember the principle upon which my interpretation of all these miracle stories is based: that the physical ailments from which the Gospel characters are suffering are mirrors of universal human spiritual conditions. This boy is deaf and dumb, and from birth onwards he has been thrown into the fire or into the water, unable to determine for himself the course of his existence, buffeted here and there by a force greater than himself. He has no voice, no power, no control. The boy's father asks if Jesus can help, and Jesus replies, 'Don't ask what I can do, ask what *you* can do! Everything is possible to one who has faith!' Or, to put it another way, 'Everything is possible to one who accepts his own innate power as a child of God.' And Jesus cures the lad. Jesus represents that power

---

[77] Frankl, page 157

within each of us which enables us to transcend those confining shackles, what William Blake calls 'mind forg'd manacles', false ideas about our nature and our abilities which shut our ears to the call of our innate divinity, and which keep our aspirations paltry, and make us slaves to fashion and circumstance. Changing our attitudes, having faith in ourselves and in all human beings, may not cure our physical ailments – to think this is, in my view, to misread the story – but it will transform our personal psychic universe, and help us to create that transfigured world for which we all long.

The Face to Faith column in yesterday's *Guardian* dealt with this very theme. Its author Canon Andrew Clitherow, says that such a faith is actually a prerequisite of a genuinely mature faith in God.

> However, while religion often tells you to have faith in God first and then to know your place in his scheme of things, developing a faith in human nature today actually precedes having an authentic faith in God. Then as we unearth the divine potential in cosmic existence, we can take increasing responsibility for ourselves and the universe in a creative and loving way.[78]

One final point: 'the divine potential in cosmic existence', the transforming power of the Christ within, has to be discovered. The kind of demon that was afflicting the young boy – that is, the demon which convinces the individual that he or she is a plaything of circumstances – cannot be driven out, merely by wishing it away. 'Only prayer will do it,' says Jesus. By which he means that we must pay assiduous attention to our spiritual practice, if we are to develop the kind of faith which will transform the individual and help to transform the world.

---

[78] Andrew Clitherow, in *The Guardian* 'Face to Faith' column, Saturday 18th August 2007.

Chapter 6: Virgo
23rd August – 22nd September

Virgo is Mutable Earth, and is the sign of the harvest, and in Luke's parallel passage (Luke 10:2) the harvest is mentioned. Virgo's symbol is the Maiden with the Wheatsheaf. In Egypt the sign was associated with the goddess Isis, who is often depicted carrying the infant Horus, and the sign has strong connections with childhood. Its keywords are service, humility, simplicity, purity, characteristics of the Virgin Mary, whose birthday is celebrated by Catholics on 8th September, when the Sun is in the centre of Virgo.

Service and Simplicity

Mark 9:33-50

They came to Capernaum, and when he was inside the house he asked them, 'What were you arguing about on the road?' But they were silent, because on the road they had been arguing about who was the greatest. When he'd sat down, he called the twelve and said to them, 'If anyone wants to be first, he will be the last of all, and the servant of all.' He took a little child, and stood him in their midst. Taking him in his arms, he said to them, 'Whoever receives a child such as this in my name, receives me; and whoever receives me, is not only receiving me, he is also receiving the one who sent me.'

John said to him, 'We saw someone casting out demons in your name, and we stopped him because he wasn't of our company.'

Jesus said, 'Don't stop him. Nobody who does a powerful work in my name will then be able to slander me. Whoever is not opposed to us is on our side. I'm telling you the truth: whoever gives you a cup of water to drink because you bear the name of Christ won't go unrewarded. But it would be better for him who puts obstacles in the way of one of these little ones who believe in me to be thrown into the sea with a huge millstone tied around his neck! If your hand causes you to fall, cut it off! It's better to enter into life maimed than with both hands to go into Gehenna, into the inextinguishable fire. And if your foot causes you to stumble, cut it off! It's better for you to enter into life lame than to be thrown with both feet into Gehenna. And if your eye causes you to fall, pluck it out! It's better for you to enter into the kingdom of God with one eye than to be thrown with both eyes into Gehenna, where the worm doesn't die, and the fire is never put out! Everyone will be salted with fire; salt is good, but if ever it loses its saltiness, what will you use to make it salty again? Have salt in yourselves and live in peace with one another.'

Story: Starfish on the Beach

While walking along the beach one day, a young man noticed that thousands of starfish had been washed up by the tide. The tide was going out, and the starfish were stranded. There was no way that they could get back to the water, and within an hour or so they would all be dead.

In the distance, he noticed an elderly woman, who was picking up the starfish from the beach and throwing them back into the sea. He approached her and asked, 'What are you doing?'

'I'm throwing these starfish back into the sea.'

'But why are you bothering? There are thousands of them, and what you are doing won't make any difference,' said the young man.

'It will make a difference to this one,' said the lady, as she hurled another starfish into the receding tide.

A new book has just been published about Mother Teresa. It's called *Mother Teresa: Come Be My Light*,[79] and it consists of extracts from letters she wrote over 66 years to her various spiritual directors. The book is set to cause a stir because, apparently, it portrays a tortured soul, expressing doubts about God's existence and the efficacy of prayer; indeed, it describes an interior life which seems very much at odds with her public persona. It has been published now, no doubt, to coincide with the 10th anniversary of her death on 5th September 1997. She died, you

---

[79] Kolodejchuk, page 73

remember, just a few days after Diana Princess of Wales, and so her expected death in old age was somewhat overshadowed by the tragic, accidental death of her younger, more glamorous contemporary, but it seems an odd coincidence that two of the most famous women in the world – if not *the* most famous women in the world - should die within days of each other. I always feel that it is unfortunate to share your death with a public icon. Aldous Huxley and C.S. Lewis both died on the same day as President Kennedy in 1963, and news of the deaths of these extraordinarily talented and influential men had to be reported on the inside pages of the newspapers.

But there was something fitting about Mother Teresa dying when she did, because whatever the details of her own private spirituality, and despite the criticisms of people like Christopher Hitchens, who see her as a manipulative, cynical, sentimental figure, she was known world-wide for her quiet humility, and dying while the world mourned Diana enabled her to slip unobtrusively into the great beyond without the fanfare which would have inevitably attended her death at any other time.

Mother Teresa died at this time of year, and she was born at this time of year too. She was born in late August, 1910, under the sign of Virgo, the sign which all the astrology text books will tell you is concerned with service. People in whom the Virgo principle operates strongly generally shun the limelight, but they are excellent workers, well able to provide a practical structure for someone else's grand, but hazy and unformed, idea. I remember asking my wife, Morag, many years ago, who the best nurses were. Surely, I said, they are the Pisceans, the ones who can empathise with the patients, hold their hands, cry with them a little. No, said Morag. The best nurses – from her point of view as a ward sister – are the Virgos, because Virgos actually see what needs doing and do it! Anyone who knows a strongly Virgoan person will testify to the truth of this. They are organisers and systematisers. Virgos like to catalogue things, put them in order, clean up the mess. They tend to be strongly conscious of hygiene, and can become pernickety about dress and diet. The English astrological writer, Charles Carter, says this about Virgo:

> It is not the sign of leadership but of service; it does not aim at brilliant results but at useful ones. It is patient and does not turn from routine drudgery; it hates show and shuns responsibility and publicity. It is not ambitious but is satisfied with a straight job and a fair wage.[80]

If we translate the elements of this somewhat unflattering psychological portrait into spiritual categories we can see that the Virgo phase of experience is characterized by service, discipleship, actually living out the precepts laid down by the spiritual master. In the modern era no one has exemplified these better than Mother Teresa, whose practical, 'hands-on' approach to religion has had such a marked influence on the contemporary world. Although her shrewd self-promotion, her high profile, and her considerable leadership qualities seem to indicate the importance of other factors, her image and her public utterances seem almost invariably to reflect her birth sign.

> A sacrifice to be real must cost, must hurt, must empty ourselves. The fruit of silence is prayer, the fruit of prayer is faith, the fruit of faith is love, the fruit of love is service, the fruit of service is peace.[81]

Leo Tolstoy (born 9th September, 1828), who, in his later years was drawn towards an analysis of the religious nature of the human being, extolled the simple, rational, practical aspects of religion, free from supernaturalism, and concentrating almost exclusively on behaviour: 'Let all the world practise the (teaching) of Jesus and the reign of God will come upon earth,' he wrote.

Virgo, the second of the Earth signs, is the sign of the harvest, and in ancient Egypt it was represented by the maiden with the wheat sheaf in her hand, or by the goddess Isis carrying the infant Horus – an image which is highly relevant to the passage of Mark which we are considering, as we shall see. This is harvest time, when work has to be done. We've been basking in the leonine sunshine for long enough; now it's time to take out the farming

---

[58] Carter, page 73
[81] Mullan, page 122

implements and get down to some productive activity. Mark's Gospel doesn't mention the harvest, but the parallel passage in Luke does; at this precise point in the narrative, Luke has Jesus say, 'The harvest is plentiful, but the workers are few. Ask the Lord of the harvest to send out workers into his harvest field',[82] which is another reason why I am convinced that the Gospel of Mark as we have it is a truncated version of a much longer document which displayed the zodiacal signatures even more clearly than the Gospel as we now have it.

    Our activities at this time of the year unconsciously reflect the Virgoan preoccupations. It's time to get down to the nitty gritty. Since the Sun entered Virgo around 21st August, we've all been getting prepared for the new year at work and particularly at school. (The Jews actually celebrate the New Year at this time – Rosh ha Shana is this year on September 12th.) School uniforms are dragged from the wardrobe; books are bought and backed; pencils are sharpened; shoes polished. There's a general air of 'eager reluctance' pervading the atmosphere.

    These are the very themes of the section of Mark's Gospel we are considering today. The apostles have just come down from the mount of Transfiguration, which, as we noticed a few weeks ago, symbolises the glory of the individual, the innate divinity of the human person. And, no doubt because they have been informed of these elevated things they are getting a little carried away with a sense of their own importance. What are they doing? They are arguing. They are arguing, as men will, about who is the greatest among them. They want to construct a league table – extraordinarily typical of the male psyche! Just another expression of the 'mine is bigger than yours' mentality of the average man! Jesus responds by explaining to them the great Virgo principle of service: 'If anyone wants to be first, he will be the last of all, and the servant of all,' he says. And, to give a graphic demonstration, he takes a little child and sets him in the midst of them – echoing the ancient Egyptian symbol of Virgo, the goddess Isis with the young Horus in her arms. What it's all about, says Jesus, is looking after these little ones, and being as free from guile and spiritual ambition as them. Never

---

[82] Luke 10:2

mind your complicated theology, your learned articles, your fancy titles, your hierarchies, your sense of self-importance: look at these children and learn a lesson from them. Yes, you are divine; you are a 'little lower than the angels', you are made in the image of God, but so is everybody else, and you can only express your own divine nature by serving the divine in other people. Jesus informs us that in order to save our life we must lose it, and that suffering and self-denial are a necessary part of following Christ: we can only realize our true divinity by relinquishing it. In the Letter to the Philippians, St Paul expresses it thus:

> **Your attitude should be the same as that of Christ Jesus, who, being in very nature God, did not consider equality with God something to be grasped, but made himself nothing, taking the very nature of a servant, being made in human likeness. And being found in appearance as a man, he humbled himself and became obedient to death – even death on a cross!**[83]

This is the principle of *kenosis*, self-emptying: our divine nature is only realized to the extent that we serve the divine in other people. In the Gospel of Mark, no sooner are we apprised of Jesus's glory (Leo) than we are given clear instructions about the necessity of humility (Virgo). Or, as the Hindus put it, 'Namaste' – the god in me salutes the god in you!

No one was more convinced of his own divine nature than Walt Whitman, who wrote:

> I believe in the flesh and its appetites,
> Seeing, hearing, feeling, are miracles, and each part and tag of me is a miracle.
> Divine am I, inside and out, and I make holy whatever I touch or am touch'd from.
> The scent of these armpits aroma finer than prayer.
> This head more than churches, bibles, and all the creeds.

---

[83] Philippians 2:5-8 (NIV)

But he also stresses, that what applies to him applies to all:

> By God! I will accept nothing which all cannot have
> their counterpart of on the same terms.

And how did he express the conviction of his own divinity? He went to tend the wounded and dying in the American Civil War.

Walt Whitman knew what following Christ meant, although he probably wouldn't have called himself a Christian. But we Christians don't seem to have much idea. We still want our league tables, even in the spiritual life, and we confer titles on ourselves just to remind everybody how important we are. Clergy titles are wonderfully ironic in the light of Jesus's teaching. There's 'monsignor', 'bishop', 'archbishop', 'cardinal', 'pope' – 'princes of the church'; they are 'Reverend', 'Most Reverend', 'Very Reverend'; they are to be addressed as 'My Lord', 'Your Grace', 'Your Holiness', 'Holy Father', all according to strict protocol, and woe betide anyone who gets it wrong! People still curtsey in front of bishops, and kiss their rings! And even Unitarians are not free from this. Why do we covet the title 'Reverend'? Why do we clamour to put titles in front of our names, and qualifications behind them? The time is surely here when we should consign all this preposterous stuff to the dustbin. We are a lay movement – that is, a movement without priests, without hierarchy; a movement in which anything a minister can do can be done by a suitably qualified and appointed member of the congregation. 'Whoever wants to be first, will be last of all, and the servant of all,' says Jesus. The most ironic title of the pope is 'servus servorum dei', 'servant of the servants of God' a title which no doubt strikes him as odd as he is carried into St. Peter's in a sedan chair, and as he reflects that he has probably never so much as boiled an egg in his life.

Nor should we be concerned with who is making the greatest contribution to our spiritual movement, or to any spiritual movement: even the person who gives a cup of cold water is making a significant contribution, and won't go unrewarded. There are some people who, in Emerson's words, are 'too great for fame'. I know them, and so do you. They will never be featured in any newspaper biopics; there'll be no mention in the Queen's Honours

List, and yet they, and countless millions like them, are people of whom the world is not worthy, the 'salt of the earth', people who live lives of such quiet heroism that our paltry efforts are shamed by comparison.

Gerard Manley Hopkins wrote a poem in 1888, here in Dublin, extolling just such virtues in St. Alphonsus Rodriguez, a Jesuit lay-brother, who did little more than act as a doorkeeper for forty years, and yet he performed his duties with such diligence that God granted him extraordinary spiritual insights.

In our own community everyone makes a contribution, and every contribution is of inestimable value. A few months ago, Michael, who does our rotas, told me that about 90 separate individuals feature on one or more of our several rotas; some look after the children in the Sunday club, some bring flowers, some read at the service, some welcome people on Sunday mornings, some provide coffee and tea. These are extraordinarily important activities without which the church would be immeasurably impoverished. Even just showing up, being present, smiling at visitors, contributes to the friendly community that has been built up over the years. When I first came here there was an elderly man in the congregation called John McCabe. He was a very quiet man. He wasn't well off, in fact he was probably quite poor, and he wasn't particularly well educated, but he had thought his way into this congregation, and attended every week without fail before his death in 1997. He didn't have the confidence to read or to do any of the other duties, and he couldn't make any real financial contribution, but he asked the committee if he could paint the vestry as his contribution to church life. It hasn't been painted since he did it, and I for one am rather reluctant to have it repainted, because the fading colour down there at present reminds me of this simple and generous man who offered his own 'cup of cold water' in a spirit of humble service.

'The first will be last, and the last will be first.' Such is the great lesson of Virgo, the great lesson we in this celebrity obsessed culture need to learn.

Beginner's Mind

Story: The Overflowing Cup

A very clever University professor went to visit Nan-in, a Buddhist holy man. The professor wanted some advice on how he should live a spiritual life. 'I have been studying for many years,' he told the holy man. 'I have read hundreds of books; I have sat at the feet of many gurus; and I have attended many different places of worship; but I have never found what I am looking for. So now I have come to see you.'

Nan-in looked kindly at the professor. 'Would you like a cup of tea?' he asked with a smile.

'Yes, please,' replied the professor.

Nan-in prepared the tea and began to pour. The professor's cup was filled to overflowing, but Nan-in continued to pour the tea until it spilled out on to the saucer, and then on to the table.

'What are you doing?' asked the astonished professor. 'The cup is full. No more will go in!'

'Just like you,' said Nan-in. 'Your head is so full of theories, scriptures, ceremonies, and philosophies that there is no room for anything else. Before I can start to teach you, you must empty your cup.'

Last Saturday, 8th September, a friend called me from Montenegro to say that the nuns in the local convent had been singing and chanting for virtually the whole day. It must be a special feast day, she thought, and she found out subsequently that her surmise had been correct. It was a special Catholic festival, the birthday of the Virgin Mary. But, one asks, why celebrate it now? Surely there's nothing in the Bible about the date of Mary's birth – there's nothing about the date of Jesus's birth, for that matter. We celebrate the birth of Jesus at the time of the winter solstice, but the Bible doesn't say explicitly that he was born then. So Mary's birthday is even more conjectural.

You, I'm sure, will not be surprised to learn that there is a certain astronomical appropriateness in celebrating the birth of the Virgin at this time of the year. Many centuries ago, when the Church calendar was drawn up, on the 8th September the stars of the constellation Virgo once again became visible before sunrise after being overwhelmed by the powerful rays of the Sun for about three weeks: 'the virgin is born'. From mid-August, the stars of Virgo had been invisible; they had, poetically, been taken up into the glory of the Sun, hence the feast of the Assumption of the Virgin into heaven which has been celebrated by Catholics for centuries on 15th August. So, the dates of two Catholic festivals are determined by the Sun's path in the sky, and we can add a third, because the feast of the Immaculate Conception – a big feast in Catholicism, a Holy Day of Obligation – occurs on 8th December, nine months before Mary' birthday on 8th September. These were, originally, references to astronomical phenomena, and had deep mystical significance, but their astronomical correspondence has been lost in the Church's fervent attempts to apply them, absurdly, to the life of an individual who may or may not have lived two thousand years ago.

But remember, as I keep stressing throughout these sermons on the correspondence of the Gospel stories with the zodiac signs, we are not dealing with history here; still less are we dealing with biology. Birth of the Virgin, or birth from a virgin, are not statements relating to physical birth in either a historical or a biological sense, in spite of what the orthodox theologians say. The original mystical message of these metaphors is that the Christ, the divine life, is *always* born of a virgin. The birth of the Christ spirit within the individual – in you and me and everybody else – is a *spiritual* birth, a rebirth, which owes nothing to flesh and blood. And it always occurs symbolically in Bethlehem, which means, in Hebrew 'The House of Bread', or Virgo, the sign of the harvest, the sign pictured by the ancients as a Woman with a Sheaf of Wheat in her hand, or as the goddess Isis with the child Horus in her arms.

So, there was a connection, in the ancient mysteries, between this time of the year and the virginal rebirth of the spirit. That's why Mark's Gospel introduces children at this point in the narrative, and why Jesus tells us that we have to become like children if we want to inherit the kingdom of God. These sayings of Jesus have always puzzled people, particularly those people (like me) who have had a lot to do with children, and who have found it difficult to sentimentalize their behaviour. We all know that children can be noisy, troublesome, demanding, selfish, impatient, and unreasonable. In fact, it may well be that this is their natural condition, so we can't think that the kingdom of God would be a place of peace and quiet if it was peopled only by the childlike. However, you will be relieved to hear, Jesus wasn't asking us to copy any of these characteristics. But there are some aspects of childhood which we could well do to rediscover. One is lack of cynicism. Whatever else a child might be, he or she is not cynical. Cynicism, world-weariness, lack of delight in the world, lack of trust in human beings, is adult, learned behaviour. The word 'cynic' comes from the Greek word for dog, and while it may once have been the name of a respected school of ancient philosophy, today the word describes a person who sees self-interest as the only real human motivator, and who is suspicious of virtue or altruism.

Children are free from this corrosive spiritual disease; they are still interested in the world, still see it as a magical place, while we have become what the Harry Potter books call 'Muggles', non-magical people, who have lost any sense of wonder and delight in the simple things of life. The contrast is brought out beautifully in chapter 4 of *The Little Prince*, by Antoine de Saint-Exupery.

> Grown-ups love figures. When you talk to them about a new friend, they never ask questions about essential matters. They never say to you, 'What does his voice sound like? What games does he prefer? Does he collect butterflies?' They ask: 'How old is he? How many brothers does he have? How much does he weigh? How much money does his father earn?' It is only then that they feel they know him. If you were to mention to grown-ups: 'I've seen a beautiful house built with pink bricks, with geraniums on the windowsills and doves on the roof...' they would not be able to imagine such a house. You would have to say to them: 'I saw a house worth

two million pounds.' Then they would exclaim: 'Oh! How lovely!'[84]

Rediscovering the child-like delight in the world is a prerequisite of entry into the kingdom of God, says Jesus. Not sophistication; not knowledge; not accumulated experience; not skill; not expertise. The Kingdom of God is not something we grow *into*; paradoxically, it's something we grow *out of*, and this gives rise to the spiritual principle, which runs completely counter to secular and even religious wisdom, that the people who understand the world best are those who have lived in it least. As Wordsworth says:

Heaven lies about us in our infancy!
Shades of the prison-house begin to close
Upon the growing Boy.
But He beholds the light, and whence it flows,
He sees it in his joy;
The Youth, who daily farther from the east
Must travel, still is Nature's Priest,
And by the Vision splendid
Is on his way attended;
At length the Man perceives it die away,
And fade into the light of common day.[85]

Sometimes it takes catastrophe or even tragedy to bring us back to this primal state of awareness, in which we can experience 'the vision splendid', which is why the spiritual writers are not so dismissive of adversity as are politicians or economists, and it is also why, as I've mentioned before from my own experience, when one thinks that one's time on earth is limited, one begins to perceive the world in a completely different way – a way akin to the way one perceived it as a child. There is no better example of this than that described by the British playwright Dennis Potter in an interview with Melvyn Bragg, just a little before his death from pancreatic cancer in 1994. He knows he's going to die soon, and yet, he says,

---

[84] Saint-Exupery, pages 21-2.
[85] Wordsworth, *Intimations of Immortality*

'the nowness becomes so vivid that, almost in a perverse sort of way, I'm almost serene. You know, I can celebrate life.' He goes on:

> Below my window in Ross, when I'm working in Ross, for example, there at this season, the blossom is out in full now, there in the west early. It's a plum tree, it looks like apple blossom but it's white, and looking at it, instead of saying 'Oh that's nice blossom'.... last week, looking at it through the window when I'm writing, I see it is the whitest, frothiest, blossomest blossom that there ever could be, and I can see it. Things are more trivial than they ever were, and more important, and the difference between the trivial and the important doesn't seem to matter. But the nowness of everything is absolutely wondrous, and if people could see that, you know. There's no way of telling you; you have to experience it, but the glory of it, if you like, the comfort of it, the reassurance .... not that I'm interested in reassuring people – bugger that. The fact is, if you see the present tense, boy do you see it! And boy, can you celebrate it![86]

Potter here mentions the second child-like virtue: the capacity to enjoy the moment, to live 'in the present tense, which is all a small child lives in. So a wet Tuesday afternoon can actually be years long, and it – childhood – is full to the brim of fear, horror, excitement, joy, boredom, love, anxiety...'

Fear, horror, excitement, joy, boredom, love, anxiety. How troublesome they are! We're better off without them! Let's just keep our lives nice and tranquil, inoffensive, trouble free. Let's just keep shopping and eating and travelling and washing the car and watching television. Is it any wonder that the Western world has come under the spell of Prozac?

'Look at these children,' says Jesus. 'Learn a lesson from them.' The third lesson they can teach us is the lesson of spiritual and intellectual humility. Aren't we so proud of our adult sophistication and our learning? Aren't we so much more intelligent and so much better informed than our forebears who were swathed

---

[86] *Great Interviews of the 20th Century*. Number 5 in a Series of 14, issued by *The Guardian* during September 2007.

in almost invincible ignorance? In some ways we are, but in many ways we're no more enlightened than they were. Just because we have words and concepts like 'Big Bang' and 'Evolution' doesn't mean we have solved the problems of existence. We still haven't got a clue about the really big questions of meaning and purpose. It's a mysterious world. Some corners of the blanket of mystery have been lifted, but there is much more to discover and, perhaps, some things that will never be discovered. Even so, this doesn't stop us filling our heads with complicated and conflicting theories, about which we argue and fight, interminably. But our clever but inadequate theories actual keep us from any real understanding. This is why, according to today's children's story, we have to 'empty our cup'. 'Emptying your cup' is what the Buddhists call 'cultivating beginner's mind', starting again, looking at the world again, getting back to that openness to experience which we had as children, but over which our pretended sophistication has thrown a veil.

On Tuesday night I was sitting in the kitchen trying to read when I became aware of a moth flying crazily between the lights in the ceiling. It seemed to me as if it was mad – angry, or drunk, or drugged – and I was disturbed by it, even picking up a newspaper to swat it in case it came too close to my head, which it seemed to be threatening to do. Then I began to ponder the amazing nature of this tiny piece of animated matter, this miracle of aerodynamic beauty, this entity with a rudimentary mind, countless tiny muscles and nerves, perfectly working organs of nutrition, reproduction, and respiration, with an unfathomable but fatal attraction for the light, and I decided against killing it. I turned off the light so that it would calm down and went off to bed.

I momentarily perceived the moth a little differently from my usual perception of such a creature, and I was reminded of Walt Whitman's opinion that 'a mouse is miracle enough to stagger sextillions of infidels'. Even the simplest creature defies our powers of explanation and understanding. I'm not arguing for creation against evolution here. Nothing could be further from my mind. At that moment on Tuesday, I wasn't concerned with how it came into being. I was simply content to experience its unfamiliarity, its strangeness, its 'mothness', and in doing so I've been prompted to consider the strangeness and unfamiliarity of myself and of those around me, and of everything.

Try it yourself. Each day take something, or someone, and try to experience it, or him, or her, as if for the first time. Look with new eyes, not the jaded eyes of your conventional sight. Consider the intricacy and beauty of their physical make up, or the mystery of their consciousness. See how your chosen subject resembles others of the same category, but consider too how each thing or person has a uniqueness which stands beyond categorisation. I love what Gabriel Garzia Marquez said about his wife of many years: 'I have been married to this woman for thirty years, and I know her so well that I haven't the slightest idea who she is.'

Marquez is a poet, and poets are people who see the world with fresh eyes. who refuse to be imprisoned in consensus reality, in the clichéd world of derived opinion. The poet is a perpetual beginner. When we allow ourselves to become beginners again, to become children again, we die to the cynical, grasping, greedy kingdom of mammon, and are reborn - virgin-born - into the kingdom of God.

Chapter 7: Libra
23rd September – 23rd October

Libra, the Balance, is the sign of the autumn equinox, when day and night are equal. It is associated with relationships, marriage, and has been called 'the sign of cosmic reciprocity'. Its ruler is Venus, the goddess of love. The Greeks called Libra 'Zugos,' *the Yoke*, and it is a word derived from this that Jesus uses to describes the bond between male and female.[87] In Egypt it was represented by the goddess Ma'at, who judged the dead, weighing their souls in the balance: those who passed her test were said to be 'light hearted'; those who failed were 'heavy hearted'.

---

[87] Συνέζευξεν: *Strong's Exhaustive Concordance* gives: 'From συν (*sun*) and the base ζευγος (*zeugos*); to yoke together, i.e. figuratively conjoin (in marriage) – join together.'

121

Getting the Balance Right

Mark 10:3-9

> Jesus then left that place and went into the region of Judea and across the Jordan. Again crowds of people came to him, and as was his custom, he taught them. Some Pharisees came and tested him by asking, 'Is it lawful for a man to divorce his wife?'
>
> 'What did Moses command you?' he replied. They said, 'Moses permitted a man to write a certificate of divorce and send her away.' 'It was because your hearts were hard that Moses wrote you this law,' Jesus replied. 'But at the beginning of creation God "made them male and female". For this reason a man will leave his father and mother and be united to his wife, and the two will become one flesh. So they are no longer two, but one. Therefore, what God has joined together, let man not separate.'

Story: The Two Foolish Cats

> Once upon a time there were two cats. One was a big, black cat; the other a small tabby. These two cats were best friends; they went everywhere together, and shared many adventures. And they very rarely quarrelled. One day, they came across the remains of a picnic which some untidy, thoughtless people had left behind on the grass, and there, among the empty bottles and uneaten sandwiches, were two pieces of cake.
>
> Now these two cats happened to share a passion for cake – unusual, I know, but these were strange cats – and this was very good cake: cream cake topped with icing and strawberry jam. 'I've not had cake like this for a long time,' said the big black cat. 'It's great!' But no sooner were the words out of his

mouth, than he noticed that his piece was smaller than his friend's piece. 'Hey!' he said, angrily. 'Your piece is bigger than mine, and it's not fair! I'm bigger than you, and so I should have the bigger piece!'

The small tabby cat could see the logic of this, and he was just about to agree to a swap, when he thought of something. 'Yes, you are bigger than I,' he said to his friend, 'but if I don't eat more than you, I'll never become big. So I should have the bigger piece.'

This made sense, too. The two cats didn't know what to do. 'I know,' said the big, black cat. 'We'll go to the wise monkey in the forest. He'll know how to solve our problem.'

So the two cats set off to find the wise monkey. 'Mr. Wise Monkey! Mr. Wise Monkey!' they called, as they approached the tree where he lived. 'I'm up here!' shouted the monkey. And there he was, sitting in his tree, with a pair of weight-scales in his hand – just what was needed to sort out the problem.

'We want you to settle an argument, Mr. Wise Monkey,' began the big, black cat. 'Yes,' interrupted the tabby. 'We have two pieces of cake, but one is bigger than the other. My friend is bigger than I, but if I don't eat more than he does, I'll never grow. I think I should have the bigger piece, and he thinks that he should have it. Can you divide them so that we get equal shares?'

'You've come to right person,' said the Wise Monkey. 'I'm just the one to make sure that you get equal shares. Let me see the two pieces.' The cats handed over the pieces of cake, and the monkey placed them on either side of his weight scales. 'Yes, I can see your problem; this one is much bigger than that,' he said, picking the bigger piece off the scale. 'I'll just even them up!' and with that, he took a big bite. Then he placed it back on the scale. This time the other piece was heavier. 'Oh, I'd better have a piece out of this one, now,' he said taking a bite. And so it went on, first a bite from one piece, then a bite from the other, and, despite protests from the two cats, he didn't stop until he'd devoured both pieces. 'There you are,' said the monkey. 'You've got equal shares

123

now! That's what you came for, isn't it? You've nothing to quarrel about now, so you may thank me and leave.'

The two hungry cats left a lot wiser than they arrived. And they never quarrelled again.

On the 23rd September this year the Sun entered the zodiacal sign of Libra. You can always tell when the Sun is approaching this point on its journey through the heavens, because people start to say (when they can think of nothing else to say), 'The nights are drawing in now, aren't they?' And indeed they are. The long days of summer are over. Now it's dark at 7.30 pm, and most of us are getting out of bed before dawn. Now day and night are of equal duration – twelve hours or so of each – with the point of exactitude occurring on 23rd September, the day of the autumnal equinox. Six months ago we had the spring equinox, and day and night were equal then, too, but there is a difference between these two points: after the spring equinox, the light begins to dominate; after the autumn equinox, the darkness begins to prevail. Soon, it will be dark when you arrive at work, and dark before you set off home.

The contrast between light and darkness, which is almost lost on us because of our electric lights and round-the-clock lifestyle, would have had a marked impact upon people in times gone by, who would have been compelled to organise their lives around the natural rhythms of night and day. Daylight was for activity and work; darkness for rest and sleep; in the daylight they could be reasonably secure from predators and so could act alone; in the night they were vulnerable and needed each other for safety and for comfort. We still say, 'Things will look different in the daylight,' meaning that the light will put a temporary end to those nameless fears which seem to beset us in the darkness. Brendan Behan once described himself as 'a daylight atheist', a theological position with which many of us will be familiar: when the Sun is shining and we've plenty to do, those nagging questions about existence which will often assail us in the darkness seem to evaporate.

The zodiac, which, as I've constantly stressed, is simply the path of the Sun in the sky, derives its imagery, in part, from this interplay of light and dark. In the spring, when the light begins to dominate, we have the sign Aries, which symbolises the growing light of individual consciousness struggling against the forces of collective darkness, and so Aries comes to represent the loner, the pioneer, the trailblazer, who heads off almost recklessly to chart new paths for the rest of us to follow. In the autumn, when the darkness begins to prevail, we have Aries's complementary sign, Libra, which symbolises intimacy, relationships, marriage – social and communal activities, as opposed to individualistic ones. Jeff Mayo, who taught me the language of astrology 40 years ago, and whose book *Teach Yourself Astrology* is still one of the best introductions to the subject, says that Libra symbolises 'the primitive urge for unity and relatedness with others .... and the need to conform to an ideal pattern of community life'. People who are strongly Libran are said to be cooperative, socially aware, with a strong sense of justice and fair play. Their 'ruling planet' is Venus, the planet of love and beauty, which tends to render them amorous, stylish, artistic, refined, but with an unfortunate tendency (they say) to laziness and self-indulgence.

The symbol of Libra is the balance, reflecting the equinoctial balance between night and day, but also symbolising the balance between all pairs of opposites: the individual and the community, male and female, work and rest, outgoing and indrawing, initiative and caution. The Libran scales are used as symbols of justice – paying what one owes to the community. On the Old Bailey courts in London, there is a statue of the goddess of Justice with scales in her hands, and in ancient Egypt, Libra was the goddess Ma'at, who was said to weigh the souls of the dead against a feather; those who passed her test were 'light hearted', those who failed it 'heavy hearted'. The word 'Libra' is the Latin word for a pound weight, and in the pre-decimal system of weights and measures the pound was abbreviated to 'lb', a contraction of Libra.

The Greeks called Libra *Zugos*, the Yoke, which refers to the wooden device fixed across the necks of oxen to keep them together as they were pulling the plough, reflecting once again the notion of harmony, balance, and working together, which are central to the symbolism of Libra.

In the Gospel of Mark, the Libran section begins, appropriately, with an argument over marriage. In an attempt to trap

Jesus into making an injudicious reply, some Pharisees ask Jesus about the legality of divorcing one's wife. Jesus, quoting from the Book of Genesis, tells them that male and female become 'one flesh' in marriage,[88] and that men shouldn't separate what God has joined together.

'Joined together' is a translation of the Greek word 'Sunezeuxen' which literally means 'yoked together', from the very same root as 'zugos' the Greek word for the sign Libra. This is added confirmation that Mark is following the sequence of the zodiacal signs in his narrative.

For its time, this gospel teaching on marriage was really radical. Marriage was not a sacred institution in the ancient world and divorce was commonplace, even among the Jews, for whom monogamy was the ideal. Theoretically, divorce was open to both parties, but given the general status of women at that time, it was hardly an option for the female. William Barclay describes the situation as follows:

> One thing vitiated the whole marriage relationship. The woman in the eyes of the law was a thing. She was at the absolute disposal of her father or of her husband. She had virtually no legal rights at all. To all intents and purposes a woman could not divorce her husband for any reason, and a man could divorce his wife for any cause at all. 'A woman,' said the Rabbinic law, 'may be divorced with or without her will; but a man only with his will.'[89]

Getting a divorce was very simple. The man had to give his wife a 'bill of divorcement' in the presence of two witnesses. This stated: 'Let this be from me thy writ of divorce and letter of dismissal and deed of liberation, that thou mayest marry whatsoever thou wilt.'

The passage from the Jewish scriptures to which the Pharisees refer in their discussion with Jesus can be found in Deuteronomy 24:1. The text states that a man may divorce his wife 'if she find no favour in his eyes, because he hath found some

---

[88] Genesis 2:24
[89] Barclay, W. (1975) page 151

uncleanness in her'. The prevailing opinion among rabbis at the time of Jesus was that this was a specific reference to adultery, but certain rabbis, following Rabbi Akiba, considered that 'finding no favour' in one's wife could simply mean that one no longer thought her attractive. The rabbinic school of Hillel taught that a man might divorce his wife if:

> she spoiled his dinner by putting too much salt in his food, if she went in public with her head uncovered, if she talked with men in the streets, if she was a brawling woman, if she spoke disrespectfully of her husband's parents in his presence, if she was troublesome or quarrelsome.[90]

Divorce, it seems, was possible on the flimsiest of pretexts.

This teaching on the sanctity of marriage is an obvious improvement on what preceded it, but the total ban on divorce, which Jesus' teaching has been used to justify, has left its own legacy of misery and injustice, and I don't think the text is really advocating this. We undoubtedly need to extend the principles of justice, fairness, and balance into our intimate lives, but there is a deeper meaning to the text which has been missed in all the legalistic moralising which a purely surface reading has occasioned. The mystical traditions preserve another dimension to marriage which transcends its function as a social institution. The union of male and female does not just refer to the coupling we call matrimony. *The 'sacred marriage' is something that occurs within the individual.* 'In the beginning,' it says in the Book of Genesis, 'God created them male and female'.[91] The original, perfect state of the human being is one of balance between spirit (male) and matter (female), which were joined in harmonious unity and balance – the image of God -, before being sundered by the Fall.

In the *Tao Te Ching*, which precedes the Christian scriptures by at least five hundred years, we read about the eternal interplay between the opposites, *yin and yang*. *Yin* refers to the characteristics of softness, passivity, femininity, darkness, the valley, the Moon, the negative polarity; *yang* refers to characteristics such as hardness,

---

[90] Barclay W., (1975), page 152
[91] Genesis 1:27

masculinity, brightness, the mountain, the Sun, the positive polarity. All reality is based upon these two opposing forces, say the Taoists. Neither is superior; both are necessary, and each contains the seed of the other. The Taoist attempts to see these forces at work in the world and in himself, and to act in harmony with them, uniting the opposite forces within himself. 'Tao' means 'The Way', and it is significant that Christianity was originally called 'The Way'.[92]

At about the same time that Lao Tzu was compiling the Tao Te Ching in China, Plato was writing in Greece. In his *Symposium*, he makes reference to a myth that was probably very ancient even then, that at one time, male and female were joined together, and the human being had four legs not two, but because in that state they were considered to present a threat to the gods, Zeus cut them in two, and now the separated halves are doomed to spend their time seeking each other. There was also a warning that, if the two-legged creatures misbehave, Zeus would cut them again! At the heart of this myth lies the notion that male and female constitute a unity, a unity that has been lost, but which can and must be re-established within the individual.

We find the same idea within Christian mysticism. We have tended to see marriage as the union of a man with a woman in mutually rewarding partnership with, traditionally, a clear demarcation of duties and responsibilities. This indeed is so, and has its place, but there is another dimension to this teaching which we find in the Gnostic Gospel of Thomas:

> When you make the two one, and when you make the outside like the inside, and the above like the below, and when you make the male and the female one and the same so that the male be not male nor the female female, then you will enter the kingdom.[93]

The 'sacred marriage' is not the public jamboree, complete with white dress, bridesmaids, posh food and an exotic honeymoon. The sacred marriage occurs when the spiritually mature individual is able to balance male and female, yang and yin, activity and passivity,

---

[92] Acts 9:2
[93] The Gospel of Thomas, saying 22

spirit and matter, science and mystery, striving and yielding, adventure and repose, and a whole host of other complementary forces, *within him or her self*.

Balancing the polarities within the self may take some doing but it doesn't require us to learn anything new or to embark upon years of spiritual training. In fact, Robert Fulghum, in his celebrated essay *All I Really Need to Know I Learned in Kindergarten* says that we were well acquainted with this principle before we started big school. What did we learn by the sand pit in the nursery?

> Share everything.
> Play fair.
> Don't hit people.
> Put things back where you found them.
> Clean up your own mss.
> Don't take things that aren't yours.
> Say you're sorry when you hurt somebody.
> Wash your hands before you eat.
> Flush.
> Warm cookies and cold milk are good for you.
> Live a balanced life – learn some and think some and draw and paint and sing and dance and play and work every day some.[94]

It's as simple as that! And yet how difficult is it in our 24/7, work-hard play-hard, striving, competitive, comparative, acquisitive world is it to put these things into practice! But the great spiritual message of Libra, is that just as day and night come naturally into equilibrium, so must we strive to bring that sense of balance into our own lives. The reward – personally and socially – for finding the balance is immense. As Plato's myth intimates, when the male and female principles are joined in harmony within an individual, she attains a state in which she could almost challenge the gods.

---

[94] Fulghum, page 6

Distractions

Mark 10:17-31

When he'd gone back on to the road, a man came running towards him. He fell on his knees before him and said, 'Good teacher, what should I do in order to inherit eternal life?' Jesus said to him, 'Why do you call me good? No one is good except God alone. You know the commandments: don't murder, don't commit adultery, don't steal, don't tell lies, don't defraud, honour your father and your mother.' He replied, 'Teacher, I've kept all these from my youth.' Jesus, gazing at him, warmed towards him, and said, 'There's only one thing you need. Sell what you have and give it to the poor, and you will have treasure in heaven. And come follow me!'

But the young man was upset by what Jesus said, and he went away sorrowfully because he was a man of great wealth. Looking round, Jesus said to his disciples, 'How difficult it is for a very wealthy person to enter the kingdom of God!' His disciples were astonished at his words, but Jesus told them again, 'Children, how difficult it is to go into the kingdom of God! It's easier for a camel to go through the eye of a needle than for a rich man to enter into the kingdom of God.' They were extremely shocked and said to one another, 'Who can be saved then?' Looking intently at them, Jesus said, 'With men it's impossible, but not with God. Everything is possible with God.' Peter began to say to him, 'Look. We left everything and have followed you.' Jesus said, 'I'm telling you the truth, there's no one who has left a house or brothers or sisters or mother or father or children or fields for my sake and the sake of the good news who won't now receive a hundred times more houses, brothers, sisters, mothers and children and fields (with persecution) and in the coming age, eternal life! Many who are first will be last, and the last first.'

Story: The Diamond

One night, Hemendra had a dream in which a voice told him that if he were to go into the park the next day he would meet a man who would give him a treasure so great that it would change his life.

When he awoke, Hemendra could not get the dream out of his head. He didn't normally pay much attention to his dreams, and anyway, he generally couldn't remember them, but this one had been so vivid that he could remember all the details even after he had eaten his breakfast. He had nothing else to do that day so, a little sceptical but with nothing to lose, he decided he'd walk in the park and see what he could see.

No sooner had he passed through the park gates than he saw an old man sitting on a bench. 'Perhaps that could be the man who is going to change my life,' he thought to himself. He approached the man and said, 'Excuse me, sir, but could it be possible that you have something precious to give me? I had a dream last night in which I was told to come into the park and seek a man who would give me something of great value.'

The old man said, 'Well, all I possess is in this little bag. I'll have a look. Maybe there's something I can give you.' He emptied out his bag on the grass, and along with a few inconsequential items there was a huge diamond! It was bigger than Hemendra's fist! 'Perhaps that's it,' stammered Hemendra, pointing at the diamond.

'Oh, the stone! I'd forgotten about the stone! I picked it up in the forest a few days ago. You can certainly have it. It's no good to me.' With that he handed over the diamond to Hemendra, who thanked him profusely and then rushed off before the old man had chance to change his mind.

All the way home Hemendra thought about what he would do with the money that the diamond would bring him.

He'd buy a big house, hire servants, eat the best food, drink the finest wine, travel to exotic places. He was so excited! It was too late for him to go to the big city to sell his treasure, so he put it under his pillow just to keep it safe, and tried to go to sleep. But he couldn't sleep. He tossed and turned in bed, and, at the first light of dawn, he got up and went back into the park. There, sitting on the same bench, was the old man. Hemendra handed him the diamond. 'Please take this back,' he said, 'and give me instead the wealth that makes it possible for you to give such a thing away.'

Victoria Coren is a very talented and versatile English woman. She writes a column in the *Observer*, presents high-brow quiz programmes on BBC 2, commentates on and writes about poker, in addition to being a world-renowned poker player. A few months ago Victoria won $1 million (£500,000) in a poker tournament, and in a recent *Observer* column she made the following honest and very perceptive comment about how this win has affected her:

> Do I feel rich? Quite the opposite. Having never had real money in the bank before, its existence has created a sudden nervousness in me about not having it. I worry about how long it will last, and what I will do when it has gone. I never wanted or needed half a million pounds; now I've got it, I wish it was a million. Or five million. I suddenly understand how footballers, the moment they can afford to fly everywhere first class, start worrying that they can't afford a private jet.[95]

How curious that her reaction to winning an enormous amount of money is exactly the opposite of what we would expect. Instead of exulting in her good fortune, she's lamenting the fact that she didn't win more. Now that she's rich, she feels the urge to become richer. It's no doubt the same feeling that lottery winners

---

[95] The *Observer*, 7th October 2007

have when they share a prize: 'I may have won two million, but if I'd been the only winner this week, it would have been eight million. Just my luck!' And it's probably something similar which drives the super-rich to compromise their integrity by advertising products they never use for sums of money they'll never need. The late, lamented Bill Hicks, said that anyone who ever endorses any commercial product automatically forfeits his or her rights to an opinion on any subject whatsoever, and when I see millionaire film actors and pop stars extolling the virtues of Tesco or Marks and Spencer, I am inclined to agree with him. What possibly motivates someone who is already rich beyond the dreams of avarice to earn a few measly hundred thousand in this way?

Yesterday's *Guardian* carried this little gem about the actress Liz Hurley:

> The multi-millionaire model, clothing designer, producer, and greatest spangly knickers wearer this country has ever produced was this week accused by Gloucestershire parishioners of breaking a promise to make a cash donation to the chapel in which her forty-two-part marriage to Arun Nayar was blessed. Rev. John Partington, apparently waived the standard thousand-pound fee in the hope that the couple would disburse a sum more commensurate with their exceptional wealth. Chapel members were hoping for enough to replace the boiler. This, they think, will prove difficult to do with the twelve hand-embroidered cassocks La Hurley sent in return for the service rendered. 'It strikes me as rather mean,' said Chapel treasurer, Sue Williams, 'especially as I understand that most of the wedding was paid for by a magazine,' proving that the art of understatement is alive and well and living in Winchcombe.[96]

And, in the same issue, the film producer Eli Roth is quoted as saying that his pet hates are the greed and envy he has found among actors: 'You meet with actors,' he says, 'and they're so

---

[96] *Guardian*, 20th October, 2007

excited to get involved in a project, then all they start worrying about is that their trailer is not big enough.'[97]

The plain fact is that, for most of us, enough is never enough. We get used to things so quickly that today's exciting novelty is tomorrow's boring commonplace. Ten years ago I would have willingly waited an hour to download an email from the other side of the world; now, if it takes twenty seconds I'm drumming my fingers with impatience. It's also true that today's privilege becomes tomorrow's entitlement. As someone has so wisely observed, 'When a man first borrows from you, he'll kiss your hand; the second time he'll doff his cap; the third time he'll nod, and the fourth time he'll chide you for being late with the payment, and the fifth time he'll ask you for twice as much'. When I was undergoing treatment in St. James' hospital in Leeds, I had to pick up a prescription from the pharmacy every Monday. There was invariably a queue, and sometimes a wait of an hour or so while the hard-pressed pharmacists sorted out the drugs. But Morag and I would wait patiently, maybe get a coffee from the machine, or go for a stroll round the hospital grounds. After all, we were getting extremely expensive drugs for nothing. There was a little sign which told you how long you could expect to wait before picking up your completed prescription. On one occasion, a young woman – no more than about 19 – was sitting with her tattooed boyfriend. They had a child in a push-chair, and another child on the way. She took one look at the expected completion time and said, 'They needn't think I'm waiting for fifty minutes,' and with that she stormed out of the hospital.

This woman's grandparents would have thought the National Health Service in Britain just about the twentieth century's greatest achievement; I know my parents did. But she had been raised on free consultations, free operations, and free medicine. Now she wanted them immediately.

I'm not blaming her. She simply exemplifies a pretty consistent human characteristic. We have no real perspective on things. We in the developed West are fabulously rich compared with our pretty recent ancestors. When Ernest Savell Hicks, the minister

---

[97] *Guardian Magazine*, 20th October, 2007

here from 1910 to 1962, first came to Dublin, he and his wife nearly caught the next boat back to England because they were horrified to see children in bare feet on a winter's day. There are no bare feet now. Poverty has changed its face. Morag and I cleared the church doorway one day last week while the caretaker was away, and in addition to the usual sheets of cardboard and blankets that had been left there by the rough sleepers, we found some unopened packets of sandwiches, and about three euros in loose change. These particular beggars didn't want change and they didn't want food. I have seen two of the people who regularly come here for money using mobile phones in the street. No money for food or rent, but money enough to make frivolous phone calls while on the move.

All of which demonstrates what we all know: poverty is relative. And because it is relative, it can never be eliminated. Once poverty meant no shoes; now it means no flat screen T.V., or no iPod. Poor people are those who want more than they have – which covers just about all of us. In fact, some of the poorest people I know, people who feel that their lives are blighted because of lack of money, are really extraordinarily well off. They have money, but they can't bring themselves to spend it.

Which brings us to today's gospel passage, the story of the Rich Young Man. 'What can I do to inherit eternal life?' the young man asks Jesus. 'You know the commandments,' replies Jesus. 'Keep them.' 'I have kept them all my life,' says the young man. 'You lack only one thing,' says Jesus. 'Sell all you have and give the proceeds to the poor. Then come follow me.' But the young man can't do it.

This particular passage is appropriately placed here, in the Libra section of the Gospel of Mark, because, as I said last week, Libra is associated with charm, style, attractiveness and flair, all characteristics of this young man. The man is loveable and Jesus 'warms towards him'. What's more, he is a law abiding citizen who has tried to do his duty to God and to his fellows, and Libra concerns the law and our legal obligations. His one failing, according to Jesus, is that he cannot relinquish his wealth, and this is keeping him from taking the next step in his development as a human being, called in the Gospel 'entry into the kingdom of God'. Real wealth is reaching a state of consciousness in which we are no longer slaves to the things we own. Remember the last line of the story I told the children: 'Give me the wealth that enables you to give away such a precious diamond.'

Last week I also said that the Egyptians associated Libra with the goddess Ma'at, who weighed the souls of the dead in the balance, and those who passed her test were 'light hearted', those who failed it 'heavy hearted'. This rich young man leaves Jesus sorrowful, 'heavy hearted'; he has just been weighed in the balance and found wanting.

Why does Jesus tell the man to give everything to the poor? Not, I think, because Jesus was on this occasion particularly concerned about the poor. He was concerned about the state of the rich man's soul. It's harder for a rich person to enter into the kingdom of God than for a camel to go through the eye of a needle, says Jesus in a wonderfully arresting image, but these are not the words of an early Che Guevara. Jesus was no politician. Of course, Jesus was not advocating living in penury. Abject poverty leaves us no time or inclination to pursue the interior life of the spirit. But Jesus knew, as all the spiritual luminaries know, that wealth keeps us from this, too. For a start, it gives us enormous headaches, as Victoria Coren is finding. How can I protect it? Why don't I have more? Why has he got more than me? What would happen to me if I lost it? To whom can I leave it? In addition, it gives us ample opportunity to squander our time in shallow and frivolous entertainment, of which we soon tire, and which ultimately proves unsatisfying. 'Getting and spending we lay waste our powers,' says William Wordsworth. Consuming, accumulating, protecting, displaying take us away from more spiritually productive activities. 'The more you possess, the greater the tedium,' says St. Teresa of Avila. Possessions and money are not wicked, but, if we are not careful, they can distract us from the things that matter. Teresa goes on:

> It's as if a person were to enter a place where the Sun is shining but be hardly able to open his eyes because of the mud in them. ... So, I think, must be the condition of the soul. Even though it may not be in a bad state, it is so involved in worldly affairs and so absorbed with its

possessions, honour, or business affairs, that even though as a matter of fact it would want to see and enjoy its beauty, these things do not allow it to; nor does it seem that it can slip free from so many impediments. If a person is to enter the second dwelling place, it is important that he strive to give up unnecessary things and business affairs. Each one should do this in conformity with his state of life.[98]

Recently, I happened to catch an item on GMTV, ITV's morning magazine show. The presenter, Fiona Phillips, was in Tanzania, meeting up with a young girl called Neema, whom she has been sponsoring for the past few years. After showing us the one room mud hut that the family of six had been sleeping in, and introducing us to the members of the family, Fiona said something like, 'These people have nothing. Just happiness, respect, and love.' And she wasn't trying to be smart or ironic. It made me wonder who should be sponsoring whom.

---

[98] Bielecki page 49

Chapter 8: Scorpio
24th October – 21st November

Scorpio is the sign of hidden power, death, regeneration, expiation, purgation, sexuality, and spiritual initiation into the deep mysteries of life. It concerns the hidden connections between living and dead. Halloween is celebrated on 31st October, when the Sun is in Scorpio. The Scorpio section of the Gospel is relatively short, but a passage from what appears to have been a longer version of Mark[99] is appropriately placed here, as is part of what is called 'the longer ending' in which Jesus tells his apostles that they will pick up serpents and not be harmed, a reference to the constellation Ophiuchus, the Serpent Holder, which is close by Scorpio. At this point in the narrative Jesus and the apostles are approaching Jericho, the lowest point on the earth's surface; this is appropriate for the 'descent into the depths' which Scorpio symbolises.

---

[99] See *The Secret Gospel*, by Morton Smith. (1973, Dawn Horse Press)

Into the Depths
Mark 10:35-45

James and John, the sons of Zebedee, approached him saying, 'Teacher, we want you to do for us whatever we ask.' Jesus said to them, 'What do you want me to do for you?' They said to him, 'Allow one of us to sit on your right hand and one on your left hand in your glory.' Jesus said to them, 'You don't know what you are asking! Are you able to drink the cup which I shall drink, or to be baptised with the baptism with which I shall be baptised?' They said to him, 'We are able!' Jesus said to them, 'The cup I shall drink you shall drink, and the baptism I shall undergo, you shall undergo but to sit on my right or on my left is not in my gift; it's for those for whom it has been prepared.' When they heard this, the other ten began to be annoyed at James and John and, calling them together, Jesus said to them, 'You know that those who consider themselves leaders among the Gentiles lord it over them, and the greatest among them exercise dominance. Well, that's not the way it is among you. No. Whoever wants to become great among you will be your servant and whoever wants to be first among you will be a slave of all. Because the son of man hasn't come to be served but to serve, and to give his life in order to purchase the freedom of many.

Story: 'Nobody'

Nasrudin gate-crashed a very posh reception and sat down at the top of the table in a very elegant chair. A guard approached and said, officiously, 'Excuse me, sir, but those chairs are reserved for the guests of honour.'

'Oh, I am more than just a guest,' replied Nasrudin.

'Really?' asked the guard, with a little more respect in his voice. 'Are you perhaps a government minister?'

'No, I'm much more important than a government minister!'

'Wow! Are you the Prime Minister?'

'No, I'm much more important than that!'

'Goodness, you must be the king himself!'

'I'm even more important than the king!'

'In this country, nobody is more important than the king!'

'That's it! You've got it! I'm nobody!'

'Adversity makes men; prosperity makes monsters.' Victor Hugo

Last week I saw a little boy, six or seven years old, walking to school with his mother. He was wearing a black cloak and a pointed hat; his face was white, except for a little trickle of red at the corner of his mouth. He was obviously involved in some Halloween festivities in school. How different from my days, I thought. Fifty years ago there was no celebration of Halloween in England, and even twenty years ago, as my teaching career was coming to an end, there was scant attention paid to the festival, and certainly none in school. It's yet another example of the Americanisation of our culture, I thought. But then, I thought again. This particular way of celebrating it – with fancy dress and 'trick or treat' expeditions – may be novel and commercialised, but this time of year has ever been acknowledged as a strange time, a time for leaving the rational behind a little and entering into the mysterious 'otherworld', the world we tend to ignore when the Sun is shining.

And it was there when I was growing up. It just took a different form. Within the Catholic tradition, this time of year is devoted to praying for the dead, the souls in purgatory, and All Souls' Day and All Saints' Day close out October and open November. In the earlier Celtic tradition, we have the feast of Samhain, marking the end of summer, which, according to Wikipedia, was time to take stock of the herds and grain supplies, and decide which animals would need to be slaughtered in order for the people and livestock to survive the winter.

There is a definite feel of encroaching winter now. The trees are bare, and the leaves seem to be piled up everywhere. The nights are longer, the Sun lower in the sky. This is the beginning of nature's fallow time, when growth above ground has come to a halt, and all of nature's activity seems to be concentrated below the surface. According to the Greek myth, this is the time of year when Persephone goes back to the Underworld, and her mother Demeter, the goddess of grain and fertility, is so distraught by her absence that she forbids any new growth upon the earth.

The Sun has entered the zodiacal sign of Scorpio, the sign which symbolises the hidden depths of the human personality, all those ungovernable emotions, secret desires, buried motivations, which we try to suppress or to ignore, but which burst through our superficial rational consciousness from time to time, to disturb or even to wreck our tranquillity. People who are strongly Scorpionic are said to be 'deep', intense, uncompromising, with a powerful will, and a tendency to strong emotion which can often manifest as jealousy and possessiveness. It is a strongly sexual sign; not with a recreational, hedonistic approach to sexuality, but with a deep feeling of sexual connectedness, an appreciation of the mystery and power of human union. Scorpios are not to be trifled with emotionally, and there is often something about the eyes which indicate a passionate and forceful character. Scorpio is said to be ruled by Mars, the god of war and bloodshed, and so it is a sign of strength, aggression and ambition, and its symbol, the scorpion, a creature of the shadows with a deadly sting in its tail, should warn us that Scorpios make very bad enemies. It may be that people born at this time of year are more aware of these things than most, but all of us have these traits within us in some measure. Robert Louis Stevenson, born 13th November, 1850, wrote his classic work *Dr Jekyll and Mr. Hyde* about this potentially very troublesome aspect of the human psyche: buried under the thin layer of sophistication and politeness lies a much more sinister and demanding character.

Scorpio is also associated with suffering and death, hence the motifs which constantly surface at this time of the year – the 'death' of the vegetation, the 'undead' who walk among us, the dead who have gone on ahead of us; the 'suffering' of the earth as it withdraws its plants; the 'suffering' of the holy souls in purgatory. It is also associated with rebirth; the earth is lying fallow, gathering its strength for another burst of life next spring, when Persephone will return to her mother, and the vegetation will be resurrected.

In the Gospel of Mark, the Scorpio section takes place as Jesus and his apostles approach Jericho. As I've said before in this series, there is nothing accidental or arbitrary about names or locations in this Gospel. Jericho is an appropriate place to teach about the things of Scorpio, because it is the lowest city on earth, 825 feet below sea level, so, descending to Jericho symbolises the descent into the depths of the human person where we have to confront our most mysterious and troublesome motivations. Near Jericho Jesus is approached by James and John, given the nickname 'Sons of Thunder' by Jesus, indicating something of their 'martial', aggressive character. These 'sons of thunder', 'sons of Mars' have a question for Jesus: 'Let us sit, one at your right hand, and one at your left, when you come into your kingdom,' they ask. What do they want? Power! It's a typical Scorpionic request, a typical *human* request. We all want glory and honour and power, not only in secular affairs, but in spiritual ones, too. But ambition of this kind should play no part in our spiritual life. Dane Rudhyar, one of the 20th century's most respected astrological writers, says this about the Scorpio phase of the spiritual life:

> (The mystical way) ... asks moreover that all forms of ambition be relinquished – and 'spiritual' ambition may be the most dangerous, withal most subtle, kind of ambition.... There should be no feeling whatsoever of competition in one's endeavours, especially if one is part of a group of seekers or disciples. It does not matter if one appears to be first or last, for the competitive spirit is a form of violence, and there can be no violence in the soul of the true disciple on the spiritual Path. The zodiacal sign Scorpio tends to be associated with violence and competition, because the Scorpio type of person is often too emotionally and personally involved in making of human relationships what to him or her is a 'success'.[100]

---

[100] Rudhyar, pages 75-6

Reading these words by Rudhyar for the first time, I had another of those 'eureka' moments, when I realised that my speculations about the Gospel of Mark were correct. He doesn't mention the Gospel, but he deals with precisely the same issue as is dealt with in the Scorpio section – the quest for personal power, the desire to control others and to achieve some kind of public accolade for one's spiritual attainments. Jesus is adamant that such things should have no part in our motivations. Each of us is on an individual path towards God; no one is above another; no one should seek to lord it over another. Once again, Jesus mentions that service to one's brothers and sisters is the highest form of spiritual activity. Just as he has come to serve, so we who seek to follow him must see ourselves as servants.

But Jesus says something else which is also connected to the things of Scorpio. He asks James and John a question: 'Are you prepared to suffer, as I am about to suffer?' This gets to the heart of things. Spiritual reward does not come just because one has been a member of some religious group or other; it doesn't come because one has believed the right things, known the right people, performed the right rituals. Spiritual advancement comes through suffering.

This is very hard to take; particularly so for 21st century people, committed to a life of ease, pleasure, and prosperity. Where does suffering fit in? Why do we have to suffer?

We suffer because we have no alternative. Suffering is part of what it means to be human. Simply knowing that we are mortal involves us in inevitable suffering. From those first painful moments of awareness when we are small children, through the deaths of family and friends, and on to the realisation that our own death is not too far away, we participate in what Wordsworth calls 'the still sad music of humanity'. We can try to ignore it, to bury it, to pretend that it doesn't affect us, but it silently operates on our psyche, often manifesting in distressing complexes and strange phobias.

We are the only species that can suffer in this way. We are the only creatures to have knowledge of our own certain demise, and this should be enough to engender within us overwhelming feelings of pity for our fellows, along with admiration for the heroism with which most people live their lives in the midst of such uncertainty, vulnerability and inevitable finality. This certainty of our own death and the deaths of those we love is one reason why all talk of some future Utopia, in which we can live together in peace and happiness because the politics and economics of life have been sorted out for us, is merely a naive and foolish pipedream. No matter how prosperous we become; no matter how peaceful we become; no matter how comfortable, educated, sophisticated, cultured, healthy, or long-lived we become, there will always be the spectre of death haunting our days, tempering all our joys with sadness.

But, you might ask, what if God, or science, removed the consciousness of death? How would that affect things?

Many years ago, I used to have a Jehovah's Witness friend, who came to visit me every second Saturday for an hour's discussion of religious topics. As a Jehovah's Witness, he believed that, one day soon, Jesus would come back to earth, the righteous dead would be resurrected, and everyone would live for ever in a world of peace. I asked him what would happen if I were to be rewarded in this way, but that someone I loved didn't make it. No problem, he said. The memory of them would be blotted out from your consciousness, so you wouldn't feel the pain of separation from them. What an appallingly dehumanising prospect! No pain, no love, no memory of certain people. Whatever beings would inhabit the Jehovah's Witness paradise would not be human beings.

Maybe the secular world will one day overcome death, or at least postpone it indefinitely. Ask yourself: Will human love be possible for those who do not fear death? To triumph over death may yet become our greatest technical achievement, but what will we lose as a consequence of it? Aldous Huxley's vision of a Brave New World from which pain and suffering have been removed and people are kept in a chemically induced state of pseudo-happiness is too terrifying even to contemplate.

But the spiritual traditions tell us that bearing the pain of our own mortality is actually a condition of our human development. Without suffering we would cease to be human. Perhaps we might welcome this. Maybe the burden of our humanity is too great to bear. I know that for some people this is so. The Russian novelist, Dostoyevsky, born under Scorpio (11th November, 1821), and so acutely aware of these things - as anyone who gets below the surface of life must be aware - deals with this whole issue in his novel *The Brothers Karamazov*, one of the greatest novels ever written, and I do recommend that you read it if you haven't already done so. In fact, the whole of Dostoyevsky's work deals with these deep issues of human existence. Dostoyevsky himself was no stranger to suffering. His father was murdered; he was arrested and came within seconds of being executed; he spent years in a Siberian prison; he had epilepsy and emphysema; his marriage was difficult; some of his children died young; he had heavy debts from gambling. And yet, his ability to plumb the depths of human experience and come to an understanding of love, grace, forgiveness, and redemption in such incomparable ways can only have come from his first-hand experience of life at its rawest. Paradoxically, Dostoyevsky came to God *through* pain and suffering, not in spite of them.

Dostoyevsky knew what all great souls know, but which we, in our hedonism and cowardice refuse to accept. William Blake put it like this in his *Auguries of Innocence*:

> Joy and woe are woven fine,
> A clothing for the soul divine.
> Under every grief and pine
> Runs a joy with silken twine.
> Man was made for joy and woe;
> And when this we rightly know
> Thro' the world we safely go.

We find a similar idea in *The Friendship Tree*, a book written about Davoren Hanna, by his father Jack. Davoren was born with terrible handicaps. He couldn't walk, he couldn't speak, and yet he had a remarkable poetic gift which was nurtured by his parents at enormous cost to themselves and their own peace and tranquillity. Davoren's mother died, partly, at least, from the strain of caring for her son, in 1990, and Davoren himself died, aged just nineteen, in 1994. At the end of his book, Jack, Davoren's father, sums it all up: 'Earth to earth, and dust to dust, we say, but in between, such roaring, such flights, such sorrows, such heart-bonding, such words of nurture and celebration, such song.' Are we up for this, do we want to sing in ecstasy, or do we just want peace and quiet, a full stomach, and longer eyelashes?

James and John wanted the prize without the pain, spiritual enlightenment without effort. But this Gospel, along with all the great works of spiritual literature, tells us that this is impossible. And this is the important lesson of Scorpio: we can't have the heights without the depths; we can't have a crown without a cross; we can't get to Jerusalem unless we are prepared to go through Jericho.

The Ransom

Mark 10:46-52

> And they came to Jericho, and when he, his disciples and a large crowd left Jericho, Bartimaeus, the son of Timaeus, a blind beggar, was sitting by the roadside Hearing that it was Jesus the Nazarene he began to cry out and say, 'Son of David, have mercy on me!' Many people told him to keep quiet, but he cried out all the more, 'Son of David, have mercy on me!' Jesus stopped and said, 'Call him.' They called the blind man, saying, 'Cheer up and get up. He's calling you.' Throwing off his coat, he jumped up and went to Jesus. Jesus said in response, 'What do you want me to do for you?' The blind man said to him, 'Rabbi, let me see again!' And Jesus said to him, 'Go. Your faith has saved you.' And at once he could see and he followed Jesus on the road.

Story: Diluting the Wine

> Many years ago, the mayor of a village in China wanted to prepare a big feast for the whole village. He called together his chief advisors and told them of his plan. 'I shall be happy to provide all the food,' he said, 'but I want you to supply the wine. Each of you must bring a wineskin filled with your finest wine. We will pour them all into a common pot so that

the people can help themselves.'

The advisors told their leader that this was a very good idea: a party makes the people happy, and happy people work hard and commit fewer crimes. 'It will bring our people closer together,' said one.

However, not everyone was pleased. One of the advisors, a young man called Chang, thought to himself: 'A wineskin full of wine will cost me a pretty penny. I'm not prepared to sacrifice my best wine so that the village rabble can get drunk. In fact, I'm not even prepared to give them my poorest wine. I'll take water instead. No one will notice if the common pot of wine is slightly diluted.' He felt very pleased with his money saving plan, and when he told his wife she congratulated him on his cleverness.

When the big day arrived, Chang went to the well, filled a wineskin with fresh water, and gave it to a servant to carry to the feast. As they approached, they could hear the merrymaking and the music, and smell the delicious aromas of the spices the cooks had used in preparing the huge vats of food. It looked like being a day to remember!

In the middle of the village square stood a gigantic pot, into which each of the mayor's advisors was invited to pour the contents of his wineskin. As they did so, the crowd cheered wildly, impressed by the great generosity of their leading citizens. Chang poured his water into the pot.

Everyone sat down and listened impatiently as the mayor gave his speech; they were eager to get down to the serious business of eating and drinking! After the speech, the people began to fill their plates with food from the long tables, and their goblets with wine from the big pot. But as each of them took a drink, the look of expectation on each face changed into one of puzzlement. 'This is not wine,' they said, 'this is water!' Sure enough, every one of the advisers had brought water, thinking as Chang did that 'no one will notice if the common pot of wine is slightly diluted.'

The mayor was disgusted with his miserly and hypocritical advisors. He stripped them of their position, and ordered them all to pay a big fine.

147

> *No man is an island, entire of itself; every man is a piece of the continent, a part of the main...any man's death diminishes me, because I am involved in mankind; and therefore never send to know for whom the bell tolls; it tolls for thee.*
> *(John Donne)*

In last Saturday's Thinking Anew column in the *Irish Times*, G.L. (the authors of these columns are always identified by their initials only) wrote: 'Jesus belongs to the world, not the church ... he died for all and not a few'.[101] It's the sort of statement that theologians and preachers will use routinely, because it encapsulates a very prominent and important strand of the orthodox Christian message: that in some way the death of Jesus has had a profound effect upon the whole human race.

Different Christian groups interpret this idea differently, from the ultra-liberal, who see Jesus as an enlightened and brave man, whose sacrifice on behalf of his principles set an example for the rest of us to follow; to the ultra-conservative, who see the death of Jesus as a cosmic transaction in which the price of human sin was paid to satisfy the requirements of God's justice, and so make 'salvation' available to those who believe.

This latter position has never had any prominence within Unitarianism for a number of very obvious reasons. First, it implies that God in some way demanded a blood sacrifice in reparation for the accumulated sins of the human race, a distasteful implication which seems to do little to exalt the image of the Creator. Second, it is difficult for us to understand how the death of one person, no matter how exalted, could have such a cosmic impact. We can understand how heroic military actions on the part of individuals can have quite far reaching effects on the outcome of a war, or how parents can sacrifice their lives for their children, but how one death two thousand years ago can affect me now is difficult for me to comprehend. Of course, millions of books and articles have been written, and millions of sermons have been preached on the topic,

---

[101] *Irish Times*, 25th November, 2007

but the very notion remains bizarre, primitive, repugnant even, to liberal Unitarian ears.

Repugnant or not, there is no getting away from the fact that such ideas have a strong scriptural warrant. They are clearly expressed in Paul's influential *Letter to the Romans*, and in the *Letter to the Hebrews*, which, although probably not written by Paul, is generally attributed to him because it is undoubtedly influenced by Pauline theology.

Traces of such thinking can be found in the Gospels, too. In what I have called the Scorpio section of Mark, Jesus says: 'For even the Son of Man did not come to be served but to serve, and to give his life as a ransom for many'.[102] The word 'ransom' is from the Greek *lutron*, which, according to *Strong's Bible Dictionary*, means 'to loosen something with a redemption price', or, to put it in more colloquial terms, 'to pay the price of someone's freedom'. We are all familiar with the idea of buying a slave out of slavery, buying oneself out of an apprenticeship, paying off a football manager before his contract is up, paying a sum to kidnappers to release someone from captivity; even redeeming an item from the pawnbroker's. All of these help us to understand the concept of 'lutron', or 'ransom'.

So, Mark is telling us that the suffering and death of Jesus will be a means of bringing about freedom for many people. Nowhere does he say that God *demands* the sacrifice, but it is still difficult for us to grasp the idea, and even more difficult for us to warm towards it.

One reason for the difficulty is that we have gradually become estranged from the thinking which gave rise to the notion. We live in a fiercely individualistic culture, which sees human beings as discrete, separate entities, forever imprisoned in our singularity. 'My life is my own,' we say, 'and I can do with it what I wish. As long as I do not act in a way which infringes the rights of another, I can do as I like'. This is one of the cornerstones of Western liberal thinking. When we hear the question, 'Whose life is it anyway?' – when the legitimacy of suicide is being discussed for example – we tend to answer, unequivocally, 'It's mine'.

---

[102] Mark 10:45

Such thinking, which has developed in the West since the time of the Renaissance, - and which found its most celebrated contemporary expression just twenty years ago, when Margaret Thatcher famously declared, 'There's no such thing as society; there are individual men and women, and there are families' - would have seemed very strange to the people who wrote the Bible. They were aware of connections among people which we have long since disregarded – to our cost, I fear. For example, the idea that we all share a common humanity is expressed very graphically in the mythological story of Adam and Eve. It may not be a very popular myth now, post Darwin, but by concentrating on its scientific implausibility, we are neglecting its spiritual insights: we are fostering division among cultures by overlooking – or even totally ignoring – the idea of human solidarity which the myth teaches, an idea which alone can save us from destructive racial conflict.

One very interesting story expressing the hidden connections among people can be found in the Book of Joshua. On the surface it is a horrible story, and our sense of justice recoils at it, but there is a principle of biblical interpretation enunciated by the great 12th century Jewish Rabbi and scholar, Moses Maimonides, which might help us to understand such passages better: 'Every time that you find in our books a tale the reality of which seems impossible, a story which is repugnant to both reason and common sense, then be sure that the tale contains a profound allegory veiling a deeply mysterious truth; and the greater the absurdity of the letter, the deeper the wisdom of the spirit'.[103]

The story of Achan in chapter 7 of the Book of Joshua is one such story. The Israelites are in the process of conquering the Promised Land, and have just taken Jericho, but they suffer grievous setbacks in their attempt to conquer the city of Ai, and Joshua asks God why he seems to have deserted them. God tells him that someone disobeyed his command not to plunder anything from Jericho, and consequently, Joshua's people are being punished. By a strange process of elimination, the culprit is found. It is Achan, of the tribe of Judah. Buried beneath the ground in his tent they find a

---

[103] Quoted at the beginning of Hodson, *The Hidden Wisdom of the Holy Bible*

beautiful Babylonian robe, two hundred shekels of silver, and a wedge of gold weighing fifty shekels. The story continues:

> They took the things from the tent, brought them to Joshua and all the Israelites and spread them out before the Lord. Then Joshua, together with all Israel, took Achan son of Zerah, the silver, the robe, the gold wedge, his sons and daughters, his cattle, donkeys and sheep, his tent, and all that he had to the Valley of Achor. Joshua said, 'Why have you brought this disaster on us? The Lord will bring disaster on you today.' Then all Israel stoned him, and after they had stoned the rest, they burned them. Over Achan they heaped up a large pile of rocks, which remains to this day. Then the Lord turned from his fierce anger. Therefore the place has been called the Valley of Achor (Disaster) ever since.[104]

A horrible story indeed, and taken purely literally it does nothing to endear the God of the Bible to us. How unjust, we think, to kill and then burn everything that belongs to a criminal – his family, his livestock and his possessions! Surely it would be enough to punish the culprit alone. But using Maimonides's principle we can look beneath the surface of the story and find the truth it is expressing. And it's a simple but important one: that 'guilt' is not to be imputed to an individual alone, and the effects of an action are not restricted to those who seem to be immediately involved. It is a commonplace of contemporary sociology to say that it takes a village to raise a child; and when things go wrong, there are more people to bear the blame than we generally think. 'No man is an island,' wrote the English poet John Donne. We are part of a whole, and what we do, and even what we think, affects the whole.

St. Paul makes a similar point in the *First Letter to the Corinthians* (chapter 12), where he compares the group of believers to a body, composed of parts which are so interconnected that 'if one part suffers, every part suffers with it, and if one part is

---

[104]Joshua 7: 23-26 (NIV)

honoured, every part rejoices with it' (vs.26). Anyone who has ever had toothache or stubbed a toe knows that the malfunction of an apparently small and insignificant member can have an overwhelming impact on the whole body!

It would appear that so called 'primitive' peoples are more aware of these inter-personal connections than we are. I recently came across an account of the greetings employed by members of the tribes of northern Natal in South Africa. The most common greeting, equivalent to 'hello', is 'Sawu Bona', which means 'I see you', and the reply is 'Sikhona' – 'I am here' -, implying that until you see me I do not exist. Mary Kay Boyd comments, 'It's as if, when you see me, you bring me into existence'. She goes on to explain that the Zulu expression 'Umuntu ngumentu magabantu' means 'A person is a person because of other people', implying that a person's identity is based upon the fact that he or she is seen by others.[105]

In our opening words this morning, we heard similar sentiments:

> May we know once again that we are not isolated beings
> But connected in mystery and miracle, to the universe
> To this community and to each other.[106]

Such 'hidden' but real connections are part of what the zodiacal sign Scorpio symbolises. Six months ago, in the spring, the flowers sprouted above the earth in individualised beauty; but, in the Scorpio season, the vegetation is ploughed back into the soil, where it rots to produce the nutrition in which the new seeds can take root. Now is the time for the 'underground' activity of tangled root fibres, and those mysterious processes which take place away from human scrutiny, but which are absolutely vital to the nourishment of biological life.

Scorpio symbolises the hidden links between past and present, life and death, individual and community, which is why the Catholic Church has designated November, the Scorpio month, as

---

[105] Quoted in Colin Greer and Herbert Kohl, page 308.
[106] Unitarian Universalist Service Book, *Singing the Living Tradition*, (1993), Beacon Press, Boston, number 434.

the time for us to remember the Holy Souls, those members of the human community who have passed into the unseen world, but who are still connected to us by invisible threads.

Such ideas will help us to explain what the Gospel of Mark means when it says that 'the son of man must give his life as a ransom for many'. The 'Son of Man' is, as I have explained before, you and I. 'Son of Man' is a Hebrew expression which means nothing more than human being, and the suffering of a human being, the experiences of a human being, the noble achievements of a human being, affect the whole human race. We are in this together; 'when one rejoices, all rejoice; when one suffers, all suffer,' says St. Paul. We all bring our individual bottles to the party. 'I am a human being, and nothing human is alien to me,' wrote the Roman poet Terence. The selfless suffering of someone like Jesus ennobles *me*; the unspeakable cruelties of someone like Hitler, diminishes *me*. I cannot dissociate myself from the collective, either spatially or temporally. What my ancestors did is still affecting me – 'to the third and fourth generation' it says in the Bible;[107] what I do affects the generations to come. Someone can suffer so that I don't have to suffer, just as my suffering can benefit others. When my brother Barry was dying in 2001, I took a profound lesson from his brave, uncomplaining attitude, which gave me untold strength when, in the following year, I came face to face with my own possible death. Einstein expressed this idea very succinctly:

> From the standpoint of daily life, however, there is one thing we do know: That we are here for the sake of others... for the countless unknown souls with whose fate we are connected by a bond of sympathy. Many times a day, I realize how much my outer and inner life is built upon the labours of people, both living and dead, and how earnestly I must exert myself in order to give in return as much as I have received.[108]

Which brings us to the very last story in the Scorpio section of the Gospel. As Jesus and his disciples are leaving Jericho –

---

[107] Exodus 20:5
[108] See: www.einstein-website.de/z_biography/credo.html

remember, as I said last time, Jericho is the lowest inhabited city on earth and therefore symbolically the ideal place to discuss the hidden depths of things – they encounter Bartimaeus, a blind man who is begging by the roadside. 'Son of David, have mercy on me!' he shouts. 'What do you want?' asks Jesus. 'Lord, give me back my sight!' he replies.

Bartimaeus is blind. Whenever we come across blindness in the Bible we should realise that we are dealing with spiritual blindness not physical blindness. Why is he spiritually blind? *Because he understands salvation as something that will come to his people from outside.* The expression 'Son of David', which he's shouting at Jesus, was a conventional messianic term; he sees Jesus as a liberator, a military leader who will throw off the shackles of Roman oppression and lead the people to freedom. But the whole of this Gospel teaches us that this is erroneous. Salvation never comes from outside. Not from politics, not from economics, not from some external divine deliverer, not from some charismatic human leader. Salvation will only come when we understand who we are, how we are linked to each other, and how our actions and even our thoughts affect each other. Jesus cures Bartimaeus of his spiritual blindness, and the once-blind beggar accompanies Jesus 'in the way', towards Jerusalem, the City of Peace. If we want to follow him there we must overcome our own blindness, by acknowledging, cherishing, and strengthening those hidden ties which bind us one to another.

Chapter 9: Sagittarius
22nd November - 21st December

Sagittarius is the Archer or the Centaur, and is the third of the Fire signs. It is associated with zeal, foreigners, travel, horses, religion. Notice how Mark says that Jesus rides into Jerusalem on a young unbroken *horse*, before zealously venting his spleen on the hypocritical religious activity of the Temple. Jesus overturns the tables and chairs of the moneychangers and 'Two small groups of stars (in Sagittarius) marking the head of the archer's arrow … … have been compared to an overturned chair', says R. A. Allen.[109] There is also a clear allusion to the nearby constellation Ara in Jesus's curse of the fig-tree. (Ara means the *Altar*, in Latin; the *Curse*, in Greek).

---

[109] Allen, page 355

Where Two Roads Meet

Mark 11:1-11

When they drew near to Jerusalem, to Bethphage and Bethany towards the Mount of Olives, he sent out two of his disciples. He said to them, 'Go into the village opposite and as soon as you enter it you will find a tethered colt on which no one has ever sat. Untie it and bring it. If anyone asks you what you are up to, tell them that your master needs it, and he will send it straight back.' They went off and found the young horse tied up by the door outside, where two road meet, and they untied it. Some of those standing there said to them, 'Why are you untying the horse?' They replied as Jesus had instructed them and they were allowed to go. They took the colt to Jesus and placed their coats on it. Jesus mounted it. And many people spread their coats on the road; others cut down branches from the fields Those going on ahead, and those who were following were shouting, 'Hosanna! Blessed is the one who is coming in the name of the Lord! Blessed is the coming kingdom of our father David! Hosanna in the highest!'

Mark 11:15-19

They came to Jerusalem and going in to the Temple area he began to throw out those who were buying and selling in the Temple, and he overturned the tables of the money changers and the seats of those who sold pigeons. And he wouldn't allow anyone to carry their goods through the Temple. He taught them: 'Isn't it written, "My house will be called a house of prayer for all the nations?" You have turned it into a den of thieves!' The chief priests and the lawyers heard of it, and they looked for a way to kill him; but they were scared because the crowd were amazed by his teaching. And when evening came, they went out of the city

Story: The Wolf and the Dog

One day a dog met a wolf in the forest. The dog said to the wolf, 'Mr. Wolf, why are you so thin? Haven't you eaten recently? You really must learn to look after yourself better!'

'I eat when I can,' said the wolf, 'but it's not always easy to get food. I'm getting older and I'm not as quick as I used to be. The animals I eat seem to be able to get away from me these days.'

'You should come and live with me,' said the dog. 'I live in a big house; it's warm and cosy; my master feeds me three times every day and I can sit and doze in front of the fire any time I like. Sometimes he lets me out for a few minutes so I can run around the forest. There he is, over there, waiting for me to go back to him. Come with me. He'll look after you.'

'I think I will,' replied the wolf. 'Why should I be out here in the cold, grabbing what food I can when I can be fed for free? Lead the way.'

As the dog went on ahead, the wolf noticed that the dog had a little circle round his neck where the fur had worn away. 'What's wrong with your neck?' he asked.

'Oh, it's nothing. It's just where my master fastens a chain around me each night to keep me in my place while he is asleep,' said the dog, a little ashamed.

'Sorry,' said the wolf. 'I won't be coming with you. I'd rather be half-starved and free than well-fed and a slave. Goodbye!'

And the wolf vanished into the forest.

> *To be in a passion you good may do,*
> *But no good if a passion is in you.*
> *(William Blake, born 28th November, 1758)*

I wonder what images were floating through your mind as I read the passage from Mark's Gospel about Jesus's entry into Jerusalem. Whatever they were, they were probably coloured by memories of hearing this story in your infancy, or perhaps by Hollywood presentations of it. Your mental picture might even have been influenced by the numerous sermons you've heard over the years, all of them emphasising the great humility Jesus showed by choosing to enter into Jerusalem in this way.

But one thing is certain: if your mental image included a donkey then you weren't really paying attention to the actual words I was reading today, because nowhere in his account does Mark mention a donkey. Matthew does – he has Jesus riding on two animals at once, which is something of a feat even for Jesus – but Mark tells us that Jesus rode into Jerusalem *on a horse*, and so does Luke.

It is also likely that, as I read the passage, you were thinking: 'Why is he reading this during December? Surely it belongs to Palm Sunday, the Sunday before Easter Sunday, and this is always in the spring.' I agree; this is when it is generally read these days. But I think that in some of the very earliest Christian communities, this passage would have been read at this time of the year, because, since November 21st, the Sun has been in the zodiacal sign of Sagittarius, which is symbolised by the Centaur, a mythological beast that is half man and half horse, the very image which, with a bit of imagination, is conjured up by the figure of Jesus as he rides triumphantly into Jerusalem.

The association of Sagittarius with horses and with centaurs goes back through the millennia. In the ancient world Sagittarius symbolised the urge to travel, either mentally or physically, and represented the desire to break through the bonds of convention, to explore, to take some risks, to gamble even, and today, strongly

Emily Dickinson

Sagittarian people are difficult to chain down. They chaff at restriction, and even when they are physically restrained by circumstances, they are prone to extended journeys of the mind. Emily Dickinson, born on 10th December 1830, rarely left her home town, or even her house, but her mental explorations were as extensive as those of the most inveterate explorer. She wrote:

> I dwell in Possibility –
> A fairer House than Prose-
> More numerous of Windows-
> Superior for Doors.

'Possibility' is where most Sagittarians would like to dwell. That's why you will often find them in the bookmaker's office, or on the race track, or the sports field. They want to see how far and how fast they can go. And sometimes they go too far too fast for the more conventional among us to comprehend or to tolerate. In another poem, Emily tells us that:

> They shut me up in Prose—
> As when a little Girl
> They put me in the Closet—
> Because they liked me "still"—

They may have liked to shut her up, but, she says, if they could have seen her brain go round they would have realised that trying to enclose her was as effective as trying to keep a bird shut up in a field. Her mind was free to roam where it wished. Pedestrian, prosaic, conventional, unimaginative responses to life were unthinkable to Emily, and, like the wolf in our children's story today, no true Sagittarian would willingly swap the life of mental and spiritual freedom for a pampered life of comfortable slavery.

The planet associated with Sagittarius by the ancients was Jupiter, the planet of expansion, benevolence and generosity. The composer, Gustav Holst – a student of astrology – whose *Planets' Suite* is one of the most popular pieces of modern classical music, called Jupiter 'The Bringer of Jollity'. William Blake, born on 28th November 1752, expressed the essence of Jupiterean expansiveness when he wrote, 'Damn braces, bless relaxes!'; 'You never know what is enough, until you know what's more than enough!' and 'The road of excess leads to the palace of wisdom'.

Blake's famous lines from Jerusalem, 'Bring me my bow of burning gold/Bring me my arrows of desire' capture another Sagittarian image, that of the archer aiming his arrows at the heavens, symbolising the seeker after wisdom reaching beyond his physical self in order to capture the things of God.

Sagittarians are also known for speaking their mind – sometimes rather unwisely and indiscreetly – but their unashamed bluntness makes them exceptionally effective satirists, and some of the world's great exponents of the art have been born under Sagittarius: Voltaire, 21st November, 1694; Jonathan Swift, 30th November, 1667; Samuel Butler, 4th December 1835; Mark Twain, November 30th 1835, and in recent years, the brilliant comedian Bill Hicks, 16th December 1961, and Hicks mentor Richard Pryor, 1st December 1940. Jesus took a 'scourge' to the money changers in the Temple: these men were scourges to the religious establishment of their day.

So, Jesus rides into Jerusalem on a horse, not a donkey. And it's not just any old horse either. At the beginning of the piece, Jesus instructs his disciples to go into the city where they will find a horse 'on which no one has ever sat', and bring it to him. Think about this for a moment. A horse on which no one has ever sat is an *unbroken* horse, an untamed horse: the animal that Jesus had deliberately chosen was more like a 'bucking bronco' than a harmless seaside donkey. And although the Gospels tell us nothing about Jesus's skill in horsemanship, it must have been considerable because he brings the beast under sufficient control that the crowd, instead of sensibly running for cover, stand calmly by and throw palm branches in his path.

And should we want any more evidence that this period of Jesus's life was not characterised by the passive humility that centuries of sentimentality have heaped upon it, the next two incidents in Mark's narrative will provide it. Jesus curses a fig tree so that it withers and dies, and then he goes into the Temple and drives out the market traders and overturns the tables of the moneychangers – John's Gospel tells us that he took a whip to them. Neither action is that of the donkey-riding, 'gentle Jesus meek and mild', about whom we learned in Sunday school.

These three related incidents – the horse-riding, the cursing of the fig tree, and the casting out of the moneychangers – are intrinsically unlikely, the first two for obvious reasons, the third because the Temple precincts were very closely guarded, and Jesus would have been given the bum's rush before he could have done any significant damage. But remember – and I cannot stress this principle enough – *the more unlikely the scriptural story the more we need to look beneath the surface meaning to find out what it is trying to tell us.* We have to stop asking the wrong questions. These are spiritual parables not historical reminiscences, and they do not simply ask us to 'believe' in them, but to respond to them. We should approach them as poems to be explored rather than as incidents to be amazed at, or, as we liberals tend to see them, as dubious stories to be dismissed as exaggerations.

To grasp the significance of Jesus's horse ride, we need to consider the role of the horse in the actual and the symbolic worlds of ancient people. The horse was the human being's greatest ally among the animals, since it was his principal, if not his only, means of land transport. Without the horse, human movement and activity were restricted; with it, we were able to undertake the arduous process of subduing the natural world, since the horse gave us the capacity to add strength, speed, and physical endurance to our considerable mental powers. The horse was everywhere invested with qualities of nobility, loyalty, and power. Men loved horses for their utility and versatility; women, then as now, were subconsciously attracted to them for the pure and beautiful virile energy that they display

But they are not born as our natural allies. They are born wild and turbulent; they instinctively rebel against human dominance, and in order for them to be any use to us at all they have to be brought into subjection. Their natural uncontrollable energies have to be harnessed to a will that is stronger than their own. They have to be 'broken' and when raw power is brought under the control of intelligence, a formidable alliance is formed.

In such a context was born the mythological image of the centaur – half man, half horse – which married the twin qualities of intelligence and strength. And it is not too difficult to see how the centaur came to symbolise the human being – part god, part animal; part creative intelligence, part destructive passion. Ptolemy, the ancient astrological writer, called Sagittarius 'bi-corporeal', 'two-bodied', half one thing, and half another, half physical, animal passion, half aspiring, questing angel, and it is surely no coincidence that Jesus's apostles find the horse their master is to ride at the place 'where two roads meet'. The place 'where two roads meet' – the animal and the divine – is the human being.

The 18th century English poet Alexander Pope describes this dual nature of the human being in his *Essay on Man*:

> Plac'd on this isthmus of a middle state,
> A being darkly wise and rudely great;
> He hangs between; in doubt to act, or rest,
> In doubt to deem himself a God, or Beast;
> In doubt his Mind or Body to prefer,
> Born but to die, and reas'ning but to err.
> Chaos of thought and passion, all confus'd;
> Still by himself abus'd, or disabus'd;
> Created half to rise and half to fall;
> Great lord of all things, yet a prey to all;
> Sole judge of Truth, in endless Error hurl'd;
> The glory, jest, and riddle of the world.

No one has described the ambiguous, 'centaur' nature of the human being better. We are all centaurs. For the most part, the centaurs were portrayed in mythology as wild and savage creatures, all the more dangerous because their dominant bestial power was mixed with human ingenuity, but one of their number, Chiron, was a friend to humans, and so great was his wisdom that many young people were entrusted to his care. 'The youths Chiron educated learned to laugh in the face of danger, to scorn sloth and greed, and to face all that came to them with courage and good cheer. They grew up skilful and strong, modest as well as brave, and were fit to rule by having learned how to obey.'[110]

Indeed, Chiron taught what he himself had accomplished: the marriage of passion with intelligence, which produces the outstanding, heroic, undaunted, creative human being.

It is images such as this which will enable us to understand the spiritual meaning of Jesus's entry into Jerusalem. In sedately riding an unbroken horse into the holy city, Jesus symbolises the mastery of the bestial by the spiritual, the mastery of what we might today call the ego (or, in Freudian terms, the Id) with its selfish cravings, by the powerful forces of self-knowledge and self-control. And it is the objective of all spiritual practice, in whatever tradition it comes down to us, to attain this level of control over the wilder aspects of our nature, to become one who, in George Bernard Shaw's words 'is a real force of nature, instead of a feverish, selfish little clod of ailments and grievances, complaining that the world will not devote itself to making you happy'.[111] The greater jihad (holy war), said Muhammad, 'is the struggle against the lower self'. In short, we should strive to become creatures of will, not of whim.

But being in control of our passions does not mean eliminating them. This is why the next scene in the Gospel story is so important. Jesus's violent conduct towards the traders in the Temple is not the automatic behaviour of one who has allowed his instinctive reactions to get the better of him momentarily. He is not likely to repent of his action subsequently with a shamefaced, 'I don't know what came over me,' type of apology. Jesus is in control of himself, and so his anger is not the 'red mist' of animal rage, but the justifiable, studied, and willed expression of indignant condemnation, which all of us are called upon to exhibit when

---

[110] Greene and Sharman-Burke, page 246
[111] Dyer, page 219

circumstances warrant it. Our passions, our desires, our bodies, are only our enemies when they control us; when we are in control of them, when they are our servants, they are the source of the greatest of human qualities and joys.

So, the great lesson of Sagittarius is that the human being is the creature – the only creature – in which two roads meet, that there is a duality in us which needs to be acknowledged and even celebrated, but we have to ensure that the low road of animal passion is brought under the control of the high road of divine aspiration.

How do we do this? Perhaps this little story from the Native American people – which I was going to tell the children, but which I couldn't find a way to spin out long enough – may help. It changes the metaphor, but the meaning is clear enough:

> 'Why is it that sometimes I feel that I want to do helpful things, but at other times I just want my own way?' a little Cherokee boy asked his grandfather one day.
> 'It's because there is a battle inside every human being,' replied his grandfather. 'The battle is between two creatures. One creature is kind and gentle, full of peace, generosity, compassion, and trust. The other is full of anger, hatred, greed, selfishness, pride, and arrogance.'
> The young boy thought for a moment, and then he asked: 'Which one will win the battle inside me?'
> 'The one you feed,' replied his grandfather.

Learning how best to nurture the peaceful, creative, aspiring, aspect of the self, while bringing the wilder aspects under control – in short, learning to put passion at the service of intelligence – is one of the great tasks of the spiritual life.

Moving Mountains
Mark 11:12-14

He went into Jerusalem to the Temple and when he'd looked round at everything he went off to Bethany with the twelve because it was already late. The next day, as they were leaving Bethany, he was hungry, and seeing a distant fig tree in leaf he went to see if he could find anything on it. But he found nothing but leaves, because it wasn't the fig season. He said to it, 'May no one eat fruit from you ever again!' and his disciples heard him.

Mark 11:20-26

Early the next day as they were passing along they saw the fig tree withered to its roots. Peter remembered and said to him, 'Rabbi, look. The fig tree which you cursed has withered!'

In reply, Jesus said to them, 'Have faith in God. I'm telling you the truth. Whoever says to this mountain "Be lifted up and thrown into the sea!" and who has no doubt in his mind but believes that what he says will happen, it will be done for him!' Because of this I say to you whatever you ask for in prayer, believe that it is yours and it will be! And whenever you are praying, if you are holding a grudge against somebody, forgive him, so that your father in heaven may forgive you your failings.'

Story: The Map and the Man

It was a particularly rainy Saturday afternoon. Two children, John and Rebecca, were becoming increasingly bored, and their father, who was under strict orders to keep them entertained while their mother went shopping, was running out of ideas. He wanted to watch the sport on television and to read his newspaper, but the children had demanded his attention. He'd tried them with paper and coloured pencils, but this barely entertained them for five minutes. He'd tried the television, but they'd seen all the cartoons a dozen times. For some reason they didn't even want to play on the computer. And there were still a couple of hours before their mother returned!

Suddenly, he had an idea. Picking up a magazine from the table, he quickly flicked through the pages until he came to a map of the world. 'Look at this, kids,' he said. 'I'm going to cut this map into pieces – a bit like a jigsaw puzzle – and if you can put it together again, I'll take you both to McDonalds for tea! Is it a deal?'

The children agreed to give it a try. Their father cut up the map, gave them a pot of glue, and set them to work on the kitchen table. He, meanwhile, put on the kettle, made himself a cup of coffee, and sat down with his newspaper in the living room. He was feeling very pleased with himself. 'It'll take them at least an hour,' he thought with a smile.

But barely ten minutes later he heard, 'Finished, dad!' He couldn't believe it. He went through into the kitchen and there, sure enough, sitting on the table, was the completed map. 'How on earth did you finish it so quickly?' he asked.

'It was easy,' said John. 'The map of the world was complicated, but on the other side was a picture of man. We just put the man together.'

Yes,' said Rebecca. 'If you get the man right, the world takes care of itself!'

> *'If the Sun and Moon should doubt*
> *They'd immediately go out.'*
> *(William Blake, born 28th November 1757)*

One of the best-selling novels of 2007 was the curiously titled *Salmon Fishing in the Yemen*,[112] by Paul Torday. It's about an apparently hare-brained scheme to introduce salmon into a completely inappropriate Middle-Eastern environment, so that the native Yemenis can learn to fish. One of the characters in the book, Sheikh Muhammad, who devises and finances the project, explains why this would be so beneficial. After describing the many divisions among his own people he says:

> In Britain there is violence and aggression, too – your football hooligans, for instance – but there is one group for whom patience and tolerance are the only virtues. I speak of salmon fishermen in particular, and all fishermen in general … … All classes and manner of men will stand on the banks side by side and fish for the salmon. And their natures, too, will be changed. They will feel the enchantment of this silver fish … … and when talk turns to what this tribe said or that tribe did, or what to do with the Israelis or the Americans, and the voices grow heated, then someone will say, 'Let us arise, and go fishing.'

The Sheikh goes on to explain his belief that the salmon is a 'magical creature' which brings us all nearer to God – 'by the mystery of its life, by the long journey that it makes through the oceans until it finds the waters of its own streams, which is so like our own journey towards God.'

The novel is a humorous but ultimately a very serious account of how this one man's vision, which, in the beginning, seems so preposterous, is eventually realised, demonstrating the enormous power of faith to overcome seemingly impossible odds.

---

[112] *Salmon Fishing in the Yemen*, by Paul Torday. Phoenix Books, London, 2007

It is indeed a novel about faith, and as I was reading it I couldn't help calling to mind the passage from Mark's Gospel which we heard this morning, in which Jesus says to his disciples: 'Have faith in God. I'm telling you the truth. Whoever says to this mountain, "Be lifted up and thrown into the sea!" and who has no doubt in his mind but believes that what he says will happen, it will be done for him! Because of this, I say to you, whatever you ask for in prayer, believe that it is yours and it will be!'

Jesus says these words in commentary upon the strange incident with the fig tree. Remember the story. Jesus, feeling hungry, sees a distant fig tree in leaf and goes to see if there is any fruit upon it. Finding none, he curses the tree with the words, 'May no one eat fruit from you ever again!' The next day, Jesus's disciples notice that the fig tree has withered to its roots.

Books have been written about this incident — about the fig tree as a symbol of Israel, about the significance of the fact that Jesus should have known there was no chance of any figs because the text clearly tells us that it wasn't the season for figs, about Jesus's almost spiteful behaviour as a consequence of this knowledge - and I am sure that much of what these learned tomes have to say is very relevant, but I am principally interested today in the way in which this action of Jesus demonstrates what has come to be called 'mind over matter'.

But, before we get on to that, I'd just like to comment on the place of this incident in the narrative. It comes in the Sagittarius section of the Gospel and Sagittarius, as I explained last time, is one of the three Fire Signs, which were, to the ancient mind, concerned with the virtue of faith. The symbolism is not all that difficult to grasp: fire is a natural symbol of that enthusiasm which galvanises people into action and which is so infectious that it spreads around urging and encouraging even the faint-hearted and the unsure. We talk of people being 'fired up', 'burning with zeal', and of their fervour and passion kindling similar responses in others.

But there is another reason why Mark places this incident here. One of the constellations surrounding Sagittarius is called Ara, and this is generally translated 'The Altar', because 'ara' means 'altar' in Latin. But, in Greek, the language in which the Gospel of Mark was originally written, the word 'ara' means 'curse'. Mark is deliberately incorporating the name of this constellation close to Sagittarius in his story. When I discovered this, I had another of those 'eureka' moments which proved to me once again that I was on the right lines, and that Mark was using the constellations of the sky to structure his Gospel.

Sagittarius symbolises the 'dual' nature of the human being. As we saw in the last sermon, the ancient astrological writer Ptolemy called Sagittarius 'bi-corporeal', 'two bodied', and I explained how Jesus riding into Jerusalem on an unbroken horse (not a donkey!) symbolises the mastery of the bestial part of our nature by the divine part. In the incident with the fig tree, Mark further explores that divine power we possess which sets us apart from the animal kingdom and which gives human beings the potential to exert, for good or ill, all manner of control over each other and over the natural world.

Such an idea is not terribly popular these days and it is becoming a commonplace of intellectual discourse to put us firmly in our place. Copernicus, they say, destroyed the idea that the earth was special, and Darwin destroyed the idea that human beings were special. We are, we are told, simply a 'strand in the web of life', one species among many; our minds are the product of our bodies, what the materialist philosophers call an 'epiphenomenon', a by-product, as Bertrand Russell said, of our brain chemistry. When the brain dies, the mind and its memories and aspirations die with it. What's more, each mind is self- contained, atomized, relating only to the specific body of which it is the product, so all such notions as 'thought transference', extra sensory perception, precognition, are dismissed as fictions. 'Why do we humans have such an exalted view of ourselves?' asked a friend of mine only two weeks ago, 'We're nothing special. Why do we consider ourselves so much better than the animals we share the earth with?'

You've probably heard similar sentiments. You may even have expressed them yourself. Whenever I hear such ideas I'm tempted to respond with 'Shakespeare, the Pyramids, Newgrange, Beethoven, Emily Dickinson, Michelangelo, Marie Curie, Leonardo da Vinci.' These – and countless millions more – demonstrate to me, at least, the unique place the human species holds among the species of the earth. The very first verses in the Bible tell us that we and we alone are created 'in the image of God' and, no matter how the distinction came about, and no matter how tarnished the image of God may be in us collectively, it is nevertheless abundantly clear that human beings are *qualitatively* different from other animals. In his celebrated essay, *Reflections on the Death of a Porcupine*,[113] D.H. Lawrence says that there is a very clear hierarchy of being in the natural world.

> Life is more vivid in the dandelion than in the green fern or in a palm tree. Life is more vivid in a snake than in a butterfly.
> Life is more vivid in a wren than in an alligator.
> Life is more vivid in a cat than in an ostrich.

And, of course, life is more vivid in a human being than in any of these other creatures, and it is mere sentimentality – and dangerous sentimentality - to pretend otherwise.

While our biological professors may attribute that human superiority to the law of natural selection alone, the religious traditions – and especially the Gnostic or esoteric elements within the religious traditions – take a different line. For them – and I obviously put the author of the Gospel of Mark in this category – the universe is not a physical entity in which mind has entered rather late in the day as a strange offshoot of the physical human body, but mind itself is the primary substance from which the physical universe has crystallized. Mind is not a product of matter; matter is a product of mind, and is therefore subject to mind. As the British physicist, Sir James Jeans, said, when confronted by the crazy properties of sub-atomic particles, the material world looks to be composed of 'mind stuff'. Or, as the Gospel of John tells us, a little more poetically, 'In the beginning was the word … … '- in the beginning was the *idea*.

If this is the case, then we as a species do not produce mind, we participate in it, and this may give us a clue about what the Bible really means when it says that we are created 'in the image of God', and it may also help us to understand how our mental processes can and do affect the physical world, and why what we call 'prayer' can

---

[113] Lawrence, page 65

be efficacious. If by prayer we mean 'focusing the mind' rather than 'pleading with God', then it is not outrageous for us to affirm that our individual and collective mental activities can have an influence upon the natural world, and to declare with Tennyson that 'there are more things wrought through prayer than this world dreams of'.

Materialistic science may dismiss such things – it has to because it has its own dogmas to preserve - but it can only do so by denying those experiences which are pretty regular occurrences of everyday life. Every single person here could give examples of strange phenomena which seem to indicate that our minds not only have some power over the material world, but also that they are somehow connected one with another. So, knowing who is calling before you answer the telephone; feeling that there is something wrong with a person and then finding subsequently that you were right; experiencing coincidences which seem to point to hidden connections and subtle laws of attraction; even the feeling of being stared at, when we get that unaccountable urge to turn round only to find a pair of eyes fixed upon the back of our head. Gardeners tell us that the plants they love seem to grow better than those they are indifferent to. Such experiences are indeed common, and just because they do not fit into our current materialist paradigm of reality is no reason to declare that they are all figments of the imagination.

I am not particularly sensitive to such things, but even I could give some examples from my own experience. Here's one. Some years ago I performed a ceremony for a couple of archaeologists who wanted their marriage blessed on the spot where they had met. So, the wedding party trudged up a muddy hillside in Ennis one very dreary mid-week afternoon. It was drizzling rain and the clouds looked very threatening. Before the whole group had reached the top, I said to bride and groom, 'Maybe we should get things moving because the rain could start at any minute and then we'd be in trouble.' They agreed, so we began. They were new-agers, 'earth spirit' people, and they wanted the ceremony to begin with an invocation to the spirits of the place, so my opening words were, 'I call upon the spirits of this place to bless our ceremony.' and at that precise moment the clouds opened and the Sun began to shine, and it continued to shine for the rest of the afternoon. It was one of the most uncanny and unexpected experiences of my life; coincidence maybe, but it certainly seemed like the answer to a prayer.

Two further points before I close. First, if we have such powers then it is incumbent upon us to use them wisely. If thoughts have power, then we have to direct them towards positive things. Black magic and Voodoo are based upon these very powers and what they aim to effect in the world is not always directed at the common good. Remember the old saying, 'Be careful what you wish for, because you just might get it'. Wise advice, which is why the Lord's Prayer contains the statement, 'Thy will be done', and why the Muslims will say, 'Inshallah', 'if God so wills it', which means that we want this particular thing to occur only if it is in accordance with the divine mind. Ralph Waldo Emerson, the Father of American Literature, and one-time Unitarian minister, makes the startling claim in his great essay *Nature*, that the turmoil of our collective consciousness actually contributes to the turmoil we see about us in the world – that, in some way, even natural disasters are linked to the disordered mind of humanity in the collective. The implication of this strange and radical idea is clear and was pointed out by today's story: get the person right and the world will take care of itself. Maybe one reason why churches exist, why monasteries and nunneries exist, is so that the collective mind can be influenced positively, so even our relatively small gathering here can make its own contribution to transformation of the world by directing its thoughts into loving channels.

And, finally, we tend to overlook the advice that Jesus gives at the very end of this piece: before we make our prayers we have to forgive anyone who has offended us. This is absolutely crucial. We cannot harbour vengeful thoughts when we make our entreaties to God. In freeing ourselves from vengeance, we contribute positively and lovingly to the collective mind, and we also ensure that we do not misuse our powers, that our prayers are not directed vindictively against another, and that the objective of our prayer is not to gain personal power over others.

If we learn to direct our God-like gifts rightly we can contribute significantly to the transformation of the world.

Chapter 10: Capricorn
22nd December – 19th January

Capricorn is the sign of the winter solstice, when the Sun changes direction once more. It is the Cardinal Earth sign, ruled by the planet Saturn and connected with political and social structures, convention, propriety, authority, the father. It was the Moon sign of the Emperor Augustus and the image of Capricorn appeared on a denarius during his reign. Capricorn also appeared on a denarius in the reign of the Emperor Titus (79-81 C.E.), who was born on 30th December with the Sun in Capricorn. Jesus asks his questioners to show him a denarius. In this section of Mark, Jesus is shown in dispute with all the authority figures in Israel, and in the corresponding passage in Matthew he says, 'Call no man on earth your father'.[114]

---

[114] Matthew 23:9

Rendering to Caesar

Mark 11: 27-33

They came to Jerusalem again and as he walked around in the Temple precincts some of the chief priests, lawyers and elders came up to him. And they were asking him, 'Where do you get your authority to do what you do? Who gave it to you?' Jesus replied, 'I'll ask you a question. Answer me and I'll tell you in what kind of authority I do all these things. Was John's baptism from heaven or from men? Answer me!' They discussed the matter with one another. 'If we say that it was from heaven, he'll ask us why we didn't believe him. But we can't really say that it was from men either ...' (They were frightened of the crowd because everybody considered John to be a prophet.) So they said in reply, 'We don't know.' Jesus said to them, 'Nor am I going to tell you by what authority I do what I do.'

Mark 12:13-17

But they sent some Pharisees and supporters of Herod to him, so that they could entrap him in his speech. They came and said to him, 'Teacher, we know that you are sincere and that you don't bother what other people think of you. You don't judge on appearances, but you teach the way of God truthfully. Is it lawful to pay the poll tax to Caesar? Should we pay it or not?' Fully aware of their hypocrisy, he said to them, 'Why are you trying to test me? Bring me a denarius. Let's look at it.' They brought one and he said to them, 'Whose is this image and inscription?' They said, 'Caesar's.' Jesus said to them, 'Give to Caesar what belongs to Caesar, and to God what belongs to God.' They were amazed at him.

Story: The Big Headed King

There was once a king in India who was so vain and so mentally unstable that, despite all evidence to the contrary, he believed himself to be the best at everything. He couldn't so much as boil an egg, but when he gathered his cooks around him to discuss the week's menus, he would ask them, 'Who is the best cook in the world?' and they would prudently reply, in unison, 'Why you are, your majesty!' He was fat and lazy and no good at sports, but occasionally he would organise a race in which he would compete against the country's top athletes, but they knew it was wise to under-perform and let the king win. 'Who is the best athlete in the world?' he would ask, as he celebrated yet another victory, and all the super-fit runners would reply, 'Why you are, your majesty!'

One day, he gathered all the country's religious leaders together and asked them a question: 'Who is greater, God or I? You have until tomorrow to come up with a satisfactory answer.' The priests and ministers were very frightened. They knew that if they answered as their conscience told them to answer they were running the risk of banishment from the kingdom, and perhaps even of execution, and yet they did not want to betray their calling by simply giving in to the king's vanity. Here was a dilemma indeed!

'What can we say?' they were asking each other, as they left the palace. Some were shaking with fear; others were weeping, thinking of banishment to some far-off land, life-long separation from their homes and families.

'I know what to say,' said one venerable priest. 'Leave it to me!'

The next day the religious leaders gathered in the palace to give the king the answer to his question. The king stood before them, flanked by heavily armed soldiers who looked menacingly at the assembly. 'Well, have you decided? Who is greater, God or I?' asked the king. There was silence for a few moments. The king looked around, smiling a wicked little smile as he watched the ministers and priests squirming with fear. Then the old priest came forward and said, 'I will answer your question, your majesty. You are the greater.' The king looked very pleased with himself; this was exactly what he wanted to hear. But then the priest continued, 'You are greater than God, because you can banish people from your kingdom, but God cannot banish people from his; for God's kingdom is everywhere and there is nowhere to go outside of it.'

There's no doubt that this is the most miserable time of the year. Christmas lifted our spirits a little – the lights, the evergreens, the carols, the jingles, the shopping, and the presents all contributed to an easing of the burden of winter. And that, of course, is their function. Christmas comes when it does in order to counteract the general feeling of gloom that the long nights and the cold weather inevitably bring. To our ancestors, who lived without central heating, electric lights or television, it would have been an almost unbearably dreary and even dangerous time. In the darkness, entertainment is limited, and you can't see the predators; in the cold people die. This is the time of year when people suffer from the aptly named SAD - seasonal affective disorder - when lack of sunlight can bring on depression and feelings of hopelessness, and even in those of us whose moods don't change quite so dramatically there is a general feeling of contraction, in sharp contrast to the expansive optimism of the springtime.

This is not all negative, of course. Winter has its own beauty and its own range of pleasures. Hot drinks, blazing fires, snow, frost, can all delight us, as they give us permission to slow down a little, to lie fallow like the earth, to recover our energies for the next burst of activity which is only a few months away.

In addition, winter makes us conscious of our vulnerability, and of our reliance on each other for the smooth continuance of our lives. In the summer we feel invincible, but things can go very badly wrong now, so we need people around us to share the burden of the darkness.

On our journey round the zodiac circle we have had occasion to mention that one of the symbolic bases for our understanding of the individual signs is their relationship to the light or the darkness. The light represents individual consciousness, the darkness symbolises the collective, so when the light is strongest – from the spring equinox to the summer solstice, from March to June, - the signs of the zodiac symbolise emerging individuality, separateness. When darkness prevails, as it does now, and we need to huddle together for warmth and safety, the signs symbolise group consciousness, the community, the state even.

These are the very themes which the ancient astrologers associated with Capricorn, which the Sun entered on 22nd of last month. Capricorn symbolises the relationship of the individual to social and political organisations, and the most ancient symbol of Capricorn was not the mountain goat, but the goat-fish, a mythical creature which lives in two environments, just as human beings live both a private and a public life. People who are strongly Capricornian – and that doesn't just mean people born at this time of the year

> take life and its responsibilities very seriously, and sometimes seem weighed down with care ... ... When in charge of any concern, they see that rules are punctiliously observed, sometimes displaying an inflexibility which becomes absurd... ...They not only cherish a deep respect for law, order and convention, but also reverence all that is ancient. .....All this ....may cause a Pharisaical attitude of mind which obeys the letter of the law rather than the spirit.[115]

So writes Joan Hodgson in her engaging little book *Wisdom in the Stars*, and we can supplement her insights with a few observations of our own. The Capricorns I know are generally serious people, often 'old beyond their years', even in youth. They tend to be responsible, cautious, prudent, quietly ambitious, industrious, sometimes with a sense of constantly fighting a tough battle against life, as if, somehow, they have chosen to follow a hard

---

[115] Hodgson. J., page 100-1

and stony path, but like the mountain goat, which is their symbolic animal, they continue to climb relentlessly to the top, undeterred by obstacles. They are conscious of status and so can be deferential to authority while expecting deference from those who stand beneath them on the social ladder. England is said to be heavily under the influence of Capricorn, as is India, and both of these countries have age-old systems of social stratification which seem quite ridiculous to outsiders. The English reserve and concern for propriety are parodied throughout the world, and there's an old joke about two Englishmen who were washed up on a desert island. Ten years later a ship picks them up; they are living on opposite sides of the island and have never spoken to one another. 'Why didn't you get together?' asks the incredulous ship's captain. 'We haven't been introduced,' was the reply.

A typical Capricornian figure was the 19th Century English politician William Ewart Gladstone. Born on 29th December 1809, he was one of the hardest working and most productive politicians of all time. In addition to running the British Empire, he translated and wrote commentaries on the classical authors, and even found time to 'save' fallen women. He would roam the streets of London at night, meeting with prostitutes, attempting to rescue them from their life of vice. He was called, in true Capricorn style, 'The Grand Old Man', and his manner was so formal that Queen Victoria said, 'He always addresses me as if I were a public meeting'. When he was 85, he bequeathed £40,000 and many of his books to found a library and, despite his advanced age, he himself hauled most of his 32,000 books a quarter mile to their new home, using his wheelbarrow.

William Ewart Gladstone

Another political Capricornian, Richard Nixon, (born January 9th 1913), was known for his incredible political ambition and his complete lack of humour. David Frost said that he had absolutely no small talk whatsoever. Sadly, as Nixon's career shows, in another of life's little ironies, those who talk loudest in public about duty and responsibility are often the ones who flout them both in private, and hypocrisy, which, in one sense, is the failure to live up to a sometimes impossible ideal, is often the besetting fault of the heavily Capricornian person.

The 'ruler' of Capricorn, the planet most closely associated with it, is Saturn, which, to the ancients, marked the boundary of the solar system. From Saturn we get our word 'saturnine' which, according to the dictionary, means 'gloomy; taciturn, showing a sullen, brooding ill humour'. Saturn was associated with the metal lead, and when we describe people or skies as 'leaden' we are not expecting much jollity from either. The colour of the Sun is gold; the colour of the Moon is silver; Mars is red, Venus is green – all lively, vibrant colours. But Saturn, like lead, is dull grey. And what's more, Saturn has rings around it, further emphasising the idea of boundaries and restrictions. Saturn symbolised the Father, not as a tender protector, but as a figure of authority and power, who lays down the law and sees that it is enforced. Saturn was also said to be associated with the bones, which give structure and form to the body

The Roman Saturnalia was celebrated as the Sun passed into Capricorn and was a riotous celebration marked by acting in defiance of everything that Saturn stood for: traditions and customs were overturned; authority figures were ridiculed; conventions and laws were suspended. It was the Roman way of cocking a snook at Saturn, of squeezing out a few drops of pleasure from life before the dourness of winter set in.

According to the English astrological writer, Charles Carter, the Jews are a Capricornian people, and he goes on to say that 'the New Testament does contain condemnations of the leaders of Jewry that certainly sound like attacks upon the traditional Capricorn – the love of high places, hypocritical formalism in religion, the desecration of holy places in pursuit of gain.'[116]

Carter is right. And what's more, this attack by Jesus on those aspects of Jewish formalism and hypocrisy, occur in what I have called the Capricorn section of the Gospel of Mark. If you read

---

[116] Carter, C., page 83

from chapter 11:27 to chapter 12:44, you will see that Jesus encounters and argues with representatives of each of the leading groups within Judaism, Pharisees, Sadducees, elders, lawyers, and in the Parable of the Tenants he savagely attacks the historic leaders of the nation, who, he says, have murdered God's representatives while pursuing their own corrupt political ambitions

The section begins, appropriately for Capricorn, with a question about the source of Jesus's authority, a question which he very cleverly avoids. Then some Pharisees and Herodians ask him whether it is right to pay taxes to Caesar, to the Roman state. What is often overlooked by commentators is the implausibility of this combination of inquisitors. The Pharisees were patriots, committed to reclaiming Palestine from Roman rule. The Herodians were collaborators, supporters of King Herod who was a puppet ruler, put and kept in place by the Roman overlords. It would have been as unlikely for Pharisees to mix freely with Herodians as for the U.D.F. to associate with the I.R.A. However, they appear together in Mark's narrative in order to put Jesus in an apparently impossible position, because whatever answer he gave would alienate him from one group or the other.

Jesus asks to be shown a denarius, a silver coin. 'Whose image is this?' he asks. 'Caesar's,' is the reply. 'Then give to Caesar what is Caesar's, and to God what is God's.' This little saying of Jesus's has been used by Christian people down the centuries to express the demarcation between one's civic obligations and one's spiritual duties, a demarcation which needs to be kept in mind by those who would argue for an established church. America recognised this demarcation in the Constitution – engineered largely by the Unitarian sympathiser, Thomas Jefferson - which kept church and state separate, but the creation of the Church of England – and numerous other state churches – was an attempt to combine the two jurisdictions, often with catastrophic results, as religious dissent became tantamount to treason. We Nonconformists have, like Jefferson, always been on the side of disestablishment, since, no matter how seriously we take our civic responsibilities – our duties to Caesar – we recognise that the law of conscience – our duty to God - must always take precedence in any conflict between the two. Two very different approaches to this dilemma can be illustrated by the respective careers of Cardinal Wolsey and Thomas More, successive Chancellors to Henry VIII. More, obeying his Catholic conscience, disagreed with Henry's divorce and was beheaded for treason. Wolsey never disagreed so radically with the King, but, at the end of his life was heard to lament:

> Had I but served my God with half the zeal
> I served my king, he would not in mine age
> Have left me naked to mine enemies.[117]

The King has power; the state has power, and ostensibly, as our children's story today showed, such power is often experienced more acutely and more directly than is the power of God. But, the ultimate crime against conscience is the deifying of state power, the confusion of jurisdictions which occurs in all kinds of totalitarian regimes, from the right and the left, and two of the twentieth century's most notorious attempts to do this were made by men born under Capricorn – Mao Tse Tung (born December 26th, 1893), and Joseph Stalin (born January 2nd, 1880).

We can readily see how the things of Capricorn feature in this little altercation between Jesus and his enemies, but there is another Capricornian signature here. Jesus specifically asked to see a denarius, and a denarius minted during the reign of Augustus Caesar actually carried a representation of Capricorn on its reverse. The Irish poet Louis McNeice, in his last book, which was about astrology, writes:

> The young Augustus, though a hard-headed and calculating person, was so impressed by the glorious future foretold for him... ...that he struck a silver coin stamped with Capricorn, the sign under which he was born.[118]

---

[117] Shakespeare, *Henry VIII*, Act III

[118] McNeice, page 122. Augustus was actually born on September 23rd 63 BCE, when the Sun was in Libra, but Capricorn was the sign in which the Moon was placed at his birth. He died in 14 CE.

We can assume that Augustus was long dead when Mark was writing, but it is quite possible that this Augustan denarius was still seen as a symbol of imperial power, since Augustus was the first of the Roman emperors, and the one under whom Roman rule in Palestine was consolidated. However, we might also note that the emperor Titus, who was born on 30th December, also issued a denarius with Capricorn on the reverse in 79 C.E., and, as far as I am aware, these are the only Roman coins with zodiac signs on them.

Denarius showing Augustus and Capricorn

We seem to have been a little hard on Capricorn this morning, associating it with authority, gloom, coldness, seriousness, industriousness, inflexibility, ambition, and the like – even its virtues seem like vices! - but we have to remember that somebody has to provide structure for society in order to prevent it falling into anarchy, and so we can be thankful that the world contains people who are prepared to shoulder this onerous burden. We just have to make sure that the worst excesses are avoided, and that personal freedom does not become sacrificed to social control.

We have to remember, too, that Capricorn, like its polar opposite Cancer, is a sign of reversal. When the Sun enters Capricorn on or around 21st December, we have the darkest time of the year. But then it starts to get light again, and Jesus, like all representations of solar deities, is said to be born at this time. In fact, according to the ancients, the enlightened human soul ascends to heaven through the gate of Capricorn. The symbolism is clear: at the darkest time of the year, the light is born anew. Kahlil Gibran, St. Theresa of Lisieux, St. Bernadette Soubirous, Paramahansa Yogananda, Albert Schweitzer, Alan Watts, were all born under this sign and these, along with countless other Capricorn natives, have reflected the light of the spirit just as effectively as natives of less sombre signs.

Call No Man Father

Story: The Blind People and the Elephant

The Buddha and his disciples were staying near the town of Savatthi. One day some of the disciples went into the town dressed in their saffron robes in order to beg alms from the citizens, when they became aware that the place was full of people from numerous conflicting religious traditions, who seemed to be engaged in a constant debate about religious matters. Some were saying, 'The world is eternal; this is the truth and everything else is delusion.' Others were arguing exactly the opposite point of view. Some were saying, 'Body and soul are really just one thing,' while members of an equally vociferous group were declaring that body and soul were distinct entities. 'The soul lives on after the death of the body,' said the representatives of one group. 'There is no life after death,' said the representatives of another. The town seemed to be in an interminable state of disputation, men and women abusing each other with words that pierced like swords.

Amazed by the ferocity and intensity of the arguments, the disciples returned to the Buddha and told him of their experiences. After listening to their story, the Buddha said, 'These people are blind. They don't know what is real or what is not real. They can't distinguish truth from falsehood, and it is purely because of this state of ignorance that they spend their time in argument. What's more, they've been at it for a very long time. Then he proceeded to tell his disciples this story.

Many years ago there was a king in this very town of Savatthi who was himself so sickened by the religious disputes that he decided to teach the people a lesson. He ordered a servant to gather together all the town's blind people and have them touch an elephant, but he was to make sure that each one touched a different part of the elephant's body.

The servant assembled the blind people in the town square. 'Here is an elephant,' he said to them, 'and I want each of you to touch it.' To one he presented the head of the elephant, to another the ear, to another the tusk; to others the trunk, the leg, side, tail, tuft of the tail, saying to each one that what he could feel was the elephant. Then he went to the king and said, 'Your majesty, the elephant has been presented to the blind people.'

'Now bring the blind people to me,' ordered the king.

When the blind people were brought before the king, he said to them in turn, 'Have you studied the elephant?'

'Yes, I have, your majesty,' each one replied.

'Then tell me your conclusions about it.'

The one who had touched the elephant's head answered, 'Your majesty, the elephant is just like a pot.'

The one who had felt the ear said, 'The elephant is just like a basket.'

'It's like a sword,' said the one who had touched the tusk.

The elephant's side was said to be like a wall;
 its leg like a pillar;
 its trunk like a pipe;
 its tail like a rope;
 the tuft of its tail like a brush.

After each one had given his opinion, the others would disagree, shouting, 'It's not like that!'

'Yes, it is!'

'No, it isn't!

At the end, the arguments became so bad that the blind people even began to hit each other!

The king was delighted with the scene.

After he had told this story, the Buddha said, 'The people in the town of Savatthi today are just like the blind men in the story: some of them may have part of the truth, but each of them is arguing as if he has the whole of it. Then the Buddha uttered these memorable words:

> O how they fight and wrangle, some who claim
> Of monk and priest the honoured name!
> For quarrelling, each to his own view they cling.
> Such folk see only one side of a thing!

About ten days ago I received two consecutive but very contrasting emails. The first was from Michelle Read, thanking the church's managing committee for donating €500 to the Dublin Buddhist Centre. Michelle is a member of our church, but she has attended yoga and meditation classes at the centre, and she had asked the committee to consider a donation to the centre's refurbishment fund. Michelle's email contained the response of Simon, the centre's representative:

> What a lovely surprise!... ... How generous of you to suggest to your management committee that they support our work; and how generous of your management committee to agree to give us €500. We really are delighted, more especially as we're such a small community, not practising within the mainstream religious traditions of Ireland, so to know that what we do is appreciated by someone like yourselves is very gratifying.

The second email contained very different news. It was an extract from an article printed in a Lancashire newspaper about the decision of three churches to boycott an event which is to take place in a Unitarian church.

> A war of words has broken out after three leading Christian churches snubbed an event to bring women together in prayer. The Church of England, Baptist, and Methodist

185

churches in Padiham rejected the invitation of the town's Unitarians for the Women's Day of Prayer service. Clergy said that they had taken the decision because Unitarians did not believe in the Holy Trinity, that is the father, the son, and the holy spirit.

The Women's Day of Prayer is a world-wide event, held on the first Friday in March each year, and, in the Lancashire town of Padiham, the churches have taken it in turns to host it. This was all well and good when the conventional churches were hosts, but not this year. 'The idea of the day is Trinitarian,' says Rev. Mark Jones of St. Leonard's Church, 'and we do not think that it is right for them to hold the service if they do not believe in Trinitarianism.' He went on to explain that he wouldn't be attending because 'Unitarians deny virtually every one of the crucial Christian doctrines.' Representatives from the Baptist and Methodist churches agreed with him.

The responses on the newspaper's website are entertaining. One, from 'Dave', says, 'A few hundred years ago, the other Churches would have burned the Unitarians alive for what they believe. I guess just snubbing them is a form of progress.' Another, from 'padihamresident', says, 'Typical that it is men who are arguing over a day of prayer that is meant to be for women.' Although one or two letters support the snub, calling it 'a stand for real Christianity', the vast majority express incredulity and dismay at the narrow mindedness of the decision.

Ironically, the theme of this year's service is 'God's Wisdom Provides New Understanding.'

But we here in Ireland can't be too smug about our tolerance levels. Last Tuesday afternoon on RTE Radio 1, there was a phone-in in progress, a debate on whether St. Patrick's Cathedral – Church of Ireland – should be selling rosary beads in its shop. 'It's a betrayal of the principles of the Reformation,' said the Northern Ireland Protestant man, who seemed to have raised the issue. He was a pleasant enough chap, but he told us that he wouldn't attend his daughter's wedding, or the funeral of a relative, if either event were to take place in a Catholic church. He agreed with Ian Paisley that the pope was the antichrist, that Catholicism wasn't a Christian religion, and that the sole guide to faith and morals was the Bible. 'Unless we believe on the Lord Jesus Christ we cannot be saved,' was his message.

The major issue raised, both by the emails and the radio broadcast, is that of authority in religious matters, the very question which Mark deals with in the Capricorn section of his Gospel, where he challenges us to reconsider our attitude to religious authority in whatever guise it is presented to us.

The planet associated by the ancients with Capricorn was Saturn, the planet of boundaries, rules and regulations, duty, and structure. Saturn represents the Father, not as a tender, loving parent, but as a stern, authoritarian potentate who brooks no dissent, who insists on conformity, and who upholds tradition. The paterfamilias in the Roman world had absolute power of life and death over his children, his wife, and his slaves, *for the whole of their lives*. At the time of the Roman Republic, the paterfamilias had the right to order an unwanted child to be put to death by exposure, and he even had the power to sell his children into slavery. His word was law, and punishment for disobeying it could be swift and merciless.

Capricorn was also associated with the goddess Vesta, the goddess of the hearth. Remember Swan Vestas matches? These are no doubt named after this goddess, but she was not the goddess of light in the sense of 'enlightenment' or 'truth'. Her 'sacred flame', kept alight by the Vestal Virgins, was the light of the fireside, the light of tradition. Whenever the Romans established a new colony, fire was brought to it from the central fire in Rome, emphasising continuity, and the extension of authority from the centre outwards. So important was this central fire that the Vestal Virgins were under threat of death should they let it go out.

Tradition was a dominant theme within the Roman Empire, and tradition has been a dominant theme within religion throughout the ages. In this section of Mark's Gospel, Jesus is shown debating with the upholders of the various traditions within Judaism – Pharisees, Sadducees, Herodians, the Elders, the Lawyers, all those who, in one way or another, mediated the religion of Moses to the people. It should come as no surprise to us to learn that these groups – and others - were constantly in dispute with one another;

plus ça change! For example, the Sadducees believed that only the first five books of the Bible – what the Jews call Torah, the Pentateuch, the Law – were authoritative; the Pharisees, on the other hand, while accepting the authority of these books, believed that certain oral and written traditions should also be granted authority. The two positions are not very different from the Protestant and Catholic attitudes to authority today; Scripture alone (like the Protestants) for the Sadducees; Scripture and Tradition (like the Catholics) for the Pharisees.

Jesus's dispute with the Sadducees concerns life after death. Because there is no unequivocal mention of an afterlife in the first five books of the Bible, the Sadducees did not accept it as part of their belief system. The question they bring to Jesus is this: 'Suppose a woman marries seven brothers successively, whose wife will she be in the afterlife?' It seems a silly question to us, but in its context it was not so silly. If a Jewish man died childless, it was incumbent upon his brother to marry his ex-sister-in-law and raise up children in the dead man's name. It was called 'levirate marriage', and so, theoretically, it was possible for a woman to marry seven brothers, if each of them had died in turn without producing offspring.

Jesus tells his hearers that such a woman would be the wife of none of the brothers, because in the afterlife there is no marriage, but then he goes on to say that the Sadducees have got it wrong about life after death. 'When God speaks to Moses from the burning bush,' says Jesus, 'he announces himself as the God of Abraham, the God of Isaac, and the God of Jacob. How can he be the God of these men if they no longer exist?' It's a strange argument, to say the least, and not a terribly convincing one, but you can see what Jesus is doing here: he's taking an episode from the books that the Sadducees considered authoritative and using it to refute their point of view. He does something similar a little later. By quoting a passage from the Psalms, he questions the universally held Jewish belief that the Messiah would be a descendant of King David. I won't go into detail, but suffice it to say that Jesus's argument is pretty specious here as well. But – and this is the point – *it was meant to be!* What the Gospel writer is saying – and what we all know to our cost - is that given enough time and enough ingenuity you can make the Bible – or the Koran, or the Bhagavad

Gita – say anything you like! Taken together, these two incidents make a very subtle case against what we might call Bibliolatry – worship of a book, the acceptance of any book as the definitive revelation from God.

Why would God in his infinite wisdom provide a written text as the basis of his self-revelation when every reader knows that *all* writing is shot through with ambiguity, and the more poetic a piece the more ambiguity it contains? Indeed, poetry *relies* on ambiguity. The only texts which strive to be free from all possible double meanings are unreadable insurance policies; the 'heretofores' and 'hereinafters' are there in profusion because insurance brokers know that ambiguity can be costly. But the Bible is poetry, and so it is a veritable cornucopia of double-meaning, contradiction, and implausibility, and I could give you, right now, off the top of my head, a dozen examples of each of these. In fact, Mark's Gospel itself contains an absolutely glaring error. At the end of chapter 2, Jesus says to his opponents, 'Haven't you read what David did when Abiathar was high priest, how he took the temple bread and gave it to his hungry men to eat?' But Jesus gets it wrong! Abiathar was not the high priest at that time. The high priest was Ahimelech – check it out for yourself in chapter 21 of the First Book of Samuel.

Did Jesus make mistake? Did Mark make a mistake? Unthinkable, say the literalists. Abiathar must have been another name for Ahimelech, or Abiathar must have been the high priest as well, or some such strained reasoning. Maybe it was a copyist's error, say some. Perhaps, but if we admit that there are copyists' errors in the text, how can we go on to say that it is infallible? I think the real explanation is quite startling, quite liberating, and quite amusing: this, and similar 'errors' in the Bible are *deliberately* put there, and *deliberately* left there, in the hope – forlorn as it appears – that readers will not be tempted to treat the whole thing as an oracle.

But, sadly, we have, and we do. Religion has been in the hands of pedants and literalists since the beginning of time, and the world pays for such pedantry with interminable argument and disastrous division.

No book – no matter how exalted, no matter how beautiful, no matter how venerable – can be the sole basis for our religious and moral life. Nor can any institution, any guru, any priest, any minister, any tradition. Matthew's Gospel – in the parallel section to the passage of Mark that we are considering - puts it very succinctly: 'Call no man on earth your father,'[119] it says, which means, give no one the kind of power over you which the paterfamilias exercised in the Roman Empire. Do not allow traditions, authorities, books, religious institutions, university professors and the like to usurp your inalienable right, and your absolute duty, to come to your own conclusions. Books, companions, traditions, teachers, are undeniably useful but they should never become idols to worship, they should never be permitted to do your thinking for you, and they should never be allowed to stand between you and the experience of the divine. Religious figures and institutions are, in the words of the Buddha, simply 'fingers pointing at the Moon', and they should not be confused with the Moon itself. The Buddhists say, 'If you see the Buddha on the road, kill him!' meaning, don't even allow the Buddha to get in your way. You have your own journey to make. The Buddha can be your companion; the Bible can be your guide; Jesus can be your mentor; the church can be your refuge, but none of these can do your thinking, your praying, your acting, your doubting, your praising, or your suffering, for you.

We cannot worship with the Unitarians because they don't believe in the Trinity,' says the Anglican rector of Padiham, allowing an inherited, sixteen centuries' old dogma to stand in the way of human decency, community spirit, female solidarity, and common sense. 'Unitarians deny virtually every one of the crucial Christian doctrines,' says the Rev. Jones. No we don't. We deny nothing. We simply affirm, with St. Paul, that now we 'see through a glass darkly', and, since our knowledge of the things of God is partial and relative – like the blind men's knowledge of the elephant - we must draw our conclusions tentatively. We refuse to be shackled by ancient dogmas, and we refuse to exclude others from fellowship on the basis of tenuous metaphysics. We respect the past and its many wonderful literary and spiritual masterpieces, but we refuse to allow tradition to tyrannize us. If we stand in any tradition, it is that of Socrates who told us that 'the unexamined life is worthless', or of

---

[119] Matthew 23:9

Brian in *The Life of Brian*, who constantly tried to dismiss the sycophantic crowds with the immortal words, 'Think for yourselves!'

Chapter 11: Aquarius

January 20th – February 19th

The Water Bearer. Aquarius is The Fixed Air sign and, like Capricorn, it is ruled by Saturn, but is more concerned with toppling structures than with building them up, hence its association with anarchy, political and social upheaval, drastic and radical change. The whole of chapter 13 is devoted to these themes, and the image of the man carrying a jar of water (14:13) is the clearest zodiacal indicator of all.

Standing out from the Crowd

Mark 14:1-9, 12-16

The Passover and the feast of Unleavened Bread was two days away, and the chief priests and the experts in Jewish law were looking for a way to arrest Jesus secretly and kill him, but they didn't want to do it during the festival in case there was a riot among the people.

While Jesus was in Bethany, eating a meal at the house of Simon the leper, a woman came in carrying an alabaster jar full of very expensive perfumed oil, pure nard. Breaking open the jar, she poured the oil on his head, to the great annoyance of some of those present. 'Why this waste of the perfumed oil? It's worth a year's wages. It could have been sold and the money given to the poor.' They were very indignant.

But Jesus said, 'Leave her alone. Why are you bothering her? She's done a lovely thing for me. The poor are always with you, and you can always do good to them whenever you want to, but you won't always have me around. She has done what she could. She has anointed my body in anticipation of my burial. I'm telling you the truth, wherever the good news is preached throughout the world, what this woman has done will be spoken of. She will be remembered for it.'

Judas Iscariot, one of the twelve, went to the chief priests in order to betray Jesus to them. They were delighted, and promised to pay him, so he began looking for a suitable time to hand him over.

On the first day of Unleavened Bread, when the Passover lamb was customarily slaughtered, his disciples said to him, 'Where do you want us to go to prepare the Passover meal for you to eat?' He sent off two of his disciples, saying, 'Go into the city where a man carrying a jar of water will meet you. Follow him, and say to the master of whichever house he enters, "Where is my guest room, where I might eat the Passover with my disciples?" He'll show you a large upper room, equipped and ready. Prepare for us there.' The disciples left for the city and found everything just as Jesus had said; and they prepared the Passover.

Story: The Miller, his Son, and the Donkey

A miller and his son were taking their donkey to the market in the hope of selling it. The miller walked on one side of the beast, his son on the other. As they walked along they came upon a group of young people who were laughing and joking. 'Just look at that stupid pair,' one said. 'They have a perfectly good donkey but neither of them is riding on it!' The miller heard this comment and told his son to get up on the donkey's back. They travelled like this for another mile or so until they met with some of the miller's friends. 'You'll spoil that lad, letting him ride while you walk. Let him stretch his legs. Why don't you get on the donkey and rest your weary bones?' So the miller took his son's place on the donkey's back and on they went.

As they approached a small village, a group of women spotted them. 'Look at that selfish old man, riding on the donkey while the poor young lad has to walk!' The miller was so ashamed that he told his son to get up on the donkey with him. Now, both of them were riding on the donkey's back, and a little further along the road they met some men who asked: 'Is that your donkey, or have you hired it?'

'It's my donkey,' said the miller. 'We're taking him to market to see if we can sell him.'

'Well you'd better stop riding him then,' said one of the men. 'By the time you get him there he'll look so weak and exhausted that no one will want to buy him. You really ought to be carrying the donkey!'

'Anything to please you,' said the miller. So father and son dismounted and, tying the donkey's legs together, they suspended him from a pole which they carried on their shoulders. It was such a strange sight that when they arrived in the market town scores of people came out to see it. Everyone was laughing and calling the pair idiots and lunatics. 'We've never seen anyone carrying a donkey before! Come, look at these madmen!'

There was such commotion in the streets that the donkey panicked and broke loose from his fetters just as the party was crossing over the river. In his distress, the donkey fell into the water and was drowned. So, the miller and his son made their way back home, reflecting that in trying to please everybody they had pleased nobody and they had lost their valuable donkey into the bargain.

'Go into the city, where a man carrying a jar of water will meet you. Follow him.' It was this instruction by Jesus to his apostles in chapter 14 of Mark's Gospel which prompted me to construct the theory of the zodiacal structure of Mark in the summer of 1989. This particular passage had intrigued me throughout the twelve or so years that I had been teaching courses on the Gospels. Who was this man? He's not named. There is no mention of him before this incident, and he disappears from the narrative immediately afterwards. The fact that Jesus knew he would be there – just as he appeared to know that there would be a horse waiting for him on which he could ride into Jerusalem – would seem to suggest either that he had remarkable powers of foresight, or that he had set the whole thing up in advance. While this latter is a possibility, the text gives no indication of it, and the historically minded among us are left wondering why such a strange meeting was necessary, and, in the absence of emails, telephone calls or previous visits, just when and how it had been arranged.

The most perplexing aspect of it, from the point of view of its plausibility as history, however, is the unusual way in which this man was to be identified. We can readily accept that the plan required him to grab the apostles' attention – much as, today, someone might say to a person they are to meet for the first time, 'I'll be standing under the station clock, wearing a pink carnation, and reading a copy of the *Daily Telegraph*', but for a man to be carrying a jar of water in those days would go beyond what was required for recognition. Meetings between strangers are generally done discreetly, especially if there is some reason for them not to arouse too much public attention. But a man carrying a jar of water would not have been a discreet sign; it would have been an announcement in Technicolor and stereo! Men didn't carry water in those days. This was woman's work, at a time when the demarcation between male and female roles was clear and rigid. It would have been the equivalent of someone today drawing attention to himself by standing completely naked, or dressing up as a harlequin!

To the student of astrology, however, the man is readily identifiable as the pictogram of the zodiacal sign Aquarius, and I had seen him as such, but I couldn't work out why he should appear at this point in the narrative. Why should one of the zodiacal signs be introduced, out of the blue? Baffling, indeed, but then, one afternoon, as I was supervising an examination and idly flicking through a Bible which happened to be on the desk (it was a Catholic school!) I realised, to my astonishment, that this was not an isolated appearance. All the other signs were there in Mark's Gospel, in perfect zodiacal order, and they were so obvious that I wondered why I had never seen them before, why, apparently, no one had ever seen them before. Some were clearer than others admittedly, and some incidents didn't seem to fit the scheme too neatly, but the sequence was unmistakeable; it had just been overlooked by generations of scholars who had been asking the wrong questions of the text.

I have spent a long time since then working on this theory and refining it, and, more importantly, trying to tease out the implications of such a zodiacal scheme for our understanding of the Gospel narrative. A zodiacal sequence does not preclude the story being historical, but it certainly reduces the possibility, and if it's not history, or a kind of history, then what is it? I have come to the conclusion that Mark was writing an account of what we might call today the 'spiritual journey', using Jesus as a representative figure –

Everyman or Everywoman – and that the stories in Mark's bizarre narrative should be read as spiritual 'parables', as lessons on the spiritual life. They are not so much about a historical figure called Jesus, but about you and me. Mark's stories are not simple, eye-witness accounts of incidents which stretch our credulity; they are immensely rich metaphors which challenge and excite our imagination.

Each section of Mark carries a lesson based on the intrinsic meaning of the zodiacal sign that it reflects, and one way of learning what the individual signs represent is to look at the lives and the characters of people born under them. We've done this before with the other signs and I repeat here what I've said so often before: I'm not making the fatuous claim that everyone born at a particular time of year exhibits all the characteristics of a certain zodiac sign, that the human race can be divided neatly into twelve invariant groups. There is infinite variety among people, and infinite variety even among people of the same sign. But, there are certain characteristics which can be identified as typical, which some individuals seem to embody so clearly that their zodiac sign can be guessed even after slight acquaintance, sometimes just by looking at them.

Aquarians are among the easiest to identify. The words most commonly used to describe them are 'eccentric', 'zany', 'original', 'independent', and, less flatteringly, 'opinionated' and 'perverse'. The typical Aquarian, like the man carrying the jar of water, is one who stands out from the crowd, one who almost makes a virtue out of being 'off-beat'. This will manifest in a number of ways. Sometimes it will be in their dress, but more often it will be in their intellectual life. Aquarians like nothing better than expressing controversial opinions, and they seem especially fond of assuming radical political or religious positions, which they will defend tenaciously.

Many Aquarians are iconoclastic, showing scant regard for traditional and customary ways of thought. Both Johnny Rotten, the lead singer in the Sex Pistols, and Malcolm McLaren, who managed the group, were born under Aquarius, and their song *God Save the Queen*, which came out at the time of Queen Elizabeth's silver jubilee in 1977, inaugurated the whole 'punk rock' movement, and scandalised the British establishment, which, of course, was its intention.

Some of the most prominent feminist thinkers have been born under Aquarius. (Aries has its share, but Aquarius has more.) Germaine Greer, Susan Sontag, Gertrude Stein, Virginia Woolf, Angela Davis, Vanessa Redgrave, and Betty Freidan, were all born in late January or early February, and these women have been among the intellectual leaders of the contemporary movement for women's liberation.

The man carrying a jar of water is presented in the Gospel as an androgynous figure, and androgyny – blurring the distinction between male and female, or combining male and female in one figure – seems to be associated with Aquarius. Gertrude Stein, born this very day (3rd February) in 1874, was a pioneer feminist, but she was also a lesbian, and her story *Q.E.D.*, written in 1903, is said to be one of the first 'coming out' stories in literature. Her relationship with Alice B. Toklas was, according to her friend Ernest Hemingway, similar to that of husband and wife. In more recent times, the singer Alice Cooper, originally called Vincent Furnier, while not a homosexual (as far as I know), deliberately defied convention by adopting a female name. He will be celebrating his sixtieth birthday tomorrow. And the brilliant Australian comedian, Barry Humphries, born on 17th February, is far better known as the insufferable Dame Edna Everidge.

One of the literary world's most celebrated Aquarians is Dublin's own James Joyce, who was born here on 2nd February 1882. (Incidentally, Joyce took astrology seriously, and ensured that all his major works were published at what he considered to be auspicious times.) *Ulysses* turned the literary world upside down, breaking all the novelistic conventions, and *Finnegan's Wake* is one of the most idiosyncratic works of world literature.

Ulysses stands almost as a text-book of the Aquarian vision of life. It breaks all the stylistic and linguistic rules, but it also presents the common man as hero, twenty-four hours in the life of a Dublin nobody as equivalent in grandeur and significance to the ten year peregrinations of the Greek hero, Odysseus.

For all their individuality and idiosyncrasy, however, the typical Aquarian has a strong community spirit and is generally prepared to become involved in environmental and political action groups. Indeed, they seem to operate best in a group situation where they can maintain some measure of detachment. They are not, as a general rule, quick to marry, often preferring less conventional, and less restricting styles of relationship. Many Aquarians seem very uncomfortable with deep personal intimacy: the quickest way to lose an Aquarian is to tell him that you want to marry him!

There are a number of lessons to be learned from this section of Mark's Gospel, not the least of which concerns the symbolism of the water that the man is carrying, but today I simply want to point out one very simple, and I'm sure by now very obvious, lesson from this story. 'Follow him,' says Jesus to the apostles, and what Jesus says to his apostles, he says to us. We have to follow the water-bearer, by being prepared, as he was, to stand out from the crowd – not by cultivating a studied and annoying eccentricity, but by discovering, and then exhibiting that which makes us unique. Your individuality is your precious gift to the world. The world does not need your conformity, it needs your creativity, it needs you to live as your genius impels you and guides you to live, and this means having the courage to break through those layers of convention, those unwritten and unspoken rules of thinking and acting, which would keep your life and your thought within the narrow confines sanctioned by our tyrannical, homogenising culture. 'Whoso would be a man,' writes Ralph Waldo Emerson, 'must be a non-conformist'. These words appear on the gravestone of Frank Lloyd Wright, the great architect, who was not afraid to defy the customs of his time, and who produced some of the 20th century's most beautiful buildings. He was, by the way, a Unitarian. (I would have loved him to be an Aquarian, too, but he wasn't. He was born on 8th June, so he was a Geminian.)

How hard it is to resist conformity, even in a so-called 'free' society. George Orwell's 'thought police' are lurking everywhere, detecting and punishing all who dare to stray from acceptable norms of consensus judgement, not with jail or death, perhaps, but with ridicule and lack of preferment.

I've suffered from this myself. I've been a student of astrology for 42 years, and I consider it to be one of the most important subjects I've ever studied, but I've often had to apologise for my interest in it to people with a dogmatic objection to it – an objection which has always been based on cultural antipathy and never on personal exploration or knowledge. Almost everyone you will ever meet who expresses hostility towards astrology will do so on the basis of inherited prejudice. And may I just say here that if you think that astrology postulates the existence of invisible rays emanating from the stars, then you know nothing about the subject whatsoever, and your opinion is not an informed opinion at all, it is a prejudice which you've picked up from your materialistic culture. Isaac Newton, one of the greatest scientists who ever lived, and a Unitarian of sorts, was rebuked for his own interest in astrology by the astronomer Edmund Halley (after whom the famous comet was named). Newton fittingly replied, 'Sir, I have studied the subject, you have not'.

A few weeks ago I was reading a biography of Goethe,[120] in which we learn that the great poet considered that he had been born at an auspicious moment, that his horoscope was a favourable one. His biographer, who tells us in the introduction to his book that he intends to show us that Goethe was one of the greatest geniuses who ever lived, dismisses Goethe's astrological claim as 'fantastic', meaning 'crazy'. So, on the one hand, Goethe is a genius; on the other, he's an idiot. James Joyce believed that the three greatest figures in European literature were Shakespeare, Dante, and Goethe, each one of these, like Joyce himself, interested in and influenced by astrology, and yet it is culturally acceptable today – indeed, it is culturally *required* today – to patronise the astrological interests of these towering geniuses as somehow indicative of an unfortunate tendency towards superstition which, sadly, even genius is not immune from.

So, the man with the water jar is prepared to stand out from the crowd, as is that other Aquarian figure in this section of the Gospel, the woman with the alabaster jar full of costly perfume. She breaks the jar and spreads the pure nard – said to be worth a year's wages - on Jesus's head, completely disregarding the protestations of the apostles who suggest, conventionally enough, that she should sell the precious liquid and give the money to the poor. Jesus's comment that the poor are always with us and we can help them at other times, seems a bit harsh. But, harsh or not, it's true. We can

---

[120] Armstrong, J., page 6.

help the poor, and we must help them, but we will only eliminate poverty – material and spiritual – by a complete transformation of our thinking. This is the real lesson of Aquarius, and this is what I'll be dealing with next week.

O Brave New World!
Mark 13:1-37

As he was leaving the temple one of his disciples said to him, 'Look teacher! Such stones and such buildings!' And Jesus said to him, 'You see these great buildings? There won't be one stone left upon another. There's none that won't be demolished!'

Sitting on the Mount of Olives opposite the temple, Peter, James, John, and Andrew asked him privately, 'Tell us, when will these things happen? What will be the sign that all these things are about to take place?' And Jesus began to tell them. 'Be careful that no one misleads you. Many will come in my name saying "I'm the one" and many will go astray. Whenever you hear of wars and reports of wars don't be alarmed. These things must take place, but the end is not yet. Nation will rise against nation and kingdom against kingdom; there will be earthquakes in various places; there will be famines. These signal the beginning of the birth pangs. Look to yourselves. They will hand you over to the courts, you will be beaten in synagogues, and you will stand before governors and kings, witnessing to them for my sake. But first the good news must be preached in all the nations. And whenever they arrest you don't bother about what to say, but say whatever is given to you at the time, because it won't be you speaking but the holy spirit. Brother will hand over brother to death, and a father will hand over his child. Children will rebel against their parents and kill them. You will be hated by everyone because of my name, but whoever holds out to the end will be saved. When you see the abomination of desolation standing where it ought not to be (let the reader understand), then let those in Judea flee to the mountains. Let the man on the housetop not come down; neither let him go into the house to take anything out. And let the man in the field not turn back to fetch his coat. Pity those who are pregnant or who are suckling babies in those days! Pray that it doesn't happen in winter, because in those days there will be distress the like of which has not occurred from the time of the creation right up until now. Nor will it happen again. And if the Lord hadn't shortened the days no human being would be saved, but because of those whom he has chosen he has shortened the days. If at that time someone says to you, "Look, the Christ is here" or "There he is", don't believe it, because false Christs and false prophets will rise up and give such convincing demonstrations of their power that, if it were possible, even the elect would be fooled! Keep watch, then! I've warned you about everything. But after the distress of those days, the Sun will be darkened and the Moon will not shine. The stars will fall from the sky, and the powers of the heavens will be shaken, and then they will see the son of man coming in clouds with great power and glory. And then he will send out the angels and gather together his chosen ones from the four corners of the earth, from the farthest bounds of earth to the farthest bounds of heaven. Learn a lesson from the fig tree: when its branch becomes tender and the leaves appear, you know that summer is near. So when you see these things taking place you will know that the end is near, at the door almost. I'm telling you the truth: this generation will not disappear until all these things have occurred; heaven and earth will pass away, but my words will not pass away. But as far as timing is concerned, no one knows, neither the angels in heaven nor the son; only the Father knows. Watch! Be alert! For you don't know when the time is. It's like a man travelling abroad; he leaves his house in the care of his servants, giving each of them a particular task; he tells the doorkeeper to keep watch. So, you keep watch, because you don't know when the lord of the household is coming - whether late in the evening, at midnight, or at cock-crow, or in the morning! You don't want him to come suddenly and find you sleeping! What I am saying to you I am saying to everyone: "Watch!"'

Story: Procrustes

Procrustes – whose name means 'He who stretches' – was a Greek blacksmith who kept a house by the roadside in which he offered hospitality to passing strangers. 'Come inside,' he would shout as people passed by. 'Enjoy a lovely meal and then sleep soundly in my special bed.' When people asked him what was so special about his bed, he would tell them that no matter how short they were, or how tall, the bed would fit them exactly. What he didn't tell them was that as soon as his guest fell asleep, Procrustes would go to work, stretching a short one on the rack or chopping off the legs of a tall one. The great Greek hero, Theseus, stayed with Procrustes but he turned the tables on him: he pushed Procrustes on to the bed and chopped off his head and his legs.

One of the greatest pains to human nature is the pain of a new idea.
Walter Bagehot (born 3rd February, 1826)

About ten days ago I received a package through the post. It was postmarked Tel Aviv, and so I opened it with a little more excitement than I can usually muster for brown envelopes. But I was disappointed to find that it contained an anti-Semitic rant from a British citizen resident in Israel who had accepted Jesus as the Messiah and who was fully expecting him to return to earth in the near future to punish the world for its iniquity. A quotation from the Gospel stood framed in black at the beginning of the diatribe:

> And you will hear of wars and rumours of wars; see that you are not alarmed; for this must take place, but the end is not yet. For nation will rise against nation and kingdom against kingdom, and there will be famines and earthquakes in various places: all this is but the beginning of the birth-pangs.[121]

The writer goes on to say that these Gospel prophecies of calamity are being fulfilled right now, and that the destruction of the twin towers, the Columbia spaceship disaster, and the flooding of New Orleans, are signs of God's anger, and sure indications that Jesus is about to return. What's more, he says, things are set to get even worse.

> On March 17th 2008 or 2009, a deluge will hit the U.S.A – starting from Lake Michigan. Until November 2013, 200 million residents of the U.S.A will die from a devastating series of deluges there. Three quarters of the present area of the U.S.A. will sink under water. The Third World War will begin in 2009 and last until 2014.

---

[121] Mark 13:7-8

Whereabouts in the Bible he gets this from, I don't know, but remember, you heard it here first!

We usually associate this kind of stuff with fringe Christian groups – the Jehovah's Witnesses, for example – but we mustn't forget that mainstream organisations preach a similar message, albeit generally without specific mention of times and places. Indeed, this very day, in Catholic and Anglican churches throughout the world, worshippers will be reciting a creed which clearly states that Jesus Christ will 'come again in glory to judge the living and the dead, and of his kingdom there will be no end'; and during Advent, Christians of all persuasions are expected to prepare themselves for the *second* coming of Christ as they celebrate his first coming in Bethlehem.

It was estimated in 2004 that 59% of Americans believe in 'the Rapture', that, immediately before Christ returns, born-again Christians will be taken up into the sky to meet him, leaving the rest of us behind to suffer and die in the great war of Armageddon. I read a few years ago, but I can't vouch for the truth of it, that some American airline would never have two born-again Christians piloting the same plane, so that no aircraft would be without a pilot in the event of the Rapture occurring.

In 1990 I saw a television programme about an eccentric Methodist minister and millionaire called Bernard Coffindaffer, who was buying plots of land up and down America and having three huge crosses erected on them, representing the three crosses that stood on Calvary at the time of the crucifixion of Jesus. Before his death in 1994, he spent $3,000,000 on his project. During our drive across the States in 1991, my wife and I actually saw one of these strange, imposing and unsettling triptychs, and wondered why on earth anyone would go to such trouble and such expense, and, more importantly, why the secular authorities would allow these sectarian icons to dominate the rural landscape. Bernard didn't erect these crosses himself; he spent his time sitting in his garden, gazing towards the east, because, he said, that's the direction from which the returning Jesus would descend. 'I'm doing it,' he said, 'so that the Lord will feel at home when he returns to earth', but why Jesus would want to see the instrument of his own cruel death Bernard didn't bother to say.

Such eccentricities may be harmless enough in the average citizen, but they become more troublesome when they are shared by politicians. I don't know about you, but I don't want the most powerful man (or woman) in the western world to be someone who believes that we are living in the last days, and that God is going to step in soon and sort out our global mess; or who thinks that war in the middle east is a sign of Christ's imminent return; or that some nation or other is controlled by Satan and so must be eliminated in the great battle of good against evil. President Reagan entertained such thoughts in the eighties, referring to Russia as the 'evil empire', and President Bush, a self-confessed, born-again Christian, came perilously close to expressing similar ideas in his early rhetoric about Iraq. I'm all for leaving the Bible out of politics.

Or, let me put it another way: I'm all for leaving these particular bits of the Bible out of politics, the bits which appear to tell us what is going to happen, because they are the most difficult to understand and to interpret. You can find them in both the Jewish and the Christian scriptures, and they seem to have been the obsession of every religious crank for two millennia. The problem is that although they look like prophecies, for the most part they are nothing of the kind. They belong to a multi-layered, poetic, highly symbolic and highly stylized genre called 'apocalyptic', a Greek work meaning 'unveiling', 'revealing', and in their Jewish context they are not so much predictions of specific incidents in the future, as general expressions of the dire consequences of collective sinfulness in the present. The fact that these dire consequences are presented in the language of cosmic upheaval – the Sun refusing to give its light, the stars falling from the sky, unprecedented natural disasters – serves to stress, in metaphorical terms, the writer's conviction that human sin invites calamity of global proportions. Apocalyptic deals with the breaking down of what appear to be permanent structures, and the apocalyptic passage in Mark's Gospel, chapter 13, begins with Jesus announcing to his apostles that the Jerusalem Temple, one of the most magnificent buildings in the ancient world, would soon crumble into ruins. The destruction of the Temple actually did occur in 70 C.E., so if Mark's Gospel was written before that time (as fundamentalist scholars claim), this statement of Jesus could be seen as a prophecy.

However, whether or not it's a genuine prophecy, it's certainly in the right place. It occurs in the Aquarius section of the Gospel, just before Jesus sends out his apostles to meet the Aquarian figure of the man carrying a jar of water, and Aquarius was associated in the ancient world with the toppling of structures. It was said to be ruled by the planet Saturn, just as was Capricorn, the previous sign, but, while the Saturn of Capricorn was associated with building up, stability, conformity, control, the Saturn of Aquarius was concerned with destruction, anarchy, and death. Saturn is the Roman equivalent of the Greek Cronos, Time, who, as The Grim Reaper, is depicted carrying a scythe, the symbol of death. According to the Greek myth, Cronos – Saturn - 'eats his own children', a perfect metaphor for the way Time eventually consumes everything it has itself generated. Goya's famous picture of Saturn devouring his son is one of the 19th century's most horrifying works of art.

So, a passage in which Jesus talks about the end of the present system of things, and the beginning of something new, is placed appropriately here in the Gospel's Aquarius section, but how are we to interpret it? Fundamentalists take it literally and see it as describing real events at some future time – our own time, they say. Liberal groups, like our own, tend to ignore such passages completely, considering them as belonging to a primitive strand in Christian thought, which has been rendered obsolete by a growing belief in a more compassionate God, and a scientific worldview in which cosmic cataclysms have no place. Jesus, they say, was probably wrong about the coming of the kingdom of God.

On this issue, as on so much else in the Gospels, I have ceased to hold the conventional liberal view. Strange as it may seem, I believe in a world and universe shattering cataclysm and, what is more, I believe that it is imminent, almost at the door.

Of course, I don't believe that these things will be external events, which could be recorded on a video camera. These are not and, I believe, never were originally intended to be, literal descriptions of external, temporal, spatial events. The major events of the Gospels – birth, death, resurrection, ascension, second coming – are *psychological* events, and the Gospels themselves indicate as much. In the Gospel of Luke we read that the kingdom

207

of God 'does not come visibly. People will not say, here it is, or there it is, *because the kingdom of God is within you.*'[122]

This is an extremely important passage, and really gives us the key to understanding the whole issue. If the kingdom of God is inside me, then it is pointless for me to expect it to come from outside, and waiting around, counting the earthquakes, looking up at the sky for Jesus to return are all fruitless distractions. If the kingdom of God is inside me then no wonder Jesus says that it is 'at hand'. This is the good news of the gospel, that all who wish to find the kingdom do not need to go anywhere in order to find it, and they do not have to wait for someone to give it to them. It is as close as you are to yourself, and it is awaiting your discovery. The kingdom of God is not the transformation of the external world brought about by the return of Jesus and the destruction of the wicked – this is just another procrustean solution to add to the countless similar solutions proposed by religious and secular leaders alike throughout history, all of which involve chopping off inconvenient pieces of the human race.

The kingdom of God is the transformation of individual consciousness, which comes unexpectedly, 'like a thief in the night', and when it does, it will turn our interior universe upside down, shattering our world view. The Sun, Moon, and stars of our interior space will tumble from their orbits; our former certainties will be destroyed, our petty aims and expectations will be totally transformed. Our world will never be the same again. This is why the Gospel writers use the language of cosmic catastrophe to describe it.

The transformation of consciousness, which Christians know as the coming of the kingdom of God, is described by all the spiritual traditions in similar terms. The Tibetan Buddhists say that it is

> like taking a hood off your head......everything opens, expands, becomes crisp, clear, brimming with life, vivid with wonder and freshness. It is as if the roof of your mind were

---

[122] Luke 17:17-19

flying off......All limitations dissolve and fall away...as if a seal were broken open.[123]

The Hindu sage Patanjali describes it in this way:

all your thoughts break their bonds;
Your mind transcends limitations,
Your consciousness expands in every direction,
And you find yourself in a new, great
And wonderful world.
Dormant forces, faculties and talents
Become alive, and you discover yourself
To be a greater person by far
Than you ever dreamed
Yourself to be.[124]

This 'new, great and wonderful world' will not be handed to us by some political messiah, nor will it be inaugurated by some god or demigod, who drops down from the sky. The world is already great and wonderful; we have just lost the ability to perceive it. Human beings have amazing capacities which lie neglected and atrophied under the dead weight of our limited self-understanding and our frantic and fruitless search to find happiness in material accumulation and competition. When we, inheritors of the Christian tradition say, 'thy kingdom come' we should not be praying, forlornly, for a political and economic Utopia, but, hopefully, for a new mind to be born within us, a new consciousness, which will see all things differently.

As William Blake says in the *Marriage of Heaven and Hell*:

If the doors of perception were cleansed everything would appear to man as it is, infinite. For man has closed himself up, till he sees all things through narrow chinks of his cavern.

The task of all spiritual systems is to cleanse the doors of our perception, to open up the chinks in the cavern of the mind. This is

---

[123] Rinpoche, pages 157-8
[124] Dyer, page 17

the meaning of the 'upper room' which Jesus's apostles are led to by the man carrying the jar of water. 'He will show you a large upper room, equipped and ready; prepare for us there,' says Jesus. The large upper room is the mind, which each of us must equip and prepare to receive the Christ, symbol of a transformed consciousness, who will not appear in the eastern skies, robed in glory and ready to destroy the wicked, but who will come 'like a thief in the night' to cleanse the doors of our perception and to turn our interior world upside down.

The Age of Aquarius

'This is the dawning of the Age of Aquarius',
Song from the 60s musical *Hair*

There's no doubt that the best-selling books these days are cookery books. *Jamie at Home: How to Cook your Way to the Good Life*, and Delia Smith's *How to Cheat at Cooking* are numbers one and two in the Amazon best-seller list, and good old Nigella Lawson is not too far behind at number 12 with *Nigella Express*. But, as we all know, 'a human being does not live on bread alone', and spiritual matters feature quite prominently in the best-sellers, too. Number seven on Amazon is *The Secret*, by Rhonda Byrne, which has had the distinction of being the best-selling non-fiction hardback in Ireland for a good few weeks. I was in Eason's a couple of weeks ago to check out the status of my own book, and I was pleased to find half a dozen copies placed at eye-level (the pope's book on Jesus was on the bottom shelf!) but there were piles and piles of *The Secret*, suggesting (to this jealous author) that Rhonda Fleming is well set to become a millionaire, if she isn't one already.

The Secret is just the latest in a long line of 'spiritual' books which fall into the very popular 'Body, Mind and Spirit' genre. When Duckworth were deliberating how to categorise my own book, they were torn between 'Religion' and 'Body, Mind and Spirit', since it comfortably fits into both, but, since publishers are concerned more with profit than with accuracy, they opted exclusively for 'Body, Mind and Spirit' since placement here would ensure better sales. Anyone who spends time in bookshops will readily appreciate the financial wisdom of this. You rarely see anyone in the 'Religion' section – maybe a few academic-looking types, or the odd cleric – but 'Mind, Body, Spirit' has a consistent stream of browsers of all ages and all types.

One reason for this, I suppose, is the wide-ranging nature of the category. It encompasses angels, crystals, spiritual healing, Tarot cards, astrology, meditation, dream interpretation, ghosts, UFOs, Jungian psychology, hypnosis, self-help, paganism, and the like, which means that there is something of interest here for all but the most hardened sceptic. But it is a relatively new category. I don't remember so much book-shop space being devoted to these subjects when I began my reading career in the sixties. Indeed, books on such esoteric subjects tended to be placed, almost apologetically, in out-of-the-way corners of the bookshop. You had to search for them in those days; now they hit you in the face.

Not too long ago, the subjects which make up the Mind, Body, Spirit category were lumped together as 'New Age', but this term, which has become associated with woolly mindedness and credulity, has fallen out of favour somewhat. And yet, in spite of the disparaging way in which it is referred to by both the conventionally religious and the conventionally anti-religious, I think that 'New Age' describes a genuinely modern movement in religious and spiritual understanding and that the term is neither redundant nor misleading. We really do seem to be on the threshold of a paradigm shift, which promises to be just as revolutionary as anything our ancestors witnessed. These are exciting times, but they are also frightening for many, because the old certainties – religious and moral – are being eroded and we don't like to feel so unsettled – hence the growth of religious fundamentalism, which is something of a reaction against the toppling of the old structures.

One interesting feature of the New Age phenomenon is that it was predicted. As I'll show in a minute, the Bible reflects it and esoteric writers since Biblical times have told us that our own day would be characterised by just such a shift in spiritual consciousness. Writing in the early 20th century, the great poet and mystic W.B. Yeats described the turmoil and anguish of these days in his poem *The Second Coming*:

> Things fall apart; the centre cannot hold,
> Mere anarchy is loosed upon the world,
> The blood-dimmed tide is loosed, and everywhere
> The ceremony of innocence is drowned;

For Yeats, the age inaugurated by Jesus Christ two thousand years ago is coming to an end, and a new age is about to begin; we are living through its birth-pangs, hence the misery, the pain, and the mayhem.

This esoteric tradition is based upon a simple astronomical fact of which we, who have cut ourselves off from the sky, are completely unaware, but which was well known to our star-gazing ancestors, and informed much of their spiritual writing. This astronomical phenomenon is called the precession of the equinoxes, a rather technical term for the fact that the earth wobbles on its axis causing a gradual shift in our relationship with the star-patterns in the sky. Because of this 'wobble' the Sun's position on the first day of spring – the spring equinox – moves gradually backwards along the zodiac, so that, in approximately 26,000 years, it will move all the way around the zodiacal circle. Since there are twelve constellations in the zodiac, it will stay in each one of them for a little over two thousand years.

But what are simple astronomical facts to the modern rational mind were full of meaning to our more intuitive forebears. For them, this 26,000-year cycle constituted The Great Year, which, like an ordinary year, has its 'seasons' and its 'months'. Their belief was that when the equinoctial constellation changed there was a corresponding change in human consciousness reflecting the characteristics associated with the new constellation, and that each of these twelve two-thousand-year ages marked significant and identifiable developments in religious symbolism and spiritual aspiration. Two thousand years ago the equinoctial point moved into the constellation Pisces. At the present time it is about to enter Aquarius. According to the ancients, then, we stand on the threshold of a new age: as the 1960s song said, 'This is the dawning of the Age of Aquarius'.

Now, I am not, for the moment at least, expecting you to believe in the literal truth of this; I only want you to appreciate that many ancient authors wrote *as if it were true*. The noted 19th and early 20th century historian of religion, Franz Cumont, considered astrology to be the most persistent superstition ever to infect the human mind, but he was wise enough to know that this 'erroneous belief' has 'exercised endless influence on the creeds and the ideas of the most diverse peoples' and that an understanding of it is necessary if we are to come anywhere near a correct interpretation of ancient religious writings. Sadly, we no longer have any appreciation of these things, so we translate stellar symbolism into history and find ourselves in hopeless confusion as a result

But Cumont is undoubtedly right. The change in religious symbolism over millennia testifies to the profound effect of astrological thinking upon the ancient world. The plain fact is that religions do seem to change according to the change in the equinoctial constellation. Go back 6000 years to the time when the equinox was in the constellation Taurus, the Bull. This was when the cow and bull cults began to dominate religious consciousness. In Egypt we find the ceremonies centred around the bull, Apis; in India, Hinduism begins, and the cow becomes sacred; the Minotaur, half-man, half-bull, becomes the sacred emblem of Crete. In this period, we see the beginnings of the bull cult which was eventually to become Mithraism, a religion which seriously vied for supremacy with Christianity, and in which bathing in the blood of a sacrificed bull was at the centre of its ritual and its symbolism.

The equinox moved from Taurus about 4000 years ago and entered Aries, the Ram, and who can doubt that the dominant symbolism changes dramatically? Now we have the Ram or the Lamb as the sacrificial animal, as Judaism begins. There was a 'Passover' from Taurus to Aries, and Abraham, the Father of Judaism, finds a ram caught in the thicket, which he offers to God in place of his son Isaac. The paradigmatic Passover story concerns Moses, whose journey from the securities of Egypt into the uncertainties of the wilderness are a poetic expression of the movement of the equinox from Taurus to Aries. The Passover ceremony is marked by the sacrifice of a lamb whose blood is to be sprinkled on the doorposts of the Jews to save them from the Angel of Death who would pass over their houses. And when Moses receives the Ten Commandments from God, he comes down the mountain to find that the people have built a *golden calf;* their 'sin' is that they have gone backwards, looking to the securities of the former age, instead of onward into the unknown future. The Israelites leave Pharaoh behind, and the word Pharaoh in Hebrew comes from the same root as the word for bull.

Two thousand years ago the equinox changed constellations once more; there was a 'new Passover', this time from Aries to Pisces, with a consequent change in the symbolism. The lamb of Aries is 'slain' ('behold the lamb of God who takes away the sins of the world' says John the Baptist on seeing Jesus), and the fish of Pisces begins to take precedence. Jesus's first disciples were fishermen whom he calls 'fishers of men'; he feeds the multitude on bread and fish; he eats fish with his disciples after the resurrection; he directs Peter to find a coin in a fish's mouth. In all, there are twenty-eight references to fish in the Gospels. Furthermore, the first Christian symbol was not the cross but the fish, and the letters of the Greek word for fish – *ichthus* – became the initial letters of the first Christian creed: *Jesus Christ, Son of God, Saviour*. Eating fish on Fridays, current in Catholicism until quite recently, was a type of communion with Christ; Friday was chosen because it is the day of Venus (*Venerdi, Vendredi*, in the Romance languages), and Venus was said to be exalted in Pisces.

And now, the two-thousand-year age of Pisces is drawing to a close, and we ask: what will take its place? Yeats asked the same question in the poem I referred to earlier:

What rough beast, its hour come round at last
Slouches towards Bethlehem to be born?

And Yeats knew the answer: 'A shape with lion body and the head of a man'. The equinox is passing into Aquarius, symbolised by the Man (whose opposite, complementary sign is Leo, the Lion) and, according to the ancients, a new religious consciousness is emerging, painfully, because the old dies hard, but inevitably, because the movement is always onward. Those of you who are familiar with the rich symbolism of the zodiac will have some idea what this presages: human-centred religion, technological and communications revolutions, ecological awareness; changes of patterns in primary relationships, egalitarianism.

Ten years ago I would have said that the changes in religious symbolism were simply the result of writers reflecting a very ancient esoteric belief system; but, witnessing the abundance of Aquarian features in the modern world – features which seem to be emerging unconsciously – leads me to accept, somewhat reluctantly I admit, that human consciousness *is* actually developing according to a pattern discerned by our sensitive ancestors. The implications of this are astonishing: it suggests that we are participants in some amazing unfolding of consciousness, that we are not the chance outcome of random mutations of matter, but part of a mysterious cosmic process, the stages of which, for reasons that are currently hidden from us, are reflected in the earth's changing relationship with the sky. Our religious images are not accidental or arbitrary. Their source is what Yeats called the *spiritus mundi* – 'the spirit of the world', what, to Jung, was the collective unconscious, and the images emerge when it is appropriate for them to do so. It is also likely that they emerge most clearly in those cultures which are developmentally ready for them, which gives a whole new meaning to the term 'chosen people'.

A new Passover is imminent. Dramatic changes are afoot in our religious and spiritual symbolism and practice. Signs of such change can be found in the increasing popularity of the Mind, Body, Spirit genre and the decreasing popularity of church going, which seem to indicate that people no longer find the old authorities intellectually convincing or the old ceremonies psychologically satisfying. What outworn approaches to spirituality do we need to leave behind? What emerging symbols and images do we need to embrace? How can our own religious system begin to adapt itself to the changing needs of a new age? Despite the fact that religion always seems to be in love with the past, the Bible is full of images of change and of instructions to welcome change. At the beginning of the Age of Pisces Jesus told us that 'New wine needs new wineskins', and 'Let the dead bury their own dead,' In the Book of Revelation God says 'Behold I make all things new.'

And the Bible also contains a warning for those who constantly look backwards: like Lot's wife in the Book of Genesis, they turn into pillars of salt.

Chapter 12: Pisces
February 20th - 20th March

The Two Fish. Pisces is Mutable Water and is the sign in which the Sun 'dies' before being 'born anew' at the spring equinox when it enters Aries once again. Ruled by Jupiter, it is a sign of extreme sensitivity and benevolence, but it was also associated in the ancient world with secret enemies, betrayal, cowardice, diffidence, sleep, dreams, all of which appear in this final, lengthy section of the Gospel. Nearby constellations are Cepheus (the King), and Andromeda (the Chained Woman), and both are clearly referred to in the story of the crucifixion.

The King Must Die
Mark 15:1-39

Very early in the morning, the chief priests, the elders, and the legal experts – the whole Sanhedrin, in fact – held a meeting. They bound Jesus and took him off and handed him over to Pilate, who asked him, 'Are you the king of the Jews?' Jesus replied, 'Those are your words.' But the chief priests were accusing him of many things, so Pilate questioned him again. 'Have you nothing to say for yourself? See how many things they are accusing you of.' But Jesus said nothing, and Pilate was amazed.

It was the custom for Pilate to release to the people a prisoner of their own choosing. There was a man called Barabbas, imprisoned with his fellow revolutionaries, who had committed murder in the rebellion. The crowd came up and began to petition Pilate to carry out the customary procedure, and he replied by saying, 'Do you want me to release the king of the Jews to you?' He realised that the chief priests had handed him over out of spite. But the chief priests stirred up the crowd to ask for Barabbas instead. Once again, Pilate answered them, 'So, what shall I do with the one you call the king of the Jews?' Again they cried out, 'Crucify him!' Pilate said to them, 'Why? What has he done wrong?' They shouted out all the more, 'Crucify him!' Pilate, wishing to please the crowd, released Barabbas to them. He had Jesus whipped and then handed him over to be crucified.

The soldiers took him into the courtyard inside the palace, the Praetorium, and they called the entire detachment of soldiers together. They dressed him in purple, plaited some thorns into a crown, and placed it on his head. They started to salute him 'Greetings, king of the

Jews!' they said, and they were cuffing him round his head with a reed and spitting on him. Kneeling before him, they paid him homage. When they'd finished making fun of him, they stripped the purple robe from him to crucify him. They forced a passer-by to carry his cross. It was Simon of Cyrene (the father of Alexander and Rufus) who was coming in from the field.

They took him to Golgotha, which means 'The Place of the Skull', and they offered him wine drugged with myrrh, but he wouldn't take it. They crucified him, and they shared out his clothing, casting lots to see who would take what. It was nine o'clock in the morning when they crucified him. The inscribed charge against him read, 'The king of the Jews.' And they crucified two thieves with him, one on his right, and one on his left. Those who passed by hurled abuse at him, shaking their heads and saying, 'Aha! You were going to tear down the temple and build it up again in three days, were you? Well, save yourself by getting down off the cross!' Similarly, the chief priests and the lawyers were joining in the fun, saying, 'He saved others, but he can't save himself! Let's see the Christ, the king of Israel come down from the cross now! We'd believe him then!' Even those who were being crucified with him were jeering at him.

At about noon, darkness fell on the whole earth and lasted until three o'clock in the afternoon, at which time Jesus cried aloud, 'Eloi, eloi, lama sabakhthani', which means, 'My God, my God, why have you forsaken me?' Some of those standing by heard it and said, 'Look! He's calling Elijah!' Someone put a sponge with sour wine on a reed and gave it to him to drink, saying, 'Let's see if Elijah will come to take him down.' But, with a loud cry, Jesus died, and the temple curtain split in two, top to bottom. A centurion standing opposite him as he died said, 'This man was certainly a son of God!'

Story: The Wise Little Bird

Once upon a time, there lived a man who was very proud of his garden. Every day he would stroll around it, admiring the beautiful flowers, the majestic trees, and the plump vegetables. He tended his garden with loving care, pruning the branches of the trees, watering the flowers, pulling out the weeds, mowing the lawn, planting and picking the vegetables at the proper season. All the neighbours admired his garden, and people would come from miles around just to have a look at such a perfect example of the gardener's skill.

One day, as he was taking his customary stroll round his garden, he noticed that some of his precious flowers had been pecked off their stems, and their beautiful petals were lying on the ground, shrivelling in the Sun. 'What can have happened?' he asked himself. 'While I was sleeping, some animal or other has got into my garden and is destroying my flowers!' Instead of going to bed that night, he decided to hide in the bushes to see if he could catch the culprit.

Just as the Sun was rising, he saw a tiny little bird alight on one of his prize rose-bushes and begin to peck away at the lovely red roses. 'Ah! I've caught you, you rascal,' he said to himself, and, creeping softly over to the rose-bush, with one swift movement he caught the little bird in his hand. 'Now, I'm going to take you home and cook you for my breakfast,' he said. 'You won't spoil my garden anymore!'

But then, something amazing happened. The little bird began to talk! 'Please don't eat me,' it said, in its little squeaky voice. 'I'm only very small and I wouldn't even make one mouthful for a big man like you. If you let me go I promise not to damage your flowers any more, and, what's more, I'll give you three pieces of advice that will help you throughout your life.'

The gardener was astonished and intrigued, as you can imagine, so he agreed to accept the bird's offer. Opening his hand, he said, 'Okay, I'll let you go. Now give me the advice.'

The little bird sat on the gardener's open hand and began to speak. 'First,' it said, 'don't worry about things that are finished. It's a waste of energy. It's like crying over milk that's been spilled; no amount of tears is going to put it back in the bottle. Second, never wish for something that you know you can never have. It will only bring you disappointment. And third, never believe what you know cannot possibly be true.'

With that, the little bird flew off into the branches of a nearby tree, where it began to speak again. 'Oh, you fool!' it squawked. 'If you had carried out your original intention and cooked me for breakfast you would have found that inside me there is a diamond as big as a goose's egg. You could have sold the diamond and never wanted for money for the rest of your life! You are such an idiot!'

'Oh, what have I done?' thought the gardener. 'I've thrown away the chance to become fabulously rich. I must try to get that bird back in my hands!'

'Little bird,' he said, in his most cajoling manner, 'please come back. I'm sorry I frightened you. I promise that I won't hurt you, and you can peck at my flowers any time you like!'

'You really are a fool,' replied the bird. 'You've already forgotten the three pieces of advice I gave you. You're regretting the fact that you let me go, but this is like crying over spilled milk, and I told you that you should never do that. And you're wishing for something that you can never have, because I'm certainly never coming back to you, no matter what you promise, so save your breath. But what shows that you are really stupid is that you've forgotten the most important piece of advice: never believe what you know can't possibly be true. I said there was a diamond as big as a goose's egg inside me, but a goose's egg is bigger than I am! How could I possibly have one inside me? You really are a fool!'

And with these words the little bird flew away. The gardener never saw the bird again, but he never forgot its wise words.

The story of the death of Jesus is probably the most famous story in the Western world. The Gospel accounts will be read in Christian churches this coming week, just as they have been read for millennia. It has inspired novels, poems, paintings, oratorios, hymns, theological tracts, meditations, historical investigations and, relatively recently, feature films. Cecil B. DeMille's seminal *King of Kings* (1927); Pasolini's political *The Gospel of St. Matthew* (1964); George Stevens' sentimental *The Greatest Story Ever Told* (1965); Zeffirelli's lengthy *Jesus of Nazareth* (1977); Mel Gibson's blood-fest *The Passion of the Christ* (2004), are just some of the many films devoted to it. Then there are the stage plays and musicals, notably *Godspel* and *Jesus Christ Superstar*, and television plays like Dennis Potter's controversial 1969 play, *Son of Man*.

There is no getting away from the fact that this is a very powerful and influential story, inspiring people as diverse as the ultra-orthodox Catholic, Mel Gibson, and the gay, Marxist, atheist, Pierre Paolo Pasolini. It is loved by those who believe the death and resurrection of Jesus to be the central events of human history, securing the salvation of the human race, and by more secular types (like us) who see the story as an account of a brave and selfless person who was prepared to give his life for what he believed in. No other story has generated as much artistic interest or as much theological controversy. It is undoubtedly unique.

And yet, the central incident – the crucifixion – is hardly unique. Crucifixion was a common method of execution among the Romans (the Jews stoned criminals) because it was cheap and easy, and because it was extremely painful and lengthy. It was cheap because all you needed were a few nails and a tree, and it was painful because the nails would be driven into the wrist, close to the nerve. Death came from asphyxiation – pulling oneself up in order to breathe would cause intolerable pain and so ultimately the person would give up, but this could take days, particularly if the criminal was tied rather than nailed. According to Mark's Gospel, Jesus was on the cross for six hours – from 9 am to 3 pm – and so, in a sense, he got off lightly. Roman citizens accused of capital crimes could opt for beheading – much quicker and cleaner – but miscreants among slaves and subject peoples (like the Jews) were crucified. The slaves' revolt, under Spartacus, about 70 years before the time of Jesus, ended in the crucifixion of 6,600 slaves along the Appian Way, the road from Brundisium to Rome, and, apparently, the order was never given for the bodies to be taken down, so travellers were forced to see the decaying bodies for months, perhaps even years, afterwards.

There are one or two other things I want to say about the story of Jesus's crucifixion before I outline what I believe to be its spiritual meaning. First, the dating of the event: the Gospel says that it took place on the day of the Passover. Now, the Passover was the biggest festival of the Jews and it was compulsory for every adult male Jew who lived within 15 miles of Jerusalem to go to the city to celebrate it. But not only local men attended; since it was the ambition of every Jew to celebrate at least one Jerusalem Passover in their life, Jews from all over the Mediterranean world would flock to Jerusalem at this time. All lodging in the city was free and Jerusalem could not contain the crowds, so the pilgrims would overflow into the surrounding villages. According to the Jewish historian Josephus, in 65 CE 265,000 lambs were slain for the Passover celebrations, and because it was customary for a minimum of ten people to share one lamb, it would seem that there were nearly 3,000,000 people in the city.[125] This is probably a gross exaggeration, but there can be no doubt that Jerusalem would be packed, nor can there be any doubt that strong patriotic feelings would be in evidence: during Passover, the Jews celebrated their release from bondage in Egypt under Moses, so it would be only natural for them to feel added resentment against their current Roman overlords at Passover time. The Romans, who were well aware that the atmosphere was volatile, drafted in extra troops in case of some impromptu nationalist rebellion.

Against that background, can you imagine the Romans being foolish enough to crucify a Jewish citizen, particularly one who had messianic pretensions, that is, one who was announcing a new kingdom, a new kind of freedom for the Jews? Even the execution

---

[125] Barclay, W., page 324

of a Jewish *criminal* would have been asking for trouble, and the Romans were anything but stupid. In addition, this was the busiest time of the year for the Temple priests. Their job was not counselling the people like prototypical social workers, or conducting worship in synagogues; they sacrificed the animals, and with countless thousands to slaughter, there would be little time for plotting the death of Jesus. If he had to die, it would be best left for a few days.

The way the story is told should also alert us to the fact that we are not dealing with history – or, at least, not primarily history. The whole account is full of allusions to the Jewish scriptures, principally the Psalms. The derision of the crowds (15:29), quotes from Psalm 22 (verse 7), Jesus's cry of dereliction from the cross 'My God, my God, why have you forsaken me?' (15:34) is the first line of that Psalm, and a little later in the same Psalm we read 'they divide my clothes among themselves, and for my clothing they cast lots' (verse 18); 'they gave him sour wine to drink' comes from Psalm 69 (verse 21); the people looking on from a distance is taken from Psalm 38 (verse 11). Is history written in this way?

We might also ask where the author of the Gospel got his information from. When Jesus goes off to pray in the Garden of Gethsemane he goes alone; his companions are sleeping, and yet Mark gives us a pretty comprehensive account of his prayer.[126] Who was listening? Was some stenographer or other hiding in the bushes noting down Jesus's words? Jesus prays in private, and yet we have his words. This part of the story is obviously fictional.

Have you ever considered just how much activity is said to have taken place in a few brief hours? There's the last supper, the Garden of Gethsemane episode, betrayal by Judas, trial before the Sanhedrin, trial before Pilate, (plus a trial before Herod according to Luke), and then the final scourging, journey to Calvary, and the actual crucifixion. It's unlikely that all this could have happened in the available time, and the unlikely nature of these incidents is further underlined by the fact that the Sanhedrin, the Jewish Council, was not allowed to meet in the hours of darkness.

---

[126] Mark 15:32-42

The story is implausible, but, according to the early Christian writer Origen, some biblical stories *are meant to be implausible*, so that we will go beneath the literal meaning in order to seek the deeper, spiritual meaning. As the bird advises in our story today, we shouldn't force ourselves to believe what we know can't be true. We don't need to 'believe' the story: we need to probe it, to examine it with our imagination. This is a deeply symbolic story which literalism renders absurd. One reason why Jesus has to die at Passover time is because his death symbolises the passing over of the Sun's position at the spring equinox from Aries to Pisces. The 'Lamb' of Aries is slain to be replaced by the Fish of Pisces

Jesus is slain as a symbolic lamb, but he is also crucified as a king. Pilate asks him if he is a king; the soldiers dress him as a king, and pay mock homage to him as a king; and the inscription above the cross reads 'The king of the Jews'. Why all this stuff about a king?

First, one of the constellations surrounding Pisces – which the Sun entered on 21st February - is Cepheus, the mythological king whose wife was Cassiopeia and whose daughter was Andromeda. Cepheus is always depicted as 'a glorious king, wearing his royal robe, bearing aloft a branch or sceptre, and having on his head a crown of stars.'[127] – precisely as Jesus is dressed by the Roman soldiers.

But in order to understand the image fully we must also consider the custom – according to Sir James Frazer, found all over the ancient world – of the ageing king being put to death in order to secure the prosperity of the people. Since the king symbolised the nation, his powers were thought to be related to national power and vigour. As the king's strength failed with age, the people feared that his physical weakness would be transferred to them, and his sterility would be reflected in the crops. So he had to die, and a new, young king had to be inaugurated in order to ensure the vitality of the people and the fecundity of the earth. The obvious time for the actual – or, later, the symbolic – enactment of this ceremony would be the springtime, when the people were preparing to sow their

---

[127] Seiss, page 85

crops and the continuing fertility of the earth was uppermost in their mind.

But the ancient people were also conscious of another cycle of decline at this time of the year. The Sun is coming to the end of its annual journey round the zodiac, a journey that began when it entered the sign of Aries on the first day of spring last year. Now it is in Pisces, the sign which symbolises the Sun's weakness. Just as the old king has to die before the new king can take over, so the 'old' solar cycle has to end before a new one can begin. The Sun 'dies' annually in Pisces before being 'reborn' again in Aries.

Pisces symbolises this period of decline and eventual death, which is why it was considered a malign sign by many ancient cultures, indicative of weakness and lack of courage. But while Piscean people can often be quiet and unassuming, their lack of self-promotion is not so much a mark of cowardice as of extreme sensitivity. Pisces is a Water sign, a sign of strong emotion and intuition, and the typical Piscean is remarkably perceptive, mediumistic even, with a marked degree of empathy for suffering humanity. They tend to be kind and gentle, but there is something of the martyr about them, and often, of the hypochondriac. The old text books say that the Pisces person is either the victim or the redeemer – the Gospel story shows us Jesus in both roles.

Pisces is associated with drugs and alcohol, counterfeit satisfactions for the spiritual succour that Pisces people crave, and astrological writers down the ages have invariably warned Piscean people to stay away from both. Contemporary Pisceans are often interested in film and photography, creative expressions of the desire to remould reality, to gain some measure of control in a world which overwhelms the sensitive Piscean soul. Sleep and dreams are also part of this network of associations, and both feature prominently in the Gospel accounts of the last days of Jesus.

The evolved Piscean soul, writes Joan Hodgson, 'will work in the most sordid conditions, and do anything to lighten the load for others. We find children of Pisces from all levels of society devoting their strength and their time to nursing, healing … … wherever the sick, the desolate and the outcast are to be found; and this with no thought of personal reward. Thus the inmost spirit begins to find that which it seeks, the secret of true heavenly peace. It learns that union with the Infinite comes only through renunciation of the self.'[128]

'Renunciation of the self', the chief characteristic of the evolved Piscean, is one of the major lessons of these final Gospel stories. The king must die; the ego must die; the false self must die before the new, transformed self can be born. 'The death of the ego is the birth of everything else,' wrote Carl Jung. It is the ego, the 'king' within the psyche, which is crucified on the cross. Just as the seed 'dies' so that the flower can be born, and as the chrysalis dies so that the butterfly can be born, so the grasping, fearful, defensive self must die in order to bring to birth the new, transformed person. As Aldous Huxley puts it:

> 'Our kingdom go' is the necessary and unavoidable corollary of 'Thy kingdom come'. For the more there is of self, the less there is of God. The divine eternal fullness of life can be gained only by those who have deliberately lost the partial, separative life of craving and self-interest, of egocentric thinking, feeling, wishing and acting.'[129]

Crucifixion is not just about one man's death, which may or may not have happened 2000 years ago. It's about the death of something which *must* happen in every person who endeavours to live a spiritual life: the old self must die before the new self can be born.

The birth of the new self from the old is the real meaning of resurrection, and it's the theme we'll be considering on Easter Sunday.

---

[128] Hodgson, page 122
[129] Huxley, page 122

Pisces/Aries: Resurrection

Mark 16:1-8

> When the Sabbath was over, Mary Magdalene and Mary the mother of James and Salome bought spices with which to anoint him. Very early in the morning on the first day of the week they came to the tomb. The Sun had risen. They were saying to each other, 'Who will roll away the stone from the door of the tomb for us?' But when they looked up they saw that the stone had already been rolled away, even though it was very large. Going inside the tomb they saw a young man dressed in white sitting on the right hand side. They were astonished. He said to them, 'Don't be so shocked! You are looking for Jesus the Nazarene, the one who was crucified; but he has been raised up. He's not here. See the place where they laid him. Go and tell his disciples and Peter that he is going on ahead to Galilee. You will see him there, just as he told you.
> When they came out they ran away from the tomb because they were trembling with astonishment. And they said nothing to anyone because they were afraid.

Story: The Elephant and the Rope

> A little girl was at the zoo with her father when she spotted some elephants. 'That's strange,' she said. 'The little elephant has a big rope tied round its leg, but the big elephant's leg is only tied with thin string. Why is that?' Her father didn't know the answer, but the zoo-keeper, overhearing the girl's question, said: 'When it's still a baby, the elephant is tied by a very thick rope which is attached to a sturdy stake in the

ground. The little elephant tries to pull itself free, but it is tethered too strongly. It keeps on trying, but it is never successful. After about a year it gives up trying, thinking that the rope will always be too strong for it. At that point, the keepers can tie the elephant's leg to a thin piece of string tied to a broom handle, and the elephant, remembering its inability to escape in the past, never even tries to get away. It could pull itself free very easily, but it's been tricked into thinking there's no point even trying.'

> *'Awake thou that sleepest, and arise from the dead, and Christ shall give thee light.' (Ephesians 5:14)*

Tolstoy's novel *Resurrection* was first published in 1899 when he was 71 years old. A couple of decades earlier, he had experienced something of a religious conversion and this novel, his final one, expresses his religious convictions more comprehensively and more clearly than any of his other works. I've read it four or five times – it's one of those novels I feel obliged to return to every now and again – and it never fails to uplift my spirits and to deepen my appreciation of the powerful images of new life which the Christian tradition presents to us at this time of the year. Tolstoy's novel is about one man coming back from the dead: not as a reanimated corpse, but as a transformed individual, one who has found strength to break the ropes of convention and selfishness that have bound him since childhood, and to leave the tomb of corruption in which he has been buried by his acquisitive and hypocritical society. He has been reborn to a new life of service, wholeness, and freedom.

The novel opens with a description of the springtime:

> The Sun shone warm, the air was balmy, the grass, where it did not get scraped away, revived and sprang up everywhere … … All were glad: the plants, the birds, the insects, and the children.' But, in contrast, 'grown up men and women did not leave off cheating themselves and each other. It was not this spring morning men thought sacred and worthy of

consideration, not the beauty of God's world, given for a joy to all creatures – this beauty which inclines the heart to peace, to harmony, and to love – but only their own devices to enslave each other.[130]

The man who gradually rediscovers the beauties of God's world is Prince Nekhlyudov, who, at the beginning of the novel is living a life of dissipation and frivolity in keeping with his wealth and his position in society. But, despite his status, he cannot escape the irksome task of jury service, so he finds himself reluctantly sitting in court one day, listening to the tedious account of a murder which has taken place in a local brothel. Three people are accused of the crime, a man and two women, and it is the younger of the two women who catches Nekhlyudov's eye. Her name is Maslova, and he recognises her as the former servant of his two maiden aunts, the woman whom he callously seduced a decade before. He had forgotten about her. He vaguely recollected that she had left his aunts' employ because she was pregnant, but now he learns for the first time about the life of degradation to which she has been reduced, and he realises the part he himself has played in her downfall. As the evidence is produced, he realises that she is obviously innocent of the crime she is accused of, but because of a mix up in the wording of the jury's verdict, and the haste with which the court president wants the case to end so that he can meet his mistress, she is sentenced to four years penal servitude in Siberia.

Nekhlyudov's feelings of shame and guilt mark the first stage in his resurrection. He decides to follow Maslova to Siberia to see how he can help her, and the rest of the novel describes the stages of his gradual transformation as they occur during his journey. He is forced to look at himself and the life he is leading, and to the mores and values of a society which grants to him power and status, but which totally neglects and exploits the poor and the vulnerable.

The legal system comes in for savage attack. Maslova's treatment by the court is shameful because she is poor and has no one to plead her cause, but everywhere he looks Nekhlyudov finds similar examples of injustice perpetrated in the name of justice. Very

---

[130] Tolstoy, page 5

early on we learn of a widow who is having her property taken from her by crafty lawyers whose knowledge of the intricacies of law enable them to swindle her perfectly legally. These men are 'legal criminals', a category which comprises millions of rich and powerful people who have shaped the laws and customs of society so that they can live in luxury on the backs of the dispossessed and powerless. How different are things now, a century after Tolstoy wrote *Resurrection*? How is it that the richest people in our society pay the least tax? How is it that the ability to pay a slick lawyer can so frequently enable the obviously guilty to walk away scot free? How is it that the children of American Senators and Congressmen are not fighting in Iraq? How is it that the person who will become the next President of the U.S.A. will be the millionaire who can spend the most on media image manipulation? As Bob Dylan said four decades ago, 'Money doesn't talk, it swears.' As Tolstoy's narrator comments: 'How can we – all of us - who are ourselves evil ever hope to correct evil'?

Nekhlyudov also begins to see through the church (Tolstoy was eventually excommunicated by the Russian Orthodox Church). In the courtroom there is an old priest who administers the oath to defendants and jurors. How ironic, muses the novel's narrator, that this priest has, over decades, required countless thousands of people to swear upon a book in which there is a condemnation of all such swearing of oaths?[131] More significantly, Tolstoy condemns a church which offers stupefying ceremonies to the people instead of teaching them the fundamental precepts of the Gospel. The procurator of the Russian Orthodox Church is a man called Toporov, who believes in nothing, but whose attitude to religion is the same as that of a poultry-keeper to the disgusting, rotting food he feeds to his hens; they seem to like it, so it is right to keep on feeding it to them. The people seem to like meaningless ceremonies and superstition, so let's keep giving it to them.

At the end of the novel, Nekhlyudov takes his copy of the Bible and reads the Gospels, particularly the Sermon on the Mount, and realises that in these few neglected pages lie all the moral guidance we human beings need in order for us to live fulfilled and

---

[131] Matthew 5:34

compassionate lives. 'A perfectly new life dawned that night for Nekhlyudov; not because he had entered into new conditions of life, but because everything he did after that night had a new and quite different meaning for him.'[132]

The Gospel of Mark, which we have been considering for a year now describes a similar kind of journey. The Gospel comprises a series of narratives, which seem on the surface to be historical reminiscences strung together almost randomly, but which, on closer examination, show themselves to be profound teachings on the spiritual life, very carefully arranged so that the interior journey of the aspirant towards transformation reflects the annual journey of the Sun in the sky.

Each of these stages is a step on the way towards wholeness – 'redemption', if you like that kind of language – and although they are presented consecutively, we are not meant to infer from this that we have to approach them sequentially. Individuals will vary in the way they assimilate these lessons. Some we will find easy; others will take a lifetime to master.

Here, by way of recapitulation, are the twelve steps towards redemption – resurrection - presented to us by the Gospel of Mark.

The lesson of **Aries**, the springtime sign, concerns our relationship with the past. We are not to let the past with its sins and its guilt, and its failures paralyse our present. 'Your sins are forgiven,' says Jesus to the paralysed man, 'so pick up your bed and walk!' This first section teaches that embarking on the spiritual life requires courage and a willingness to break free from debilitating personal habits of thought and behaviour, and from social and family relationships which hinder our resolve to pursue the spiritual life.

In the **Taurus** section we learn that steadfastness, sticking to our resolve is vital to our spiritual growth; we must not be like the seed that grows well for a while but which then is choked by thorns – the physical appetites, and the cares and concerns of the world. Taurus also teaches us that light will come if only we persevere.

Gemini, the Twins, highlights the fragmented nature of the psyche; that in each of us there is a whole crowd of personalities

---

[132] Tolstoy, page 483

jostling for attention, and we have to try to create a harmony between them, 'to get them to sit down at the same table' as Art Lester puts it. This section also teaches us that our ordinary condition is that we are asleep, reacting to circumstances rather than choosing our actions. Waking up from this sleep – as Jairus' daughter is awakened by Jesus – is a necessary step on the way to wholeness.

Cancer teaches us that we are closed off from others like the crab is enclosed in its shell, but we must break through this carapace and be prepared to encounter 'the other'. We are semi-blind, the story tells us; we can see other people, but they seem like trees walking about. We need to learn to see others as ends in themselves and not as means to our own ends.

In **Leo**, which includes the scene of the Transfiguration, we are taught about the true nature of the human being. We are all children of God, divine beings, eagles who think we are chickens. Each of us is a glorious emanation from God with a vital and unique part to play in the drama of the universe.

However, no sooner are we told this than we are taught the virtues of humility and service, the great lessons of **Virgo**. 'Don't get above yourself,' says Jesus to his apostles. 'Never mind arguing with each other about who is the greatest. Serve one another, and, in addition, cultivate the mind of a child and learn to perceive the world afresh.'

The equinoctial sign of **Libra**, which the Sun enters when day and night are equal, carries the lessons of mutuality and reciprocity, of entering into caring and supportive relationships with people. Here we learn about the 'sacred marriage', the union of male and female, of yang and yin, within the individual psyche. We are taught, too, that wealth can be a severe hindrance to our spiritual progress, deflecting us from the life of the spirit by fostering self-indulgence and distraction.

In the **Scorpio** section, which comes as Jesus and the apostles approach Jericho, the lowest inhabited place on earth, we are warned not to seek power over others, and taught about those hidden connections which bind us one to another, so that no individual acts to and for himself alone; our actions, for good or ill have consequences for ourselves and for others.

At the beginning of the **Sagittarius** section, Jesus rides into Jerusalem on an unbroken horse, symbolising the mastery of the bestial by the divine, mastery which each of us is called to attain. Each of us is a 'place where two roads meet'. Here we learn about the power of prayer and of faith to bring about remarkable changes in our world.

In **Capricorn** we learn about the attitude we should cultivate towards all religious authority – bishops, priests, ministers, traditions, church councils, holy books and the like. We must not cravenly follow the lead of others. We must take responsibility for our own spiritual progress.

The **Aquarius** section teaches the importance of standing out from the crowd, and of being willing to offer our unique gifts to society. We also learn that coming to a state of enlightened transformation will turn our interior universe upside down.

Finally, in the lengthy **Pisces** section, we see a dramatic presentation of the crucifixion of the false self which has kept us enslaved in our own egotism and craving but which has never been able to deliver the happiness it has constantly promised.

In the final few verses of the Gospel of Mark we read about the Resurrection, the empty tomb, which happens on the first day of the week – Sunday -, just as the Sun has risen. These references to the Sun are not accidental or peripheral. The yearly journey of the Sun in the sky reflects the life journey of the spiritual aspirant. Just as the Sun is 'resurrected' each year at the equinox, and each day at dawn; just as winter is transformed into spring; just as the caterpillar is transformed into the butterfly; just as Nekhlyudov is transformed by his journey to Siberia, so the spiritual journey outlined by Mark results in the birth of a new creature, a resurrected creature, someone who has overcome the sleep of the unlived life and who is now prepared to enter into life with new attitudes, new visions, new hopes. Jesus's disciples are to meet him in Galilee, that is, back where it all started. Galilee comes from the Hebrew word 'galil' which means *circle*. Resurrection doesn't take us away from the cycle of ordinary life, it sends us back on to it once more, but this time, in the words of T.S. Elliot, 'we'll know the place for the first time'.

All valid religion is a call to resurrection. Not to life after death, but to a new kind of life *achievable now*. As Balzac says, at the end of his novel *Louis Lambert*, 'The resurrection is brought about by the winds of heaven which sweep the worlds. The angel borne upon the blast saith not, "Arise, ye dead!" but "Arise, ye living!"'

This is the message of the Gospel. This is the real message of Easter.

Bibliography

Allen, R.H., (1963), *Star Names: Their Lore and Meaning.* Dover Publications, New York.
Andrews, B.M. (2000), *Thoreau as Spiritual Guide*. Skinner House Books, Boston.
Armstrong, J., (2007) *Love, Life, Goethe: How to be Happy in an imperfect World.* Penguin Books, London, England.
Ballou, R.O. (1959), *The Pocket World Bible.* Readers Union, Routledge and Kegan Paul, London.
Barclay, W. (1975), *The Gospel of Matthew, Volume 1.* The Westminster Press, Philadelphia.
Barclay, W., (no date), *The Daily Study Bible: Mark.* The Saint Andrew Press, Edinburgh.
Bielecki, T., (1996) *Teresa of Avila: Ecstasy and Common Sense,* Shambhala, Boston and London.
Carpenter, E., *The Origin of Pagan and Christian Beliefs.* Random House, London.
Carter, C. (1965), *Essays on the Foundations of Astrology.* Fowler, London.
Cassetari, S., (1992), *Pebbles on the Road,* Angus and Robertson, Australia.
Cooke, D. (1996) *Persecuting Zeal: A Portrait of Ian Paisley.* Brandon Books, Ireland.
De Botton, (1998) *How Proust Can Change Your Life,* Picador, Macmillan, London,
Darlison, B., (2007), *The Gospel and the Zodiac: The Secret Truth about Jesus,* Duckworth/Overlook, London, New York.
Dyer, W., (1998), *Wisdom of the Ages,* Thorsons, London.
Emerson, R.W., (1982) *Selected Essays.* Penguin, London.
Fox, M., (1988), *The Coming of the Cosmic Christ,* Harper and Row, San Francisco.
Frankl, V., (1946) *Man's Search for Meaning.* Washington Square Press.
Fulghum, R. (1989) *All I Really Need to Know I Learned in Kindergarten,* Grafton Books, London.
Goldstein, J., (1983), *The Experience of Insight.* Shambhala, Boston.

Greene, L., and Sharman-Burke, J., (2000) *The Mythic Journey*, Simon and Schuster, London.
Greer, C., and Kohl, H., (1995), *A Call to Character*, Harper Perennial,
Haddon, C., (2003), *One Hundred Lamps for the Soul*. Hodder and Stoughton, London.
Hodgson, J. (1943), *Wisdom in the Stars*, White Eagle Publishing Trust, Hampshire, England (1995 edition).
Hodson, G., (1967), *The Hidden Wisdom in the Holy Bible*, Volume 1. Published by the Theosophical Publishing House, London.
Huxley, A., (1994), *The Perennial Philosophy*, Flamingo, London.
Kolodejchuk, B., (2007) *Mother Teresa: Come be my Light*. Doubleday.
Lawrence, D.H., (1950) *Selected Essays*, Penguin Books, London
McNeice, L., *(1964), Astrology*, Doubleday, New York.
Ouspensky, P.D. (1957), *The Fourth Way*, Vintage Press, New York.
Pagan, I., (1911), *From Pioneer to Poet*, Theosophical Publishing House, London.
Rinpoche, S., (1992), The Tibetan Book of Living and Dying. Rider, London.
Rudhyar, D., (1979), *Astrological Insights into the Spiritual Life*. Aurora Press, New York.
Rushdie, S., (1989), *The Satanic Verses*, Picador,
Saint-Exupery, Antoine de (1944), *The Little Prince*. Wordsworth Classics, Wordsworth Editions, published 1995.
Seiss, J. (1882), *The Gospel in the Stars*, Kregel Publications, Grand Rapids (1972 edition).
Staal, J.D.W., (1988), *The New Patterns in the Sky*, McDonald and Woodward, Blacksburg, Virginia.
Thoreau, H.D., (1854), *Walden and Other Writings*. Bantam Books, New York.
Tolstoy, L., (1899), *Resurrection*. Translated by Louise Maude. Oxford University Press. 1994 edition.
Torday, P., (2007) *Salmon Fishing in the Yemen*, Phoenix Books, London
Unitarian Universalist Service Book, (1993), *Singing the Living Tradition*, Beacon Press, Boston.
Whitman, W. (1855) *Leaves of Grass*, Bantam Classics, (1983 edition).

Printed in Great Britain
by Amazon